DISTRICT OF COLUMBIA
Original Land Owners
1791-1800

Wesley E. Pippenger

HERITAGE BOOKS
2007

HERITAGE BOOKS
AN IMPRINT OF HERITAGE BOOKS, INC.

Books, CDs, and more—Worldwide

For our listing of thousands of titles see our website
at
www.HeritageBooks.com

Published 2007 by
HERITAGE BOOKS, INC.
Publishing Division
65 East Main Street
Westminster, Maryland 21157-5026

Copyright © 1999 Wesley E. Pippenger

All rights reserved. No part of this book may be reproduced or transmitted in any form or by any means, electronic or mechanical, including photocopying, recording or by any information storage and retrieval system without written permission from the author, except for the inclusion of brief quotations in a review.

International Standard Book Number: 978-1-58549-153-7

TABLE OF CONTENTS

PREFACE v

    Replica of the Title Page from Faehtz and Pratt's *Embryo* viii
    Sketch of Washington in Embryo ix

INTRODUCTION 1

EVENTS LEADING TO THE FOUNDATION OF WASHINGTON CITY 3

PART FIRST — HAMBURGH

    Plan of Hamburgh 23
    View of the City of Washington in 1792 24

    HAMBURGH 25
        I. — TABULAR STATEMENT, "Hamburgh Lots Conveyed for Washington Lots" 27

PART SECOND — CARROLLSBURG

    Plan of Carrollsburg 33
    Expanded Section from the View of the City of Washington in 1792 34

    CARROLLSBURG 35
        II. — TABULAR STATEMENT, "Carrollsburg Lots Conveyed for Washington Lots" 37
        III. — TABULAR STATEMENT, "Lottery Ticket Holders for Carrollsburg Lots" 45

PART THIRD — CITY OF WASHINGTON

    Expanded Central Portion from the Plan of the City of Washington, 1792 48
    Plan of the City of Washington, 1792 49

    CITY OF WASHINGTON 51
        IV. — TABULAR STATEMENT, "Square Division by the Trustees" 53

CONCLUSION 127

APPENDIX A, "List of Certificates for Washington Lots Purchased from the Commissioners" 131

INDEX 143

PREFACE

Students of District of Columbia land records may already be familiar with a work done in 1874 by Ernest F.M. Faehtz and F.W. Pratt, that had the exhaustive title, *Washington Embryo, or the National Capital from 1791 to 1800, the Origin of all Rights and Titles to Property in Washington, D.C.: An Exhaustive Manual For Reseaches into the Derivation of Titles. Containing all the original squares and lots laid out at the foundation of said City, the names of their origin owners, the dates and mode of conveyance of them, the laws authorizing and directing such transfers, and other documents and information of importance to those interested in real estate matters.* Also in 1874, Faehtz and Pratt devised a real estate "directory" atlas of the City of Washington which contained a separate plat of each square in the city.

Faehtz and Pratt's *Embryo* study was followed by another documentation effort that was commissioned in 1909 by the Federal Government in support of title in the United States to the lands within the District of Columbia. The U.S. Senate, 60th Congress, 2nd Session, published Document No. 653, which included several tables with lot ownership and conveyance data, along with three huge folding maps. The 1909 study shows in Exhibit B a partial list of lots sold by the United States to individual purchasers. The exhibit is sorted by Square number and shows lot sales made up through the 1860's.

The compiler of the present work has used the *Embryo* for the foundation commentary, structure, and data content. The original data presented is expanded to provide space for users to note where specific records for the transactions of Hamburgh (Montgomery County, Maryland) and Carrollsburg (Prince George's County, Maryland) can be found. Unfortunately, not many of the certificates of lot ownership that were issued by the Commissioners have been located among the land records of the District of Columbia. The original deed books that document the original purchases of lots for Hamburgh and Carrollsburg are at the Hall of Records in Annapolis, Maryland. Conveyances to purchasers of Hamburgh lots are all in the name of Jacob Funck (and Funk) as the grantor, and begin in Prince George's County Land Records, Liber AA No. 2, at folio 285 et seq.

The compiler has reduced for this edition maps of Carrollsburg and Hamburgh, and presented a map (that did not appear in the *Embryo*) that shows the contemporary lot structure and numbering system for the City of Washington. An appendix has been added to include a partial list of certificates for lot ownership that were issued by the Commissioners. And, most importantly, the work contains an every-name and place name index.

This compilation is significantly useful for researchers because much confusion resulted from the annexation of land from Maryland and Virginia to create the Territory of Columbia. Further chaos stemmed from the, sometimes disagreeable, taking or swapping of properties from lot-holders in the former towns of Hamburgh and Carrollsburg for equitable lots in the City of Washington; the caveats and rights various lot-holders tried to hang onto while swooped up under this movement; and the subsequent division, redivision, and subdivision of lots within each square.

After Pierre Charles L'Enfant and Andrew Ellicott devised a plan for dividing the land into squares and lots, some 10,136 lots became the share of the Government, in addition to such sites as were designated for public buildings and other public purposes. These lots were in the hands of the Commissioners who would occasionally sell lots to defray the expense in constructing public buildings. The first public auction for this purpose was in October 1791. A number of lot sales from subsequent auctions can be found listed in the Appendix.

For those of you who are occasionally stumped by not being able to find a particular square number, take note — the Tabular Statement for the City of Washington details for us there are no such squares numbered 34, 45, 46, 64, 108, 130, 187, 201, 261, 262, 301, 392, 418, 443, 474, 659, 745, 746, 848, 850, 851, 852, 993, 998, 1016, 1081, 1099, 1101, 1103, 1124, 1131 or 1147. Why? It's probably very complicated.

Enclosed is a replica of the title page from Faehtz and Pratt's *Embryo*, and it is followed by a copy of "Sketch of Washington in Embryo," which shows the division of tracts for major land owners taken to establish the seat of the Federal Government, and the proximity of Georgetown, Hamburgh, Carrollsburg, and the City of Washington.

Wesley E. Pippenger
Arlington, Virginia
September 1999

[Replica of the Title Page from Faehtz and Pratt's *Embryo*]

WASHINGTON IN EMBRYO

Or

The National Capital from 1791 to 1800

**THE ORIGIN
of all
RIGHTS AND TITLES TO PROPERTY
in
Washington, D.C.**

An Exhaustive Manual

For Reseaches into the Derivation of Titles. Containing all the original squares and lots laid out at the foundation of said City, the names of their origin owners, the dates and mode of conveyance of them, the laws authorizing and directing such transfers, and other documents and information of importance to those interested in real estate matters.

PREPARED
WITH THE SPECIAL ASSISTANCE OF BRAINARD H. WARNER, ESQ.
Real Estate Broker, corner 7th and F streets, N.W.

BY

E.F.M. FAEHTZ AND F.W. PRATT
Authors and Publishers of the Real Estate Directory of Washington
1874

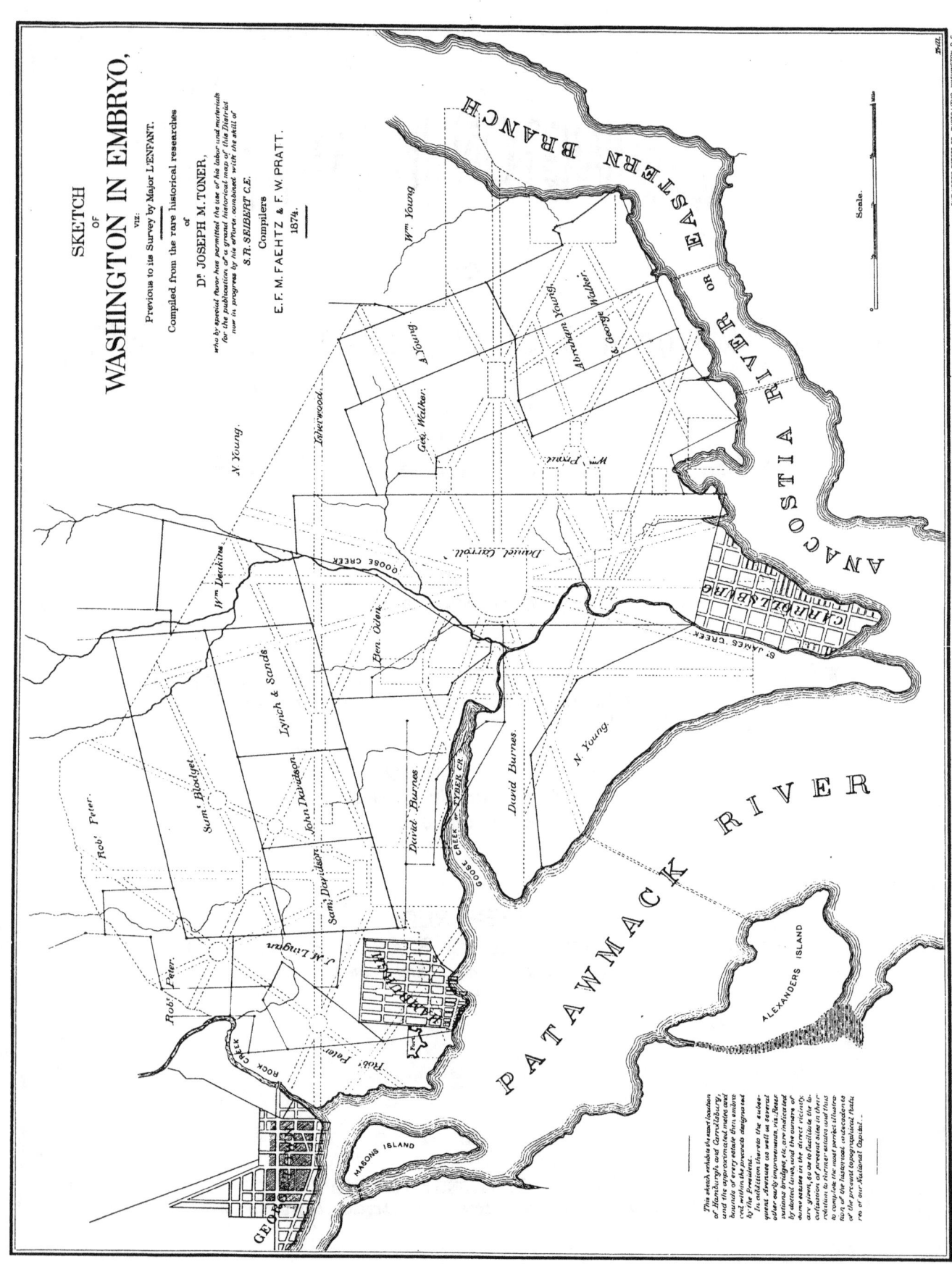

INTRODUCTION

EVEN before competing the publication called the "REAL ESTATE DIRECTORY OF WASHINGTON CITY," it became manifest to the authors that, next to the correct delineation of metes and bounds, it must be of the gravest importance to courts and lawyers, property-holders and others interested in it, to possess a reliable manual showing the original property-relations of, and titles to, the various lots and pieces of ground in that city, to serve as a safe guide or starting point from which to derive the origin of subsequent claims, titles, or rights.

To produce such a work would probably be impossible in other cities, having grown into their present dimensions at different times and from various causes, by sundry strides of gradual development, and even in our National Capital, which completed all her present boundaries at the very moment of rising into existence, it was an exceedingly difficult task, as this happened in a turbulent period, near the end of the last century, and the records of it are not in the best condition, and in some cases confused or defective.

However, the fact that contemporaneously with the foundation of the Federal City all rights and titles to property in it were regulated by law, whenever an amicable agreement could not be effected, and such agreement was realized in all cases but one, has rendered the labors of the undersigned less difficult and perfectly reliable. Hence they are confident of having produced in the following pages another compilation of great usefulness, which they herewith commend to public favor.

In making this announcement, it is due in justice to state that, previously to them, Mr. John J. Bogue, of Georgetown, had conceived a similar plan, and compiled a great amount of useful information; but before he had completed his purpose, the undersigned purchased from him the material collected, as well as the copyright obtained by him, and, after revising and augmenting the same largely, they re-arranged and embraced most of it within their present work.

In these efforts several prominent gentlemen assisted them with kindness and ability, and to great advantage, among whom, especially, Messrs. B.H. Warner, Wm. H. Ward, and Dr. Jos. M. Toner, of this city, and Mr. Henry Brooke, of Marlborough, Md. Mr. Warner greatly facilitated the success of the enterprise by encouragement and general assistance; Mr. Wm. H. Ward, by his familiarity with public records and experience in complicated examinations, furnished some excellent explanations and suggestions; Dr. Joseph M. Toner, highly reputed for his historical studies, contributed, besides other valuable information, the accompanying plats of Hamburgh and Carrollsburg, which are faithful copies of those filed in the land records of Prince George's County, Maryland; and Mr. Henry Brooke, chief clerk of the Circuit Court in that county, and as such in custody, or at least within immediate reach, of the said land records, has supplied extracts therefrom, and other important material, as will become evident from the perusal of one of his letters, which, on account of its conciseness and official character, has been rendered *verbatim*; and for these favors and courteous services the undersigned desire to express their grateful appreciation by giving these gentlemen public credit for the same.

The present compilation, in regard to facts and data connected with the cession of this territory to the United States, the foundation of the city now called Washington, and the acquisition of property within her precincts, is merely a faithful transcript of the public records; but as such property was mostly acquired by transfer, or allotment, of lots or premises situated in the Federal city for pieces of property located in settlements or estates previously existing within the same territorial outlines, some fragments of the former history of that area had to be introduced to convey the necessary comprehension of subsequent transactions, yet these historical portions are strictly limited to events directly bearing upon real-estate matters, and not as history.

From diligent researches it is safe to presume, that although there are historical data remaining in the narratives of Captain Smith as far back as 1607, which, however, concern only climatic and other contingencies within our District, they are few, if any, official records of regular real-estate transactions of prior date than 1669, of which year some deeds are preserved in the archives of the Court-house in Marlborough, Maryland; but as nothing therein affects any property within the subsequent city of Washington, they are not further noticed in this compilation, and all information needed for the understanding of property relations in Hamburgh and Carrollsburg, or any of the adjacent states, previous to their exchange for property in this city, is limited to the following letter of Henry Brooke, Esq., in answer to inquiries made by the compilers:

1. The property in Carrollsburg was subdivided into lots, streets, alleys, etc., about the latter part of 1770, by virtue and authority of a deed of trust dated the 2d day of Nov. 1770, from Charles Carroll, Jun., to Henry Rozer, Daniel Carroll, and Notley Young (see Liber AA, No. 2, fol. 299, et seq.). These conveyances authorize the grantees to subdivide 'Duddington Manor' and 'Duddington Pasture,' containing in the aggregate of 160 acres of land, more or less, into 268 lots, to sell the same (except 6 lots to be selected by the grantor, his heirs or assigns, for his or their own proper use), and to draw or cause to be drawn for by ballot or lottery. This deed is recorded on Nov. 20, 1770, and the plat, courses, and distances of the town are also of record in the Land and Special Record. Immediately following are innumerable deeds from the above grantees to different parties for lots in Carrollsburg, which the deeds recite having been drawn by the

INTRODUCTION

grantees respectively in a lottery of the same. It was a custom apparently in those days to dispose of property by lottery; in my researches of the old records I have found several such, including the St. Elizabeth Asylum of your city, which was drawn by an old sea captain. In the Elizabeth matter, as in this, the owner conveyed the property to the trustees, who sold the tickets, attended the drawing, and deeded the prize to the lucky owner. There is no mention whatever in any of the conveyances of this Carrollsburg property of any contemplated cession to the United States.

2. Hamburgh was surveyed and laid off by the owner, Jacob Funk, and his plat recorded here October 28, 1771 — a year and four days after the Carrollsburg subdivision, in Liber AA, No. 2, fol. 397. A plat of Hamburg is at fols. 398 and 399. Funk appears to have purchased the land in fee simple from Thomas Johns in [March 1768[1]] (see deed in Liber BB, No. 2, fols. 227-228), and to have taken out a commission in 1770 to perpetuate the bounds of 'Widow's Mite' and then to have laid it off and sold it out as lots in Hamburgh, giving the deeds to the purchasers himself. None of these deeds recite that the lots have been drawn by lottery or ballot. The deed of trust for Carrollsburg is the only authority I can find for a lottery, but that may be explained by the fact that not until 1792 did the statutes require a lottery to be specially authorized by the Legislature of Maryland (see Acts of 1792, Chap. 58, Sec. 1).

3. The title to Carrollsburg was in Rozer, Carroll and Young, who deeded the same to the parties drawing the lots, by deeds duly executed and recorded here.

4. The title in Hamburgh was in Jacob Funk, who deeded, etc. etc. I find no act of incorporation for either of these towns in 'Kilty's Laws of Maryland,' and hence infer they were never incorporated, as the acts incorporating other villages and towns in the State are quire numerous in 'Kilty's.'

Truly yours,
(signed) Henry Brooke.
Upper Marlborough, Md., Sept. 29, 1874.

The above letter, giving proper reference for every fact stated therein, will enable any one so disposed to carry his researches regarding property, back to the period next pre-existing the assumption of authority over this District by the United States. Its inferences appear to be well supported, and as, their nature is not essential to subsequent property-relations in our city, will not cause much controversy, yet they are very serviceable in explanation of data not directly proven by record, and the compilers for the same purpose add to them a few surmises of their own, viz:

The names of "Hamburgh" and "Carrollsburg" appear the first time in relation to the subdivision of these settlements into lots, streets, alleys, etc., and the former seems to have passed previously under the name of "Funkstown," whilst the latter was styled "Duddington Manor" and "Duddington Pasture."

In Carrollsburg all lots of its subdivision are accounted for on its map, but in Hamburgh[2] there are fifty-two lots—namely, from 57 to 67, from 117 to 131, from 191 to 204, and from 253 to 266, inclusive—not designated on the plat, nor are they assigned in the records, hence the natural inference is that they were embraced in the adjoining tracts, now forming the United States Naval Observatory, and, perhaps, Reservation No. 6, although nothing is positively stated anywhere, as far as known, to that effect.

These assumptions the authors are willing to leave standing upon their own merit, as they will not, even if erroneous, injure in any manner the reliability of the extracts from public records herewith submitted.

Very Respectfully,
E.F.M. Faehtz
F.W. Pratt

Washington, D.C., October 1874

---

[1] The property Jacob Funck (Funk) purchased is described as that previously sold by Henry Watson and Lucy his wife to James Dick, attorney in fact for William Black of London, merchant, by deed 8 FEB 1754, and by Black sold to Johns, 4 JUN 1749. Also see deed of Lucy Watson, 6 AUG 1763.

[2] Prince George's Co., Md., Land Records, Liber AA No. 2, fols. 397-399, original at Hall of Records, Annapolis, Md.

EVENTS LEADING TO THE FOUNDATION OF WASHINGTON CITY

THE subject of a permanent Capital for the General Government of the United States was first approached in Congress on the 30th day of April 1783, and less than a month thereafter New York offered the town of Kingston for this purpose, which proposition was followed, a few days later, by a tender from Maryland to Annapolis, and of an appropriation of $180,000.

These proposals gave rise to various discussions and motions concerning the site, area, and other contingencies of such a selection, until Congress, on the 6th day of October, in the same year, resolved to select one of the then existing States located not further north than New Jersey; and in the subsequent ballot this State and Maryland received the highest number of votes, without, however, effecting a final choice. The following day of the Delaware, in the vicinity of Trenton, and on the 21st day of that month another committee was authorized to examine and report on a location on or near the lower falls of the Potomac, and it was decided that, until one of these two sites should be chosen, Congress should meet alternately at Trenton and Annapolis.

This was soon found inconvenient; the said committees reported; *that on the Delaware*, favorably; *that on the Potomac, unfavorably*. On December 20, 1784, it was decided not to erect buildings in more than one place, and three days afterwards a commission was appointed to select and lay out a district of not less than two, and not more than three miles square, on either shore of the Delaware, within eight miles above or below the falls. The following Commissioners were selected: Messrs. Thomas Johnson, Daniel Carroll, Gustavus Scott, — White, and William Cranch, all of Maryland; William Thornton, of Pennsylvania, and David Stuart, of Virginia.

These Commissioners entered upon duty, but no decisive step was taken by Congress for some years.

In the meantime the Constitution of the United States (adopted 1787) gave Congress, in Art. 1, sec. 8, the following powers:

To exercise legislation in all cases whatsoever over such district (not exceeding ten miles square) as may, by cession of particular States and the acceptance of Congress, become the seat of the Government of the United States, and to exercise like authority over all places purchased by the consent of the legislature of the State in which the same shall be, for the erection of forts, magazines, arsenals, dock-yards, and other needful buildings.

Already, in the first session of Congress assembled under this Constitution, districts of ten miles square, with the right of exclusive jurisdiction, were tendered for the seat of Government by the following States, viz: Maryland, in December 1788; Pennsylvania, in September 1769; and Virginia, in December 1789. Also, petitions were received from several cities in New Jersey, Pennsylvania, and Maryland, to be selected as the national capital.

In the second session the "Capital" question was again prominently introduced, and various sites were suggested and discussed; but an act was finally passed and approved July 16, 1790, by which Philadelphia was selected as temporary seat of the Government, and the site on the Potomac, between the mouths of the Anacostia and the Conogocheague, was ordered to be prepared so as to be ready for the sessions of Congress by the first Monday in December 1800.

In the meantime, Maryland and Virginia had ceded the territory in question by the following acts:

AN ACT to cede to Congress a district of ten miles square in this State (Maryland), for the seat of the Government of the United States. Approved December 23d, 1788.

Be it enacted by the General Assembly of Maryland, That the representatives of this State in the House of Representatives of the Congress of the United States, appointed to assemble at New York on the first Wednesday of March next, be, and they are hereby, authorized and required, on behalf of this State, to cede to the Congress of the United States any district in this state not exceeding ten miles square, which the Congress may fix upon and accept for the seat of government of the United States.

AN ACT for the cession of ten miles square or any lesser quantity of territory within this State (Virginia), to the United States in Congress assembled, for the permanent seat of the General Government. Approved December 3, 1789.

1. Whereas the equal and common benefits resulting from the administration of the General Government will be best diffused and its operations become more prompt and certain by establishing such a situation for the seat of said government as will be most central and convenient to the citizens of the United States at large, having regard as well to population, extent of territory, and free navigation to the Atlantic Ocean through the Chesapeake Bay, as to the most direct and ready communication with our fellow-citizens in the Western frontiers; and whereas it appears to this Assembly that a situation combining all the considerations and advantages before recited may be had on the banks of the river Potomac, above tide-water, in a country rich and fertile in soil, healthy and salubrious in climate, and abounding in all the necessaries and conveniences of life, where, in a location of ten miles square, if the wisdom of Congress shall so direct, the States of Pennsylvania, Maryland and Virginia may participate in such location:

2. *Be it therefore enacted by the General Assembly*, That a tract of country, not exceeding ten miles square, or any lesser quantity, to be located within the limits of this State, and in any part thereof as Congress may by law direct, shall be, and the same is, forever coded and relinquished to the

Congress and Government for the United States, in full and absolute right and exclusive jurisdiction, as well of soil as of persons residing or to reside thereon, pursuant to the tenor and effect of the eighth section of the first article of the Constitution of the Government of the United States.

III. *Provided*, That nothing herein contained shall be herein construed to vest in the United States any right of property in the soil, or to affect the rights of individuals therein, otherwise than the same shall or may be transferred by such individuals to the United States.

IV. *And provided also*, That the jurisdiction of laws of this Commonwealth over the persons and property of individuals residing within the limits of the cession aforesaid shall not cease or determine until Congress, having accepted the said cession, shall by law provide for the government thereof, under their jurisdiction, in the manner provided by the article of the Constitution before recited.

These cessions of territory from the States of Maryland and Virginia were accepted by the following act of Congress, approved, as before stated, July 16, 1790:

AN ACT for establishing the temporary and permanent seat of the Government of the United States.

Sec. 1. *Be it enacted by the Senate and House of Representatives of the United States of America in Congress assembled*, That a district or territory not exceeding ten miles square, to be located as hereafter directed on the river Potomac, at some space between the months of the Eastern Branch and Conogocheague, be, and the same is hereby, accepted for the permanent seat of the Government of the United States: *Provided, nevertheless*, That the operations of the laws of the State within such district shall not be affected by this acceptance until the time fixed for the removed of the government thereto, and until Congress shall otherwise by law direct.

Sec. 2. *And be it further enacted*, That the President of the United States be authorized to appoint and, by supplying vacancies happening from refusals to act or other causes, to keep in appointment as long as may be necessary three Commissioners, who, or any two of whom, shall, under the direction of the President, survey and by proper metes and bounds define and limit a district of territory, under the limitations above mentioned; and the district so defined, limited, and located shall be deemed the district accepted by this act for the permanent seat of the Government of the United States.

Sec. 3. *And be it enacted*, That the said Commissioners, or any two of them, shall have power to purchase or accept or accept such quantity of land on the eastern side of said river within the said district as the President shall deem proper for the use of the United States, and according to such plans as the President shall approve; the said Commissioners, or any two of them, shall, prior to the first Monday of December, in the year one thousand eight hundred, provide suitable buildings for the accommodation of Congress, and of the President, and for the public offices of the Government of the United States.

Sec. 4. *And be it enacted,* That for defraying of the expenses of such purchases and buildings, the President of the United States be authorized and requested to accept grants of money.

Sec. 5. *And be it enacted*, That prior to the first Monday in December next, all offices attached to the seat of the government of the United States shall be removed to, and until the said first Monday in December, in the year one thousand eight hundred, shall remain at the city of Philadelphia, in the State of Pennsylvania, at which place the session of Congress next ensuing to the present shall be held.

Sec. 6. *And be it enacted*, That on the said first Monday in December, in the year one thousand eight hundred, the seat of government of the United States shall by virtue of this act be transferred to the district and place aforesaid; and all offices attached to the said seat of government shall accordingly be removed thereto by their respective holders, and shall, after the said day, cease to be exercised elsewhere, and that the necessary expense of such removal shall be defrayed out of the dutie on imports and tonnage, of which a sufficient sum is hereby appropriate.

GEORGE WASHINGTON.
President of the United States

July 16, 1790.

The immediate effect of the foregoing act of Congress was that among all parties concerned in its provisions a lively interest was manifested in measures for the speedy establishment of permanent metes and bounds, and for the early erection of public buildings and premises necessary for the permanency of the newly-elected seat of government of the United States.

Hence, the State of Maryland, during the subsequent session of its legislature in December of the same year, passed an act providing for the condemnation of land if necessary for public buildings (which is not rendered here, because it never was enforced, the amicable agreement of the property-holders in the new District with the United States Commissioners, inserted in one of the following pages, preventing all necessity of condemnation of land for the said purpose), and the State of Virginia, on the 27th day of the same month, passed the following act:

AN ACT concerning the advance of money to the Government of the United States for public buildings. Passed December 27, 1790.

Whereas the General Assembly of Maryland has acceded to a proposition of the General Assembly of this Commonwealth, contained in their resolution of the 10th day of December 1789, concerning an advance of money to the General Government to be applied towards the erection of public buildings at the permanent seat of the Government of the United States, should Congress deem it expedient to fix it on the banks of the Patowmack; and whereas Congress have passed an act for establishing the said seat of Government on the Patowmack—

Be it enacted by the General Assembly, That 120,000 dollars shall be advanced by this Commonwealth to the General Government, payable in three equal yearly payments, and to be applied toward erecting public buildings at the permanent seat of government of the United States on the banks of the Patowmack, and the auditor of public accounts is hereby directed to issue his warrants on the treasurer to the amount of 120,000 dollars, payable in the manner hereinbefore director, to the order of the President of the United States.

Also, under virtue of the above recited act of Congress of July 16, 1790, the President of the United States, by letters patent bearing date January 22, 1791, appointed Thomas Johnson and Daniel Carroll, of Maryland, and David Stuart, of Virginia, Commissioners.

The letters patent read in the following words:

[SEAL] GEORGE WASHINGTON, *President of the United States.*
To all who shall see these presents, greeting:

Know ye, that reposing special trust and confidence in the integrity, skill, and diligence of Thomas Johnson and Daniel Carroll, of Maryland, and David Stuart, of Virginia, I do, in pursuance of the powers vested in me by the act entitled: 'An Act for establishing the temporary and permanent seat of the Government of the United States,' approved July 16, 1790, hereby appoint them, the said Thomas Johnson, Daniel Carroll, and David Stuart, Commissioners for surveying the district of territory accepted by the said act for the permanent seat of the Government of the United States, and for performing such other offices as by law are directed, with full authority for them, or any two of them, to proceed therein according to law, and to have and to hole the said office, with all the powers, privileges, and authorities to the same of right appertaining each of them, during the pleasure of the President of the United States for the time being.

In testimony whereof I have caused these letters to be made patent, and the seal of the United States thereto affixed.

Given under my hand at the city of Philadelphia, the twenty-second day of January, in the year of our Lord one thousand seven hundred and ninety-one, and of the independence of the United States the fifteenth.
GEORGE WASHINGTON
By the President
Thomas Jefferson

Daniel Carroll, of Maryland, one of the aforesaid Commissioners, being at the issuing this commission one of the delegates appointed from the State of Maryland in the House of Representatives of Congress of the United States, refused to act as Commissioner, and hence there were only two Commissioners on duty from that time until March 4, 1791, when, Mr. Carroll's time of serving in Congress having elapsed, a new commission was sent him, and he agreed to serve as Commissioner.

In further pursuance of the aforesaid act, approved July 16, 1790, the President also issued a proclamation, dated January 24, 1791, designating the experimental boundary lines of the District to be accepted for the permanent seat of the Government, and directing the Commissioners to run the said lines, and survey the define, by proper metes and bounds, and part within the same which he directed for immediate location and acceptance, to wit:

WHEREAS the General Assembly of Maryland, by an act passed on the 23d day of December 1788, entitled 'An act to cede to Congress a direct of ten miles square in this State for the seat of the Government of the United States,' did enact that the Representatives of the said State in the House of Representatives of Congress of the United States appointed to assemble at New York on the first Wednesday in March then next ensuing, should be, and they were thereby, authorized and required, on behalf of the said State, not exceeding ten miles square, which the Congress might fix upon and accept for the seat of government of the United States;

And the General Assembly of the Commonwealth of Virginia, by act passed the 3d day of December 1789, and entitled 'An act for the cession of ten miles square, or any lesser quantity of territory, within this State to the United States, in Congress assembled, for the permanent seat of the General Government,' did enact that a tract of country not exceeding ten miles square, or any lesser quantity, to be located within the limits of the said State, and in any part thereof, as Congress might by law direct, should be, and the same was thereby, forever ceded and relinquished to the Congress and the Government of the United States, in full and absolute right and exclusive jurisdiction, and well of soil as of persons residing or to reside thereon, pursuant to the tenor and effect of the eighth section of the first article of the Constitution of government of the United States;

And the Congress of the United States, by their act passed on the 16th day of July 1790, and entitled, 'An act for establishing the temporary and permanent seat of government of the United States,' authorized the President of the United States to appoint three Commissioners to survey, under his direction, and by proper metes and bounds, to limit a district of territory not exceeding ten miles square, on the river Potomac, at some place between the Eastern Branch and Conococheague, which district so to be located and limited and accepted by the said act of

Congress as the district for the permanent seat of the Government of the United States:

Now, THEREFORE, in pursuance of the powers to me confided, and after duly examining and weighing the advantages and disadvantages of the several situations within the limits aforesaid, I do hereby declare and make known that the location of one part of the said district of ten miles square shall be found by running four lines of experiment in the following manner: That is to say, running from the Court-house of Alexandria, in Virginia, due southwest half a mile, and thence a due southeast course till it shall strike Hunting Creek, to fix the beginning of the said four lines of experiment. Then beginning the first of the said four lines of experiment at the point of Hunting Creek where the said southeast course shall have struck the same, and running the said first line due northwest ten miles; thence the second line into Maryland due northeast ten miles; thence the third line due southeast ten miles, and thence the fourth line due southwest ten miles, to the beginning on Hunting Creek.

And the said four lines of experiment being so run, I do hereby declare and make known that all that part within the said four lines of experiment which shall be within the State of Maryland and above the Eastern Branch, and al that part within the same four lines of experiment which shall be within the Commonwealth of Virginia, and above a line to be run from the point of land forming the upper cape of the mouth of the Eastern Branch due southwest, and no more, is now fixed upon and directed to be surveyed, defined, limited, and located for a part of the said district, accepted by the said act of Congress for the permanent seat of the Government of the United States; hereby expressly reserving the direction of the survey and location of the remaining part of the said district, to be made hereafter contiguous to such part or parts of the present location as is or shall be agreeably to law.

And I do accordingly direct the said Commissioners, appointed agreeably to the tenor of the said act, to proceed forthwith to run the said lines of experiment, and the same being run, to survey, and by proper metes and bounds to define and limit the part within the same which is hereinbefore directed for immediate location and acceptance; and thereof to make due report to me, under their hands and seals.

IN TESTIMONY WHEREOF, I have caused the sea of the United States to be affixed to these presents, and signed the same with my hand. Done at the city of Philadelphia, the 24th day of January, in the year of our Lord 1791, and of the independence of the United States the fifteenth.

    (signed)   GEORGE WASHINGTON.
[seal]
By the President:
Thomas Jefferson

The lines designated in the foregoing proclamation were approved by Congress, but as the original act of July 16, 1790, required the location of the District, "above the mouth of the Eastern Branch or Anacostia River," it was necessary to conform the law to the experimental lines, and hence the conflicting portions of the said act were repealed in the following act, approved March 3, 1791, which however provided the public building to be erected on the Maryland shore of the Potomac only, viz:

AN ACT to amend an act establishing the temporary and permanent seat of government of the United States.

That so much of the act entitled "An act for establishing the temporary and permanent seat of government of the United States" as requires that the whole of the district of territory, not exceeding ten miles square, to be located on the river Potomac for the permanent seat of the Government of the United States shall be located above the mouth of the Eastern Branch, be, and the same is hereby, repealed, and that it shall be lawful for the President to make any part of the said territory below the said limit, the above the mouth of Huntington [sic] creek, a part of the said district, so as to include a convenient part of the Eastern Branch and of the lands lying on the lower side thereof, and also the town of Alexandria; and the territory so included shall form a part of the district not exceeding ten miles square for the permanent seat of the Government of the United States, in like manner and to all intents an purposes as if the same had been within the purview of the above-recited act: Provided, That nothing herein contained shall authorize the erection of the public buildings otherwise than on the Maryland side of the river Potomac, as required by the aforesaid act.
Approved March 3d, 1791.

After such completion of the necessary legislation on this subject, President Washington at once prepared to proceed in person to the new seat of government, in order to initiate such measures as might be needed for the immediate location and speedy erection of public buildings, which is indicated in the following letter:

PHILADELPHIA, March 11, 1791.
DEAR SIR: I write to you by this post in conformity with my promise so to do. But it is not yet in my power to determine whether I can set out on Monday or not. If I find the roads do not mend much between this time and that, I shall not be anxious about beginning on that day, even if business should permit. As my fixing the day for meeting the Commissioners at Georgetown must depend upon my departure from this place, I cannot determine upon the former until the latter is decided. I shall write to you again by Monday's post, and in that letter shall be able to say with certainty when I leave this city. With very great esteem, I am, sir, your

EVENTS LEADING TO THE FOUNDATION OF WASHINGTON CITY

most obedient servant,
(signed) GEORGE WASHINGTON.
DANIEL CARROLL, Esq.

Soon after this letter had been dispatched on March 11, 1791, namely on March 28th, the President reached Georgetown, and on the 29th he rode over the entire new District, in company with the three Commissioners and the two surveyors, Andrew Ellicott and Major Pierre Charles L'Enfant.[3]

On the evening of the same day a meeting was held for the purpose of effecting a friendly agreement between the property-holders the next day, and thereby the rights of, and titles to, property within this District and city may be said to have been decided on that evening.

The following is an exact copy of the said agreement:

We, the subscribers, in consideration of the great benefits we expect to derive from having the Federal city laid off upon our lands, do hereby agree and bind ourselves, heirs, executors, and administrators, to convey in trust to the President of the U.S., or Commissioners, or such person or persons as he shall appoint, by good and sufficient deeds in fee simple, the whole of our respective land which he may think proper to include within the lines of the Federal city, for the purposes and on the conditions following:

The President shall have the sole power of directing the Federal city of squares he may think proper for any public improvements or other public uses, and the lots only which shall be laid off shall be joint property between the trustees on behalf of the public, and equally divided between the public and the individuals as soon as may be after the city shall be laid off.

For the streets the proprietors shall receive no compensation, but for the squares or lands in any form which shall be taken for public buildings or any kind of public improvement or uses, the proprietors whose land shall be so taken shall receive at the rate of £25[4] per acre, to be paid by the public.

The whole wood on the lands shall be the property of the proprietors, and should any be desired by the President to be reserved or left standing, the same shall be paid for by the public at a just and reasonable valuation, exclusive of the £25 per acre to be paid for the land on which the same shall remain.

Each proprietor shall retain the full possession and use of his land until the same shall be sold and occupied by the purchase of the lots laid out thereupon, and in all cases where the public arrangements as the streets, lots, etc., will admit of it, each proprietor shall possess his buildings and other improvements and graveyards, paying to the public only one-half the present estimated value of the land, on which the same shall be, or £12 10 sh. per acre; but in cases where the arrangements of the streets, lots, squares, etc., will not admit of this, and it shall become necessary to remove such buildings, etc., the proprietors of the same shall be paid the reasonable value thereof by the public.

Nothing herein contained shall affect the lots any of the parties of this agreement may hold in the towns of Hamburgh or Carrollsburg.

In witness whereof we have hereunto set our hands and seals this 30 day of March, in the year of our Lord 1791.

Signed and sealed in presence of Mr. Thomas Beale, making an exception of the land he sold A.C. Young, not yet conveyed.
    Witness to all subscribers including Wm. Young
    WM. BAILEY

    WM. ROBERTSON
    JOHN SUTER

    SAM. DAVIDSON, witness to Abraham Young signing.
    BENJAMIN STODDERT, witness to Peirce's signing.
    JOSEPH E. ROWLES, for Jno. Warring
    WM. DEAKINS, Jr., for Wm. Prout and Wm. King
    As attorney-in-fact for Eliphas Douglass

ROBERT PETER [seal]
DAVID BURNES [seal]
JAS. M. LINGAN [seal]
URIAH FORREST [seal]
BENJAMIN STODDERT [seal]
NOTLEY YOUNG [seal]
DANIEL CARROLL of Duddington [seal]
OVERTON CARR [seal]
THOMAS BEALE of George [seal]
CHAS. BEATTY [seal]
ANTHONY HOLMEAD [seal]
WM. YOUNG [seal]
EDWARD PEIRCE [seal]
ABRAHAM YOUNG [seal]
JAS. PEIRCE [seal]
WM. PROUT [seal]
ROBERT PETER [seal]
BENJAMIN STODDERT [seal] for Jas. Warren, by written authority from W. Warren.
WM. KING [seal]

The following names appear either in some of the conveyances to the Trustees or in the earlier conveyances of the United States Commissioners, being either original proprietors who joined in the above agreement at a subsequent date, or owners of lots in Carrollsburg or Hamburgh, or became property-holders at a very early date after the said agreement was executed, either by inheritance, assignment, or other kind of legal transfer, and hence are often counted among the original property-holders, viz:

Robert Morris   James Greenleaf   John H. Stone
Samuel Blodget   Thomas Johnson   Comfort Sands
William Bailey   Robert Lingan   Benjamin Oden
Samuel Davidson   Dominick Lynch   John P. Van Ness
William Deakins, Jr.   John Nicholson
George Walker, and the legal guardians of Elizabeth Wheeler (including Thomas Beall and John M. Gantt)

---

[3] This is the first occasion on which the names of the two engineers appear on the records, who played so conspicuous a figure in the demarcation of outlines and the laying out of streets, avenues, and squares of our present city; and the compilers regret very much that they did not find in the records within their reach any account of particulars in regard to the date and manner of their official employment. Biographical notices can be found in any good encyclopedia, but would be out of place in these lines.

[4] Means Pennsylvania currency, then adopted in Pennsylvania, New Jersey, Maryland, ad Delaware, and equivalent to $66.66, the pound of said currency being equal to $2.66 of the current currency.

The general form of the conveyances to be executed by the several proprietors under this agreement will be found on folio 330 of *Burch's Digest*.

After such encouraging proceedings, which, as stated before, removed all necessity of condemnation of lands for any public purpose, the President did not hesitate any longer; and, without leaving Georgetown, issued the same day, viz., March 30, 1791, the following proclamation:

Whereas by proclamation bearing date the 24th day of Jan., of this present year, and in pursuance of certain acts of the States of Maryland and Virginia and the Congress of the United States, therein mentioned, certain lines of experiment were directed to be run in the neighborhood of Georgetown, in Maryland, for the purpose of locating a part of the territory of ten miles square, for the permanent seat of government of the United States, and a certain part was directed to be located within the said lines of experiment on both sides of the Potomac, and above the limits of the Eastern Branch, prescribed by the said act of Congress;

And Congress, by an amendatory act, passed on the 3d day of this present month of March, have given further authority to the President of the United States, to make any part of the said territory below the said limit and above the mouth of Hunting Creek a part of said district, so as to include a convenient part of the Eastern Branch, and of the lands lying o the lower side thereof, and also the town of Alexandria;

Now, therefore, for the purpose of amending and completing the location of the whole of said territory of ten miles square, in conformity with the said amendatory act of Congress, I do hereby declare and make known that the whole of the said territory shall be located and included within the four lines following, that is to say:

Beginning at Jones's Point, being the upper cape of Hunting Creek, in Virginia, and at an angle in the outset of forty-five degrees west of the north, and running in a direct line of ten miles, for the first line; then the beginning again at the same Jones's Point, and running another direct line, at a right angle with the first, across the Potomac ten miles, for the second line; thence from the termination of said first and second lines, running two other lines of ten miles each, the one crossing the Eastern Branch aforesaid and the other the Potomac, and meeting each other in a point.

And I do accordingly direct the Commissioners named under the authority of the said first mentioned ac of Congress to proceed forthwith to have the said four lines run, and by proper metes and bounds defined and limited, and thereof to make due report, under their hands and seals; and the territory so to be located, defined, and limited shall be the whole territory accepted by the said act of Congress as the district for the permanent seat of the Government of the United States.

In testimony whereof I have caused the seal of the United States to be affixed to these presents, and signed the same with my own hand. Done at Georgetown aforesaid the 30th day of March, in the year of our Lord 1791, and of the independence of the United States the fifteenth.

[seal]

(signed) GEORGE WASHINGTON.
By the President:
Thomas Jefferson

After issuing the foregoing proclamation George Washington proceeded to make a brief visit to his own home, from where he wrote the following letters to the Commissioners:

MOUNT VERNON, *April 3, 1791*
GENTLEMEN: *As the instrument[5] which was subscribed at Georgetown by the landholders in the vicinity of that place and Carrollsburg was not given to me I presume it has been deposited with you. It is of the greatest moment to close the business with the proprietors of the lands on which the Federal city is to be, that consequent arrangements may be made without more delay than can be avoided.*

The form of the conveyances, as drawn by the Attorney-General, will, I presume, require alterations or a counterpart, as the present agreement essentially differs from the former. If Mr. Johnson could, conveniently, undertake to prepare such a deed as he thinks would answer all the purposes of the public and grantors, I am sure it would answer all the purposes of the public and grantors, I am sure it would be effectually done. If this cannot be, then it might be well to furnish the Attorney-General of the U.S. with a copy of the agreement, with papers I left with you, and such other information as will enable him to do it.

To accomplish this matter so as that the sales of the lots, the public buildings, etc., may commence with as much facility as the nature of the case may admit, would be, I conceive, advisable under any circumstances. Perhaps the friends of the measure may think it materially so from the following extract of a letter from Mr. Jefferson to me, dated 27th ult: "A bill was yesterday ordered to be brought into House of Representatives here for granting a sum of money for building a Federal hall, house for the President, &c." This (though I do not want any sentiment of mine promulgated with respect to it) marks unequivocally, in my mind, the designs of that State, and the necessity of execution to convey the residence law into effect agreeably thereto. Yours, &c.

G°. WASHINGTON.
THOS. JOHNSON, D. STUART, D. CARROLL, *Esqs.*

---

[5] See the agreement of 19 property-holders, March 30, 1791.

EVENTS LEADING TO THE FOUNDATION OF WASHINGTON CITY

The President a few days after proceeded to Richmond, Virginia, for the purpose of consulting with Governor Randolph whether the payment of the $120,000 appropriated by the legislature of that State towards the erection of public buildings could not be anticipated for urgent emergencies, and the Governor consented to advance the money earlier than was originally intended, of which result President Washington notified the Commissioners.

The Commissioners held their first official meeting in Georgetown, April 12, 1791, and on the 15th day of the same was the corner-stone of the lines of the Federal territory laid in their presence and with great solemnity, a large number of persons, especially from Alexandria, being present.

It will be noticed that in the foregoing pages the laying out of the National Capital as a city has only been alluded to in the President's letter dated April 3, and that he calls it on that occasion, "the Federal City." The next more definite allusion to its foundation is found in the following letter from his pen, in which he gives some direction:

ON THE CITY BOUNDARIES AND NAME
CHARLESTON, May 7, 1791

GENTLEMEN: I have received your letter of the 14th of last month. It is an unfortunate circumstance, in the present stage of the business relative to the Federal City, that difficulties unforseen and unexpected should arise to darken, perhaps to destroy, the fair prospect which it presented when I left Georgetown, and which the instrument then signed by the combined interest (as it was termed) of Georgetown and Carrollsburg so plainly describes. The pain which this occurrence occasions me is the more sensibly felt, as I had taken pleasure during my journey through the several States to relate the agreement, and to speak of it on every occasion in terms which applauded the conduct of the parties, as being alike conducive to the public welfare and to the interest of individuals, which last it was generally thought would be most benefitted by the amazing increase of the property reserved to the landholders.

The words cited by Messrs. Young, [Peter], Lingan and [Forrest], and Stoddert may be nearly what I expressed; but will these gentlemen say this was given as the precise boundary, or will they, by detaching these words, taken them in a sense unconnected with the general explanation of my ideas and views upon that occasion, or without the qualifications which, I am much mistaken, were added of running about so and so, for I had no map before me for direction! Will they not recollect my observation that Philadelphia stood upon an area of three by two miles, and that if the metropolis of *one State* occupied so much ground, what ought that of the United States occupy! Did I not, moreover, observe that before the city could be laid out, and the spot for the public buildings be precisely fixed on, the water-courses were to be leveled, the heights taken, &c. &c.!

Let the whole of my declaration be taken together and not apart only, and being compared with the instrument then subscribed, together with some other circumstances which might be alluded to, let any impartial man judge whether I had reason to expect that difficulties would arise in the conveyances.

When the instrument was presented I found no occasion to add a word with respect to boundary, because the whole was surrendered upon the conditions which were expressed. Had I discovered a disposition in the subscribers to contract my views, I should then have pointed out the inconveniencies and the impolicy of the measure. Upon the whole, I shall hope and expect that the business will be suffered to proceed, and the more so as they cannot be ignorant that the further consideration of a certain measure in a neighboring State stands postponed, for what reason is left to their own information and conjecture.

I expect to be with you at the time appointed, and should be exceedingly glad to find all difficulties removed. I am, with great esteem, gentlemen, your most obedient servant,

G°· WASHINGTON.

JOHNSON, STUART, AND CARROLL.

On the 29th day of June 1791, following a final settlement with the property-holders was realized, all having by this time declared their willingness to join in the amicable arrangement proposed in the terms of the agreement executed on March 30, except one, viz. Mrs. Elizabeth Wheeler, who, being *non pompos mentis* on account of insanity, was however, provided with proper guardians for her interests, and Thomas Beall of George, and John M. Gantt, both of Maryland, or their heirs, were chosen with universal approbation as trustees to whom the lands ceded to the General Government by the State of Maryland were conveyed in trust for the United States, and this arrangement, as well as the original cession of the land, through the Representatives authorized thereto by the act of Dec. 23, 1788, was subsequently (Dec. 19, 1791) ratified by an act of the Legislative Assembly of Maryland. In this trust the streets, squares, parcel, and lots proposed to be laid out for the United States were to be conveyed by these trustees to the United States; the residue of the land was to be divided equally. For their share, or half, the United States were to pay £25, or $66.66, an acre, the streets and squares designed for public purposes, however, to be free. The property-holders were allowed the occupancy of their land till required for public use, and other stipulations were made respecting the sale of lands and the payment of sums due the proprietors, and other matters.

Major L'Enfant was entrusted to prepare plans for the laying out of the city into streets, avenues, squares, lots, etc., and the President, in August 1791, approved his plan as submitted without any serious alterations, and the plan was carried out under the direction of Mr. Andrew Ellicott, who, without delay, formed the basis of execution for the entire plan by establishing the "meridian line" through the site selected for the erection of the Capitol.

At the next meeting of the Commissioners some regulations were established in regard to the erection of private buildings, and the present names of this District and city were adopted, which was communicated to Major L'Enfant in the following letter:

GEORGETOWN, Sept. 9, 1791

SIR: We have agreed that the Federal district shall be called the *Territory of Columbia* and the Federal city the *City of Washington*. The title of the map will, therefore, be, 'A MAP OF THE CITY OF WASHINGTON, IN THE TERRITORY OF COLUMBIA.'

We have also agreed the streets to be named alphabetically one way and numerically the other, the former divided into north and south letters, the latter into east and west numbers, from the Capitol. Major Ellicott, with proper assistance, will immediately take and soon furnish you with soundings of the Eastern Branch, to be inserted in the map. We expect he will also furnish you with the direction of the post road, which we wish to have noticed on the map.

We are, sir, etc., THOS. JOHNSON
DAV. STUART
DAN. CARROLL

The Commissioners had at this time advanced in their preliminary labors to such an extent that they could proceed to the sale of lots, but before relating their first steps in this direction a very brief review of the chief merits and demerits of the original framework of our city will be appropriate, as they appear in the future development of her destiny as the most powerful factors of propitious and adverse events.

The main defect of that plan was that notwithstanding the direct advice of George Washington, little attention was paid in its formation to the courses of natural drainage. All waters falling upon the vast surface of the city had their discharge either in the Eastern Branch, Tiber and James Creeks, or into the Rock Creek and Potomac river, through low passages, hollows, and small valleys or ravines, which ought to have received the gravest consideration in the laying out of the avenues, streets, and squares. But they are not properly regarded, and the rectilinear streets and avenues as well as the rectangular squares had little or no reference to the natural surface, and with the only view to the sites of the public buildings, they were mostly adapted to artificial objects. Hence, deplorable differences in elevation, amounting in some cases to 40 feet and more, could be found within the briefest distances, and thereby the value of entire sections was depreciated, their settlement retarded, and enormous expenses were caused in subsequent efforts of grading and draining, which, a least in part, might have been obviated. This defect was also the main cause why the western part of the city, now the most beautiful and most improved, was for many years the object of neglect, contempt, and merriment over magnificent distances in mire and desolation.

Yet these very proverbial magnificent distances are the chief merit of the original plan, and have secured to Washington capacities of development by far superior to those of any city in the world, as have become apparent by the progress of recent improvements, and these capacities will soon be the object of admiration and envy to her most famous sister cities.

This brief digression was mainly introduced here in partial explanation of the great divergencies in prices realized for lots in the very first sale, which differences have continued in many cases up to recent dates without any cause for such inequality which might not have been obviated.

It must be remembered that in the division of property between the original land-owners and the Government, as provided for in the terms of the foregoing agreement, 10,136 lots were the share of the said Government, in addition to such sites as were designated for public buildings and other public purposes. These lots were in the hands of the Commissioners; and for the purpose of raising funds to defray the expenses of erecting buildings and other public structures, for which the appropriations of the States of Virginia and Maryland were neither sufficient nor even available at the time, Congress authorized them to sell at public auction from time to time such as may be deemed desirable. The first public auction of this kind took place at Georgetown, October 17, 1791. A large number of purchasers convened on the occasion from all sections of the country, but only thirty-one lots were sold at prices ranging from £10 to £115, Maryland currency, or $266.66 to $306.50 per lot, as appears from the following report of the Commissioners to the President and other records:

From the Commissioners to the President
Oct. 21, 1791

SIR: The number 3, in square 107, at £80; No. 8, in square 87, at 55; No. 15, in square 105, at 92, and No. 16, in the same square, at £76, fall again to the public. Those bids were to protect its interest, so that sales are of thirty-one lots, averaging £97 7s. 9d. To accommodate some strangers, we were obliged, after the payment of the ¼ deposit, to agree that the land should stand as security, subject to the forfeiture of the deposits if the payments are not made. The gentlemen in town have come to a resolution not to be security—perhaps it was almost necessary—and it has happened that the purchasers had no acquaintances of whom they could desire such a favor. It makes it worth consideration whether in future the terms ought not to be varied. Since our sale there has been a few private sales, which we believe will not injure the public. Opportunities we expect will present for the Commissioners to dispose of lots at private sale. We shall do so unless you perceive any impropriety in it. We have consulted Maj. L'Enfant and Maj. Ellicott as to the time against which things will be in readiness for another sale. They expect it may be by the middle or last of June, though we wish it may be earlier, because of the ideas strangers have against coming to the southward so late as July. Yet it is our present intention not to publish a further sale till we see that the [map] plate is in circulation and the work so far complete that everybody may have a chance for the object of their choice, and in no way have cause of complain that the whole circumstances are not fully before them. We have been under some difficulties from the imperfect state furnished, which has subsided; but we wish to avoid the like in future. From several intimation we considered the business as resting more on us than heretofore. This is an additional motive for us to wish a clear understanding of the terms on which Maj. L'Enfant renders his assistance. We therefore requested him today to mention to us the sum by the year, including the time past, which would be satisfactory for his services, or, if it was not his choice, though not so agreeable to us, we would propose the sum we intended—six hundred pounds; but Maj. L'Enfant desired to be excused from entering on the subject to the present. We requested him to prepare a draft of the public buildings for your inspection, and he has promised to enter on it as soon as he finds himself disengaged. He can have recourse to books in Philadelphia, and cannot have that assistance here. We cannot expect much of your time, nor wish to encroach upon it. Yet we cannot but request you will take occasion to impress Maj. L'Enfant with the necessity of being explicit on the subject of consideration. We shall feel ourselves happy in your advice at any time you may be pleased to communicate it to

     THOS. JOHNSON
     D. STUART
     D. CARROLL

The conditions of sale mentioned in the foregoing report are the only ones which could be obtained from any of the records within the reach of the compilers.

With this sale, as might be expected, the attention of the public in all parts of the country was directed to the immediate building of the city, and so many persons rushed to the site with various plans and schemes that regulations were required for the manner of building, which the President supplied on October 17, 1791, in the following directions:

Terms and conditions declared by the President of the United States, this seventeenth day of October 1791, for regulating the materials and manner of the buildings and improvements on the lots in the city of Washington.

1. That the outer and party-wall of all houses within the said city shall be built of brick or stone.

2. That all buildings on the streets shall be parallel thereto, and may be advanced to the line of the street, or withdrawn therefrom at the pleasure of the improver; but where any such building is about to be erected, neither the foundation or party-wall shall be begun without first applying to the person or persons appointed by the Commissioners to superintend the buildings within the city, who will ascertain the lines of the walls to correspond with these regulations.

3. The wall of no house to be higher than forty feet to the roof in any part of the city, nor shall any be lower than thirty-five feet on any of the avenues.

4. That the person or persons appointed by the Commissioners to superintend the buildings may enter upon the land of any person to set out the foundation and regulate the walls to be built between party and party, as to the breadth and thickness thereof; which foundation hall be laid equally upon the lands of the persons between whom such party-walls are to be built, and shall be of the breadth and thickness determined by such person proper; and the first builder shall be reimbursed one moiety of the charge of such party-wall, or so much thereof as the next builder shall have occasion to make use of, before such next builder shall any ways use or break into the wall. The charge or value thereof to be set by the person and persons so appointed by the Commissioners.

5. As temporary conveniences will be proper for lodging workmen and securing materials for building, it is to be understood that such may be erected, with the approbation of the Commissioners, but they may be removed or discontinued by the special order of the Commissioners.

6. The way into the squares being designed in a special manner for the common use or convenience of the occupiers of the respective squares, the property in the same is reserved in the public, so that there may be an immediate interference on any abuse of the use thereof by any individual to the nuisance or obstruction of others. The proprietors of lots adjoining the entrance into the squares, on arching over the entrance and fixing gates in the manner the Commissioners shall approve, shall be entitled to divide the space over the arching, and build it up with the range of that line of the square.

7. No vaults shall be permitted under the streets, nor any encroachment of the footway above by steps, stoops, porches, cellar-doors, windows, ditches, or leaning walls; not shall there be any projects over the street, other than the eaves of the house, without the consent of the Commissioners.

8. These regulations are the terms and conditions under and upon which conveyances are to be made, according to the deeds in trust of the lands within the city.

GEORGE WASHINGTON

These building regulations were at subsequent periods greatly modified, but they are here inserted because they exercised great influence over the sale of lots, in as far as every purchaser was required to comply with them if he desired to improve his new property, and hence they rather delayed than fostered rapid sales, as may be inferred from the next following letter from George Washington's pen, viz:

President Washington to Commissioners
PHILADELPHIA, Nov. 13, 1792

GENTLEMEN: I have received your letter of the 13th October, enclosing a list of the sale of lots in the Federal city, with the prices of which I am more gratified than with the number which have been disposed of. I am pleased to find that several of your mechanics were among the purchasers of lots, as they will not only, in all probability, be among the first improvers of them, but will be valuable citizens.

I agree with you in common that the ground in such eligible places as about the Capitol and the President's House should not be sold in squares, unless there are to be some great and apparent advantages to be derived from specified buildings, immediate improvements, or something which will have a tendency to promote the advancement of the city. The circumstances under which Mr. [Blodget] bid off the square [blank] near the Capitol were such as occur at almost every public sale, and, in that instance, his having done so appeared very proper for the interest of the public. I agree, however, with you, that it would be best for the circumstance not to be generally known. How far the idea which Mr. Blodget suggests of having an agent to pass through the several States to dispose of lots might be beneficial or not I am unable to say; but it appears to me that if a respectable character, in the principal tow of each State, could be authorized to dispose of the public lots, as purchasers might appear, provided the matters could be so arranged that no confusion or inconvenience should arise from the same lot being disposed of by two or more agents (which might possibly be done by monthly returns being made from the several agents to the Commissioners, ascertaining the day, and even hour of each sale, to be by them confirmed previous to any payment; a small *per centum* to be allowed the vendor, and all private sale to cease a month before any public sale), it would be the means of accommodating persons in different parts of the Union, and would expedite the sale of the lots.

But this, as well as Mr. Blodget's suggestion (which rather appears to me to be hawking the lots about), must be weighed ad determined upon according to your best judgment and information. I think that a further public sale in the spring or early in the summer would be advantageous. For it is desirable that every opportunity which could be made convenient on account of the season and other circumstances, to dispose of lots in this way, should be embraced.

In proportion as numbers become interested in the Federal city, and the public works advance, a constant attendance at the spot will be more and more requisite on the part of those who superintend or direct the business thereof; and I am of opinion, as neither of the Commissioners reside there, that some active and competent character, vested with proper authority by them, should be constantly on the ground to superintend the business carrying on there. But who this person shall be is altogether with yourselves to chuse, and the various and essential qualifications requisite in him will readily occur to you.

With great esteem, etc.
GEO. WASHINGTON

From the foregoing document it is manifest that the Father of our Country, after whom the National Capital is named, devoted a great deal of his energy to remove impediments which might retard its speedy progress as a city. Yet, notwithstanding his efforts, there were still some legislative measures required to establish all property relations within he precincts on a firm footing, and to authorize the issue of clear and indisputable titles to property-holders therein, namely: Maryland, having ceded her part of the territory only by proxy, had to consummate such cession by ratification and by fixing positive metes and bounds of the ceded territory; and the agreement of the property-holders with the Commissioners needed legislative authorization or sanction, inasmuch as said property-holders still were citizens of Maryland, and as such subject to her laws. All this was accomplished in the following acts of legislature of Maryland, to wit:

AN ACT concerning the Territory of Columbia and the city of Washington. Passed December 19, 1791.

Whereas the President of the United States, by virtue of several acts of Congress and acts of the assemblies of Virginia and Maryland, by his proclamation dated at Georgetown, on the 30th day of March 1791, did declare and make known that the whole of the territory of ten miles square for the permanent seat of government of the United States shall be located and included within the four lines following, that is to say, beginning at Jones's Point, being the upper point of Hunting Creek, in Virginia, at an angle in the outset of forty-five degrees west of the north, and running a direct line of ten miles for the first line; then beginning again at the same Jones's Point, and running another direct line at a right angle with the first across the Patowmack, ten miles for the second line; then from the terminations of te said first and second lines, running two other direct lines ten miles each, the one crossing the Eastern Branch and the other Patowmack, and meeting each other in a point which has since been called the Territory of Columbia.

And whereas Notley Young, Daniel Carroll of Duddington, and many others, proprietors of the greater part of the land hereinafter mentioned to have been laid out in a city, came into an agreement, and have conveyed their lands in trust to Thomas Beall, son of George, and John Mackall Gantt, whereby they have subjected their lands to be laid out as a city, given up part to the United States, and subjected other part to be sold to raise money as a donation to be employed according to the act of Congress for establishing the temporary and permanent seat of the Government of the United States under and upon the terms and conditions contained in each of the said deeds; and many of the proprietors of lots in Carrollsburg and Hamburgh have also come into an agreement, subjecting their lots to be laid out anew, giving up one-half of the quantity thereof to be sold, and the money thence arising to be applied as a donation as aforesaid, and they to be reinstated in one-half the quantity of their lots in the new location, or otherwise compensated in land in a different situation within the city, by agreement between the Commissioners and them, and in case of disagreement that then a just and full compensation shall be made in money. Yet some of the proprietors of lots in Carrollsburg and Hamburgh, as well as some of the proprietors of other lands, have not, from imbecility and other causes, come into any agreement concerning their lands within the limits hereinafter mentioned, but a very great proportion of the landholders having agreed on the same terms, the President of the United States directed a city to be laid out, comprehending all the lands, beginning on the east side of Rock Creek, at a stone standing in the middle of the road leading from Georgetown to Bladensburg; thence along the middle of said road to a stone standing on the east side of the Reedy Branch of Goose Creek; thence southeasterly, making an angle of sixty-one degrees and twenty minutes with the meridian, to a stone standing in the road leading from Bladensburg to the Eastern Branch ferry; then south to a stone eighty poles north of the east and west line already drawn from the mouth of Goose Creek to the Eastern Branch; then east, parallel to the said east and west line, to the Eastern Branch; then with the waters of the Eastern Branch, Patowmack river, and Rock Creek to the beginning, which hath since been called the city of Washington;

And whereas it appears to this general assembly highly just and expedient that all the lands within the said city should contribute, in due proportion, in the means which have already very greatly enhanced the value of the whole; that an incontrovertible title ought to be made to the purchasers, under public sanction; that allowing foreigners to hold land within the said territory will greatly contribute to the improvement and population thereof, and that many temporary provisions will be necessary till Congress exercise the jurisdiction and government over the said territory;

And whereas, in the cession of this State, heretofore made, of territory for the Government of the United States, the lines of cession could not be particularly designated, and it being expedient and proper that the same should be recognized in the acts of this State:

2. That all that part of said territory, called Columbia, which lies within the limits of this State, shall be, and the same is hereby, acknowledged to be forever ceded and relinquished to the Congress and Government of the United States, in full and absolute right and exclusive jurisdiction, as well of soil as of persons residing or to reside thereon, pursuant to the tenor and effect of the eighth section of the first article of the Constitution of government of the United States: *Provided*, That nothing herein contained shall be so construed to vest in the United States any right of property in the soil so as to affect the rights of individuals therein otherwise than the same shall or may be transferred by such individuals to the United States: *And provided also*, That the jurisdiction of the laws of this State over the persons and property of individuals residing within the limits of the cession aforesaid shall not cease or determine until Congress shall by law provide for the government thereof, under their jurisdiction, in manner provided by the article of the Constitution before recited.

3. That all the lands belonging to minors, persons absent out of the State, married women, or persons *non compos mentis*, or lands the property of the State, within the limits of Carrollsburg and Hamburgh, shall be, and are hereby, subjected to the terms and conditions hereinbefore recited as to the lots where the proprietors thereof have agreed concerning the same; and all the other lands belonging as aforesaid within the limits of the said city of Washington shall be, and are hereby, subjected to the same terms and conditions as the said Notley Young, Daniel Carroll of Duddington, and others, have, by their said agreements and deeds, subjected their lands to, and where no conveyances have been made the legal estate and trust are hereby invested in the said Thomas Beall, son of George, and John Mackall Gantt, in the same manner as if each proprietor had been competent to make, and had made, a legal conveyance of his or her land, according to the form of those already mentioned, with proper acknowledgments to the execution thereof, and, where necessary, of release of dower; and in every case where the proprietor is an infant, a married woman, insane, absent out of the State, or shall not attend on three months'

advertisement in the *Maryland Journal and Baltimore Advertiser*, the *Maryland Herald*, and in the Georgetown and Alexandria papers, so that allotment cannot take place by agreement, the Commissioners aforesaid, or any two of them, may allot and assign the portion or share of such proprietor, as near the old situation as may be, in Carrollsburg or Hamburgh, and to the full value of what the party might claim under the terms before recited; and as to the other lands within the said city, the Commissioners aforesaid, or any two of them, shall make such allotment and assignments within the lands belonging to the same person, in alternate lots, determining by lot or ballot whether the party shall begin with the lowest number: *Provided*, That in case of coverture and infancy, if the husband, guardian, or next friend will agree with the Commissioners, or any two of them, then an effectual division may be made by them by consent; and in case of contrary claims, if the claimants will not jointly agree, the Commissioners may proceed as if the proprietor was absent; and all persons to whom allotments and assignments of lands shall be made by the Commissioners, or any two of them, on consent or agreement, or pursuant to this act without consent, shall hold the same in their former estate and interest, and in lieu of their former quantity, and subject in every respect to all such limitations, conditions, and incumbrances as their former estate and interest were subject to, and as if the same had been actually reconveyed, pursuant to the said deed, in trust.

4. That where the proprietor or proprietors, possessor or possessors, of any lands within the limits of the city of Washington, or within the limits of Carrollsburg or Hamburgh, who have not already, or who shall not within three months after the passage of this act, execute deeds in trust to the aforesaid Thomas Beall and John M. Gantt of all their lands within the limits of the said city of Washington, and on the terms and conditions mentioned in the deeds already executed by Notley Young and others, and execute deeds in trust to the said Thomas Beall and John M. Gantt of all their lots in the towns of Carrollsburg and Hamburgh, on the same terms and conditions contained in the deeds already executed by the greater part of the proprietors of lots in the said towns, the said Commissioners, or any two of them, hall and may, at any time or times thereafter, issue a process directed to the sheriff of Prince George's county, commanding him in the manner of the State to summon five good, substantial freeholders, who are not of kin to any proprietor o proprietors of the lands aforesaid, and who are not proprietors themselves, to meet on a certain day and at a certain place within the limits of said city, to inquire of the value of the estate of such proprietor or proprietors, possessor or possessors, on which day and place the said sheriff shall attend, with the freeholders by him summoned, which freeholders shall take the following oath or affirmation on the land to be by them valued, to wit: "I, A.B., do solemnly swear (or affirm) that I will, to the best of my judgment, value the lands of C.D., now to be valued, so as to do equal right and justice to the said C.D. and to the public, taking into consideration all circumstances," and shall then proceed to value the said lands; and such valuation, under their hands and seals and under the hand and seal of the said sheriff, shall be annexed to the said process and returned by the sheriff to the clerk appointed by virtue of this act, who shall make record of the same, and the said lands shall, on the payment of such valuation, be, and is hereby, vested in the said Commissioners in trust, to be disposed of by them, or otherwise employed to the use of the said city of Washington; and the sheriff aforesaid, and freeholders aforesaid, shall be allowed the same fees for their trouble as are allowed to a sheriff and jurymen in executing a writ of inquiry; and in all cases where the proprietor or possessor is tenant in right of dower, or by the courtesy, the freeholders aforesaid shall ascertain the annual value of the lands and the gross value of such estate therein, and upon paying such gross value, or securing to the possessor the payment of the annual valuation, at the option of the proprietor or possessor, the Commissioners shall be, and are hereby, vested with the whole estate of such tenant, in manner and for the uses and purposes aforesaid.

5. That all the squares, lots, pieces, and parcels of land within the said city, which have been or shall be appropriated for the use of the United States, and all the lots and parcels which have been or shall be sold to raise money as a donation as aforesaid shall remain and be to the purchasers according to the terms and conditions of their respective purchase; and purchases and leases from private persons claiming to be proprietors, and having, or those under whom they claim having, been in possession of the lands purchased or leased in their own right five whole years next before the passing of this act, shall be good and effectual for the estate, and on the terms and conditions of such purchases and leases, respectively, without impeachment and against any contrary title now existing; but if any person hath made a conveyance, or shall make a conveyance or lease, or any lands within the limits of the said city not having a right and title to do so, the person who might be entitled to recover the land under a contrary title now existing may, either by way of ejectment against the tenant or in an action for money had and received for his use against the bargainer or lessor, his heirs, executors, administrators, or devisees, as the case may require, recover all money received by him for the squares, pieces, or parcels sold and rents received by the person not having title as aforesaid, with interest from the time of the receipt, and on such recovery in ejectment when the land is in lease the tenant shall thereafter hold under and

pay the rent reserved to the person making title to and recovering the land, but the possession *bona fide* acquired in none of the said cases shall be changed.

6. That any foreigner may, by deed or will, hereafter to be made, take and hold lands within that part of the said territory which lies within this State, in the same manner as if he was a citizen of this State, and the same lands may be conveyed by him, and transmitted to and inherited by his heirs or relations, as if he and they were citizens: *Provided*, That no foreigner shall, in virtue hereof, be entitled to any further or other privilege as a citizen.

7. That the said Commissioners, or any two of them, may appoint a clerk for recording deeds of lands within the said territory, who shall provide a proper book for the purpose, and therein record, in a strong, legible hand, all deeds duly acknowledged of lands in the said territory delivered to him to be recorded, and in the same book make due entries of all divisions and allotments of lands and lots made by the Commissioners in pursuance of this act, and certificates granted by them of sales, and the purchase money having been paid, with a proper alphabet in the same book of the deeds and entries aforesaid, and the same book shall carefully preserve and deliver over to the Commissioners aforesaid, or their successors, of such person or persons as Congress shall hereafter appoint, which clerk shall continue such during good behavior, and shall be removable only on conviction of misbehavior in a court of law; but before he acts as such he shall take an oath or affirmation well and truly to execute his office, and he shall be entitled to the same fees as are or may be allowed to the clerks of the county courts for searches, copying, and recording.

[The above section has been superseded by laws of Congress establishing courts, and afterwards by establishing the office of register of deeds.]

8. That acknowledgments of deeds made before a person in the manner and certified as the laws of this State direct, or made before and certified by either of the Commissioners, shall be effectual, and that no deed hereafter to be made of or for lands within that part of the said territory which lies within this State shall operate as a legal conveyance, nor shall any lease for more than seven years be effectual, unless the deed shall have been acknowledged as aforesaid, and delivered to the said clerk to be recorded within six calendar months from the date thereof.

9. That the Commissioners aforesaid, or some two of them, shall direct an entry to be made in the said record book of every allotment and assignment to the respective proprietors in pursuance of this act.

10. And for the encouragement of master-builders to undertake the building and finishing houses within the said city, by securing to them a just and effectual remedy for their advance and earnings: *Be it enacted*, That for all sums due and owing, on written contracts, for the building any house in the said city, or the brick-work, or carpenters' or joiners' work thereon, the undertaker or workman employed by the person for whose use the house shall be built shall have a lien on the house and the ground on which the same is erected, as well as for the materials found by him: *Provided*, The said written contract shall have been acknowledged before one of the Commissioners, a justice of the peace, or an alderman of the corporation of Georgetown, and recorded in the office of the clerk for recording deeds herein created, within six calendar months from the time of acknowledgment as aforesaid; and if, within two years after the last work is done, he proceeds in equity, he shall have remedy as upon a mortgage, or if he proceeds at law within the same time, he may have execution against the house and land, in whose hands soever the same may be; but this remedy shall be considered as additional only nor shall, as to the land, take place of any legal incumbrance made prior to the commencement of such claim.

[The foregoing section has been superseded by acts of Congress. See act of Feb. 2, 1859, Statutes at Large, vol. 2, p. 376.]

11. That the treasurer of the western shore be empowered and required to pay the seventy-two thousand dollars agreed to be advanced to the President by resolutions of the last session of assembly, in sums as the same may come to his hands, on the appointed funds, without waiting for the day appointed for the payment thereof.

12. That the Commissioners aforesaid, for the time being, or any two of them, shall from time to time, until Congress shall exercise the jurisdiction and government within the said territory, have power to license the building of wharves in the waters of Patowmac and the Eastern Branch, adjoining the said city on the materials, in the manner, and of the extent they may judge durable, convenient, and agreeing with general order; but no license shall be granted to one to build a wharf before the land of another, nor shall any wharf be built in the said waters without license, as aforesaid; and if any wharf shall be built without such license, or different therefrom, the same is hereby declared a common nuisance. The may also from time to time make regulations for the discharge and laying of ballast from ships or vessels lying in Patowmack river above the lower line of the said territory and Georgetown, and from ships and vessels lying in the Eastern Branch. They may also from time to time make regulations for landing and laying materials for building the said city, for disposing and laying earth which may be dug out of the wells, cellars, and foundations, and for ascertaining the thickness of the

walls of houses, and to enforce the observance of all such regulations by appointing penalties for the breach of any one of them, not exceeding ten pounds current money, which may be recovered in the name of said Commissioners by warrant before a justice of the peace, as in case of small debts, and disposed of as a donation for the purposes of the said act of Congress, and the said Commissioners, or any two of them, may grant licenses for retailing distilled spirits within the limits of the said city, and suspend to declare the same void; and if any person shall retail or sell any distilled spirits, mixed or unmixed, in less quantities than ten gallons to the same person, or at the same time actually delivered, he or she shall forfeit for every such sale three pounds, to be recovered and applied as aforesaid.

[The foregoing section has ceased to be operative by lapse of time and by reason of the United States Government having taken charge of the District.]

That an act of assembly of this State, to condemn lands, if necessary for the public buildings of the United States, be, and is hereby, repealed.

December 22d 1792
A SUPPLEMENT to the act entitled "An act concerning the territory of Columbia and the city of Washington."
Where doubts have arisen upon the act to which this is a supplement, whether it be essential to the validity of deeds and other conveyances of lands in that part of the territory of Columbia which lies within that State, that the same be recorded in the manner prescribed by the laws of this State before the passage of the said act; to remove which doubts

Be it enacted, That all deeds and other conveyances of lands lying within the said territory, and recorded agreeably to the directions and provisions of the said act by the clerk appointed in the manner therein provided for the recording of deeds within the said territory, shall be as good, valid, and sufficient in law for the purposes of passing the estates therein mentioned, and for all other purposes, as if the same were also recorded in the manner prescribed by the laws of this State before the passage of the said act for the recording of deeds and other conveyances of land within this State.

December 28, 1793
A FURTHER SUPPLEMENT to the act concerning the territory of Columbia and the city of Washington.
1. That the certificates granted, or which may be granted, by the said Commissioners, or any two of them, to purchasers of lots in the said city, with the acknowledgment of the payment of the whole purchase-money, and interest, if any shall have arisen hereon, and recorded agreeably to te directions of the act concerning the territory of Columbia and city of Washington, shall be sufficient and effectual to vest the legal estate in the purchasers, their heirs and assigns, according to the import of such certificates, without any deed or formal conveyance.

2. That on sales of lots in the said city by the said Commissioners, or any two of them, under terms or conditions of payment being made therefor at any day or days after such contract entered into, if any sum of the purchase money or interest shall not be paid for the space of thirty days after the same ought to be paid, the Commissioners, or any two of them, may sell the same lots at public vendue, in the city of Washington, at any time after sixty days' notice of such sale in some of the public newspapers of Georgetown and Baltimore town, and retain in their hands sufficient of the money produced by such new sale to satisfy all principal and interest due on the first contract, together with the expenses of advertisements and sale, and the original purchaser, or his assigns, shall be entitled to receive from the said Commissioners, at their treasury, on demand, the balance of the money which may have been actually received by them, or under their order, at the said second sale; and all lots so sold shall be freed and acquitted of all claim, legal and equitable, of the first purchaser, his heirs and assigns.

3. That the Commissioners aforesaid, or any two of them, may appoint a certain day for the allotment and assignment of one-half of the quantity of each lot of ground in Carrollsburg and Hamburgh, not before that time divided or assigned, pursuant to said act concerning the territory of Columbia and the city of Washington; and on notice thereof in the Annapolis, some one of the Baltimore, the Easton and Georgetown newspapers, for at least three weeks, the same Commissioners may proceed to the allotment and assignment of ground within the said city on the day appointed for that purpose, and therein proceed at convenient times till the whole be finished, as if the proprietors of such lots actually resided out of this State: *Provided*, That if the proprietor of any such lot shall object in person, or by writing delivered to the Commissioners, against their so proceeding as to his lot, before they shall have made an assignment of ground for the same, then they shall forbear as to such lot, and may proceed according to the before-mentioned act.

4. That the Commissioners may make a seal of office of the clerk for recording deeds within the District of Columbia, which shall be kept by him, and that the like fees shall be paid for, and the like credit be given to, certificates under that seal s to the like acts under the seal of a county court; and the said clerk shall be entitled to demand and receive his fees when the services enjoined him by this act and the act to which this is a further supplement shall be performed.

The foregoing two acts of the Maryland legislature, although one or two years subsequent to

EVENTS LEADING TO THE FOUNDATION OF WASHINGTON CITY 17

the time to which this narrative of events had advanced, were inserted here because they are supplementary, and hence full of references to the one passed in November 1791; and for the purpose of rendering a chronological account of the development of the new capital it is necessary to return to the close of that year or the beginning of that time.

The proceedings of the Commissioners at that time are still existing in manuscript, and show how busily they were engaged in pursuance of their duties. A large correspondence was carried on by them; bids were invited, and proposals received; contracts were awarded for building materials and other necessary supplies, and every effort was made for an auspicious commencement of operations with public buildings at the very earliest opening of spring, and every encouragement was given for the speedy erection of private residences and business establishments.

Many letters and communications, still existing among the records of that time, are very interesting, yet, being too numerous and lengthy, are not embraced in these pages, which are exclusively devoted to matters directly bearing upon the then established relations of property. Hence, only the objects of such communications are here briefly mentioned, and among them there is some attention due to the letter of Thomas Jefferson to the Commissioners, dated Philadelphia, November 21, 1791, submitting to them the scheme of Samuel Blodget in regard to the building of a entire street. The Commissioners granted the permission requested by him, but the plan failed entirely for want of adequate means. The same speculator, however, after raising some funds by means of a lottery enterprise, succeeded in the partial erection of a large hotel, still he could not complete even this structure, and it remained unfinished, until, some years after, when general government purchased and modified it for the purposes of the Patent and Post Offices.

Many other persons rushed to the new city during the spring and summer of 1792, with various projects and enterprises, but in most cases were unsuccessful, among which there was Lee's proposition for the erection of an equestrian statue as a national monument, also communicated to the Commissioners by Thomas Jefferson on April 9, 1792.

Another letter to them, written by President Washington, January 8, introduced to their notice Mr. James Hoban, the subsequent architect of the President's House and a part of the Capitol, and the Commissioners answered this letter by reporting their contract with the said Mr. Hoban on July 19, 1792.

There are several anecdotes and incidents related of that busy year, and of the characters then prominent, but the serious scope of this work forbids the introduction of irrelevant matters, and hence it must suffice to mention that streets were opened, corner-stones laid, and improvements commenced, the second of which belongs to the period when they were completed.

No legislative measure was enacted involving any interest of the new district or city, excepting the first act of the State of Maryland, supplementary to he ratification act of the cession, and an order passed by that State for the payment of $72,000 previously donated in connection with said cession.

The next few years were all more or less similar in events and incidents; scarcity of funds, and other difficulties and embarrassments on the part of the Commissioners, yet energetic activity in all parts of the New Capital, without any great results except in preparation of future successes.

Among the experiments of some magnitude in 1793, the contract of the Commissioners with Robert Morris, James Greenleaf, and John Nicholson may be noticed, for the sale of 6,000 city lots, at $80.00 per lot, in seven annual instalments without interest, upon the condition that the purchaser should erect in each of the six succeeding years twenty brick houses, but the said parties utterly failed to comply with any part of the contract, and the Commissioners found themselves very seriously embarrassed by this failure. In addition to this purchase, James Greenleaf purchase from Uriah Forrest and Benjamin Stoddert, September 20, 1794, all of the Widow's Mite—containing 207,993 feet, and on May 13th 1796, Greenleaf conveyed this property to Morris and Nicholson.

Among the correspondence of the Commissioners during that year there are three letters of the President to them of great interest, namely, the first and second, both dated March 3, treat upon the original plans of the Capitol and President's House, and the third, dated July 25, states his objections to Thornton's plan of the Capitol.

Among the legislative enactments of that year the only one relating to the object of this compilation is the last act of Maryland supplementary to her ratification act of the cession of this territory, introduced in one of the previous pages.

The Commissioners had to contend with many difficulties, and one of the gravest among them was the scarcity of skilled labor. There was abundant supply of rude handicraft in the numerous slaves of the adjacent States of Maryland and Virginia, but to obtain artisans they had to employ expensive agencies in the North, or to resort to importations from Europe.

During the following years, 1794, 1795, and 1796, there were less venturesome schemes advanced, and more actual progress was perceptible. An increased confidence lessened somewhat the impediments by which the Commissioners were surrounded, and gradually a more desirable population of quiet settlers and steady business men was attracted.

On the 7th day of July 1794, the Commissioners, with the approval of the President, issued a modification of the previous building regulations, which were further amended July 25, 1795; but they are not inserted here, because they did not affect the rights to, or the values of, property, and since then have been superseded by entirely different directions.

The greatest obstacle, however, to a speedy progress was, during all these years, the insufficiency of funds. The grants from Maryland and Virginia, and other resources, as the purchase-money realized from the sale of city lots, were soon absorbed by the requirements of the expensive improvements under progress, and work had to be nearly suspended until Congress, upon the request of President Washington, at last authorized the Commissioners in 1796 to contract a loan of $300,000, and at the same time assumed in a certain manner the direct control of the management by ordering the Commissioners to report their operations every six months to the Secretary of the Treasury. Sill, although these measures enhanced to some degree the credit of the Commissioners, they found it very difficult to negotiate this loan, until finally, after several unsuccessful efforts, the State of Maryland came to the rescue and advanced to them $100,000.

It is supposed that the election of John Adams as President had created apprehensions on account of the opposition of New England to the location of the Capital, yet these fears were soon dispelled when John Adams declared that he would follow Washington's example in his efforts for the city named after him.

There is but little more to be told of this city's growth under Washington's administration. The streets and avenues, as well as the public reservations, had never as yet been conveyed by the Trustees, Thomas Beall of George, and John M. Gantt, to the U.S. Commissioners, as provided in the agreement of the original property-holders, and hence President Washington, two days before his term expired, issued the following proclamation:

GEORGE WASHINGTON,
PRESIDENT OF THE UNITED STATES OF AMERICA
TO
THOMAS BEALL OF GEORGE, AND JOHN M. GANTT
MARCH 21, 1797

You are hereby requested to convey all the streets in the city of Washington as they are laid out and delineated in the plan of the said city hereto annexed, and also the several squares, parcels, and lots of ground following, to wit:

1. The public appropriation beginning at the intersection of the south side of North H street and the west side of a street 90 feet in width drawn parallel to the west side of the square numbered two hundred and twenty-one, and running due south with the west side of the said street until it intersects the south side of said square numbered 221, being 90 feet wide; thence east with the south side of said street until it intersects the west side of 15th street west; thence south with the west side of said 15th street west until it intersects the north side of Canal street; thence westerly with the north side of said Canal street until it intersects the east side of 17th street west; thence north with the east side of 17th street west until it intersects the south side of an east and west street 95 feet wide, from the square numbered one hundred and sixty-seven; thence east with the south side of said street until it intersects the east side of a north and south street 90 feet wide, from the east side of square numbered 167 aforesaid; thence north with the east side of said street until it intersects the south side of North H street; thence east with the south side of said street to the beginning.

2. The public appropriation, beginning at the intersection of the north side of an east and west street, ninety feet wide from the north front of square numbered six hundred and eighty-eight, and the west side of First street east; thence west along the north side of said street until it intersects the west side of a north and south street, drawn at a distance of ninety feet from the west front of said square numbered 688; thence south with the west side of said street until it intersects the north side of South B street; thence west with the north side of South B street until it intersects the east side of 1st street west; thence north with the east side of said 1st street west until it intersects the north side of Maryland avenue; thence southwesterly with the north of said Maryland avenue, until it intersects the north side of South B street; thence west with the north side of South B street until it intersects the east side of 16th side west; thence north with the east side of said 16th street west until it intersects the south side of Canal street draw at a distance of eighty feet on the south side of said canal; thence east with the south side of said Canal street until it intersects the side of Pennsylvania avenue; thence with the south side of said Pennsylvania avenue until it intersects the east side of 1st street west; thence north with the east side of said First street west until it intersects the south side of North B street; thence east with the south side of said North B street until it intersects the west side of a north and south street of 90 feet wide, drawn parallel to the west front of square numbered six hundred eighty-seven; thence south with the west side of said street until it intersects the south side of an east and west street 90 feet wide from the south front of square numbered 687; thence east with the south side of said street until it intersects with the west side of 1st street east; thence south with the west side of said street to the beginning.

3. The public appropriation beginning at the intersection of the south side of Canal street drawn

on the south side of the canal and the west side of 15th street west; thence south with the west side of 15th street west until it intersects the Potomac river; thence northwesterly until it intersects the canal; thence east with the canal to the beginning.

4. The public appropriation bounded on the north by the south side of North E street; on the east by the west side of 23d street west; on the west by the east side of 25th street west, and on the south by the Potomac river.

5. The public appropriation bounded on the north by South T street; on the east by Canal street; on the south by the Eastern Branch or Anacostia river, and on the west by the Potomac river.

6. The public appropriation bounded on the north by North B street; on the west by 21st street west; on the east by 20th street west, and on the south by the Potomac river.

7. The public appropriation beginning at the intersection of the north side of Canal street and the east side of 9th street west; thence north to the south side of the avenue drawn in front of square numbered three hundred eighty-two; thence northeasterly with the south side of said avenue until it intersects the south side of Pennsylvania avenue; thence with the south side of the said avenue until it intersects the west side of 7th street west; thence with the west side of said street until it intersects Canal street; thence west with the north side of said Canal street to the beginning.

8. The public appropriation beginning at the intersection of the east side of 9th street west and the north side of an east and west street of 100 feet wide from the north side of the squares numbered four hundred and six and four hundred thirty; thence north with the east side of said 9th street until it intersects the south side of an east and west street of 95 feet wide, from the south fronts of the squares numbered four hundred and five and four hundred twenty-nine; thence east with the south side of said street until it intersects the west side of 7th street west; thence south with the west side of said 7th street west until it intersects the north side of the east and west street first mentioned; thence west the north side of said street to the beginning.

9. The appropriation beginning at the intersection of the east side of 5th street west and the south side of North G street; thence east with the south side of said G street until it intersects the west side of 4th street west; thence south with the west side of said 4th street west until it intersects with the north side of an avenue; thence westerly parallel with the north front of squares numbered five hundred and thirty-three and four hundred and ninety, until it intersects the east side of 5th street west, leaving he street equally wide; and thence with the east side of 5th street west to the beginning.

10. The appropriation beginning at the intersection of the east side of 4½ street west and the south side of North C street; thence with the south side of said C street until it intersects the west side of 3d street west; thence south with the west side of said 3d street west until it intersects the north side of North B street; thence west until it intersects the north side of Pennsylvania avenue; thence with the north side of the said avenue until it intersects the east side of 4½ street; thence north with the east side of 4½ street to the beginning.

11. The appropriation beginning at the intersection of the east side of 3d street west and south side of North C street; thence east with the south side of said C street until it intersects the west side of 2d street west; thence south with the west side of 2d street west until it intersects the north side of North B street; thence west with the north side of North B street until it intersects the east side of 3d street west, with the east side of said 3d street west to the beginning.

12. The appropriation bounded on the north by B street north; on the east by 2d street west; on the southwest by Pennsylvania avenue, and on the west by 3d street west.

13. The appropriation bounded on the north by the south side of South B street; on the west by the east side of 19th street east; on the south by the north side of South G street, and on the east by the Eastern Branch or Anacostia river.

14. The appropriation bounded on the west by the east side of 7th street east; on the northwest by the south side of Georgia avenue; on the north by the south side of M street south; on the east by the west side of 9th street east, and on the south by the Eastern Branch or Anacostia river.

15. The public appropriation bounded on the north by South K street; on the south by South L street; on the east by 6th street east, and on the west by 5th street east.

16. The public appropriation bounded on the north by K street south; on the south by L street south; on the west by 6th street east, and on the east by an alley of 60 feet wide bounding square numbered eight hundred and eighty.

17. The appropriation beginning at the intersection of the west side of 1st street east and the south side of South E street; thence south with the west side of said 1st street east until it intersects the south side of an east and west street 100 feet wide from the south front of square numbered seven hundred and thirty-six; thence east with the south side of said street until it intersects the west side of 3d street east; thence south with the west side of 3d street east until it intersects the north side of an east and west street 100 feet in width from the north front of square numbered seven hundred and thirty-seven; thence west with the north side of said street until it intersects the west side of a north and south street 70 feet in width from the west front of said square 737; thence south with the west side of said street until it intersects the north side of Canal street; hence with the north side of Canal street until it

intersects the south side of South E street; thence east with the south side of said street to the beginning; as the same are laid out and delineated in the said plan, to Gustavus Scott, William Thornton, and Alexander White, Commissioners appointed under the act of Congress entitled "An act for establishing the temporary and permanent seat of the Government of the United States," to hold the said Gustavus Scott, William Thornton, and Alexander White, and their successors in office as Commissioners aforesaid, to the use of the United States forever, according to the terms of the act of Congress aforesaid.

U.S. Seal

Given under my name and the seal of the United States this second day of March, in the year of our Lord one thousand seven hundred ninety-seven.
(signed)   GEORGE WASHINGTON.

By the President:
Timothy Pickering, Sec. State

On the next day, the last one of Washington's Presidency, he addressed the following characteristic letter to the Commissioners about the city he loved so well and remembered to the very last minute of his official life:

To the Commissioners
dated Philadelphia, March 3, 1797

GENTLEMEN: Three things relative to the city of Washington call for my decision, ad this is the last day I have the power to give any.

The first respects the dispute with Mr. Law, touching the conveyance of lots; the second, to my approbation of the plan of the Executive offices; and the third, to the instrument you transmitted to me in your letter of the 31st of January.

With regard to the first, however hard and unexpected the case may be, as it affects the public interest, and whatever my private opinion on some points may be, I think it safest, and, all things considered, perhaps the best, to let the opinion of the law officer of the Government, herewith enclosed, prevail; and I advise it accordingly. The second not only meets my approbation, but is much approved also by the heads of the Departments, and may, when the funds and other circumstances will permit, be carried into effect; for which purpose the plans are returned with my approving signature. On the other, or third, point, the bill for incorporating the Commissioners of the city of Washington has not been passed into a law, in consequence of the superior claim of more important matters upon the attention of Congress in the close of the present session. The instrument you transmitted to me, as mentioned before, having been altered according to the advice of the Attorney-Gen., you will herewith receive formally executed.

With esteem, I am, always, ours,
Go. WASHINGTON
Com'rs of the City of Washington

By a singular inadvertency the plan of the city referred to in the last official act of President Washington concerning it had not been annexed, and hence the conveyance of streets and reservations as directed was not made, which caused the following act of his successor, President John Adams:

JOHN ADAMS, PRESIDENT OF THE UNITED STATES OF AMERICA
TO
THOMAS BEALL OF GEORGE, AND JOHN M. GANTT, TRUSTEES

Whereas, George Washington, late President of the United States, by his act bearing date the 2d day of March 1797, did request you the said Thomas Beall of George, and John M. Gantt, to convey all the streets in the city of Washington as they were laid out and delineated in the plan of the said city mentioned to be thereto annexed,[6] and also several squares, parcels, and lots of ground appropriated to the use of the United States, particularly described in the said act, to Gustavus Scott, William Thornton, and Alexander White, Commissioners appointed under the act of Congress entitled, "An act for establishing the temporary and permanent seat of the government of the United States," the annexing of which plan was at that time omitted:

NOW KNOW YE, that I have caused the said plan to be annexed to the said act of the late President of the United States and to this writing, and I do hereby request you, the said Thomas Beall of George, and John M. Gantt, to convey all the streets in the said cit of Washington as they are laid out in the said city of Washington, hereto annexed, and all the squares, parcels, and lots of ground described in the said act of the late President of the United States, as public appropriations to the said Gustavus Scott, William Thornton, and Alexander White, and their successors in office, as Commissioners aforesaid, to the use of the United States forever, according to the tenor of the act of Congress aforesaid.

Given under my hand and seal of the United States this twenty-third day of July, in the year of our Lord one thousand seven hundred and ninety-eight.
[U.S. Seal]   (signed)   JOHN ADAMS.
By the President:
Timothy Pickering, Sec. State

The reservations designated in the request of President Washington of March 2, 1797, and alluded to in the act of President Adams of July 28, 1798, were those enumerated in the following statement:
1. President's Square, 83a. 1r. 22p.
2. Capitol Square and Mall E. of 15th street W., 227a. 8p.
3. Park S. of Tiber creek and W. of 15th W., 29a. 3r. 9p.

---

[6] It was necessary to send another plan or instrument with all the squares, reservations and streets, as Ellicott's map did not contain them.

4. University (Observatory) Place, S. (squares 33 and 34 to Potomac river), 19a. 1r. 2p.
5. The Fort at Turkey Buzzard or Greenleaf's Point (Arsenal), 28a. 2r. 31p.
6. West Market, on Potomac (covered with water), S. of square E. 88.
7. Centre Market, 2a. 3r. 23p.
8. National Church (Patent Office) Square, (given to the city and sold), 4a. 25p.
9. Judiciary Square, 19a. 1r. 27p.
10. N. of Pennsylvania Avenue, between 3d and 4½ streets W. (given to the city and sold), 6a. 31p.
11. Between North B and C and 2d and 3d W. (given to the city and sold), 3a. 2r. 34p.
12. N. of Pennsylvania Avenue, between 2d and 3d W. (given to the city and sold), 1a. 1r. 4p.
13. Hospital Square (Magazine), 77a. 26p.
14. Navy Yard Square, 12a. 3r. 15p.
15. Eastern Branch Market Square, 1a. 21p.
16. Eastern Branch Market Square, 1a. 23p.
17. Town-House Square, 23a. 1r. 18p.

Total, 541 acres, 1 rod, 29 poles.

To these public reservations were added, in subsequent times, at different dates, several valuable tracts of land, as follows:

Square 297 (Marine Barracks), 2a. 3r. 13p.
Square 249 (Fountain Square), 4a. 24p.

(This square is now called Franklin Square, and was purchased for the purpose of supplying the Executive office or President's House with water.)

Winder's Building (square 169), and several others, among which, recently, the squares 687 and 688.

It is also proper to mention that several tracts, in possession of the Government for years, had been returned to the city or sold to private holders, as those designated on the present map of Washington as Reservations A, B, C, D, and 10, 11, and 12.

It is however curious, that, for reasons now not easily to be discovered, none of the streets and reservations have, notwithstanding the foregoing requests of Presidents Washington and Adams, been actually conveyed to the United States by any proper document up to the present day; yet their control over them is nevertheless unimpeachable and absolute, according to the decisions of the Supreme Court and the highest law officers of the United States.

In addition to these grants of land for public purposes the following is a statement of property sold to original proprietors for their improvements, grave-yards, &c.

Notley Young: Squares 329, 355, 356, 389, 390, 391, 415, south of 415 and 439, containing 12a 21.37p., at £12 10s. per acre, £151 13s. 5d.

Daniel Carroll of Duddington: Square 736, containing 4a. 3r. 19.86p., at £12 10s. per acre, £60 18s 5d.

Wm. Prout: Squares 906 and 907, containing 1a. 3r. 27p., at £12 10s. per acre, £23 19s. 8d.

Ruth Ann Young: Square 1,106, containing 3a. 1r. 29.15p., at £12 10s. per acre, £42 18s.

Abraham Young: Half of squares 1,053 and 1,054, containing 3a. 2r. 24½p., at £12 10s. per acre, £45 13s. 3d.

David Burnes: Squares south of 173 and 375, containing 10a. 8.9½p., at £12 10s. per acre, £125 13s. 10d.

John Davidson's "heirs:" Square 284, containing 2a. 2r. 4-7/10p., at £12 10s. per acre, £31 12s. 4d.

Samuel Davidson: Lots 14 and 15, square 183, containing 2r. 4-4/10p., at £12 10s. per acre, £6 11s. 10d.

George Walker: Square 862, containing 5a. 8.32p., at £12 10s. per acre, £63 3s.

James M. Lingan: Lots 13, 14, 15, and 16, square 139, containing 2r. 7.58p., at £12 10s. per acre, £6 16s. 9d.

Lynch & Sands: Square 370, containing 2a. 1r. 17-9/10p., at £12 10s. per acre, £29 10s. 5d.

(signed) WASHINGTON BOYD.
March 26, 1798.

The merest glance over the aggregate area and cost price of these original land grants develops the fact that the Government obtained for less than $40,000 a domain right in the heart of the city of nearly 600 acres, which, if estimated according to the price recently paid for the last acquisition of that kind, viz. squares 687 and 688, would represent a present dollar value [1874] of forty millions of dollars, or a thousand-fold its cost price.

But these Government reservations have at various times been enlarged, and now amount to more than 750 acres so that, if it is further considered that the Government also owns, so to say, in fee simple, all the streets and avenues, which embrace over 2,500 acres, it is not an exaggeration that it now possesses the largest and probably the best half of the entire territory of the National Capital, namely, nearly 3,300 out of 6,100 acres.

This brief and general account of historical references to the past property-relations in this city has now advanced so far that few remain untold which preceded the actual removal of the seat of the Government to Washington.

In 1799, Congress again authorized the Commissioners to contract a loan of $100,000, and again Maryland advanced that amount, and shortly after added another $50,000 upon the personal security of the Commissioners, all of which was used for public purposes; hence Congress, in February 1800, ratified and guaranteed every one of those obligations, amounting to $300,000, besides the last $50,000, which they secured by such city property as had been conveyed and sold, which however was not yet paid for, and hence as yet not deeded away.

After this transaction there still remained 4,682 city lots belonging to the United States and unsold, and, moreover, some valuable water frontage.

Of the public buildings, the north wing of the Capitol, the Treasury building and the President's House were completed and ready for occupation; hence Congress directed, on the 24th day of April 1800, that the public archives should be removed from Philadelphia, and, together with the Executive offices, transferred to the new Capital in June 1800. This was effected within a few weeks thereafter, and on February 27, 1801, Congress convened here for the first time, where one of the first measures enacted was the order that, until otherwise ordered, the laws of Maryland and Virginia should continue in force in the respective portions or tracts ceded by them.

In the meantime the progress of private improvements were slow, and limited to a number of private dwellings in the vicinity of the President's House, the Capitol, and around Greenleaf's Point. Several streets and avenues had been opened, yet Pennsylvania avenue was the chief thoroughfare between the President's House and the Capitol, and this avenue alone was ditched along the rough sidewalks, but not paved.

This condition of Washington, in regard to comfort and business accommodations, was anything but satisfactory, but the rights of and to property were entirely regulated and established even then, as the subsequent tabular statements will exhibit, which, for the sake of easy comprehension and greater accuracy, have been so arranged that, first, is to show how, when and to whom each lot in Hamburgh and Carrollsburg was disposed of; and then, how, when and to whom each lot in the city was acquired; thus proving the correctness of the given data by a tally with corresponding accounts.

It would have been very desirable to apply such a tally also to such estates as were not comprised in either of these settlements, yet were embraced in the city. This, however, was impossible, because these estates had not been previously subdivided into parcels which could be transferred intact in metes and bounds. But as long as every lot within the city is accounted for by metes and bounds, and the date, title, and method of each conveyance is established, and the correctness of such account is vouched for or endorsed by a positive record, it is immaterial to know its exact former location; and subsequent claims, titles, or rights may be derived from such record.

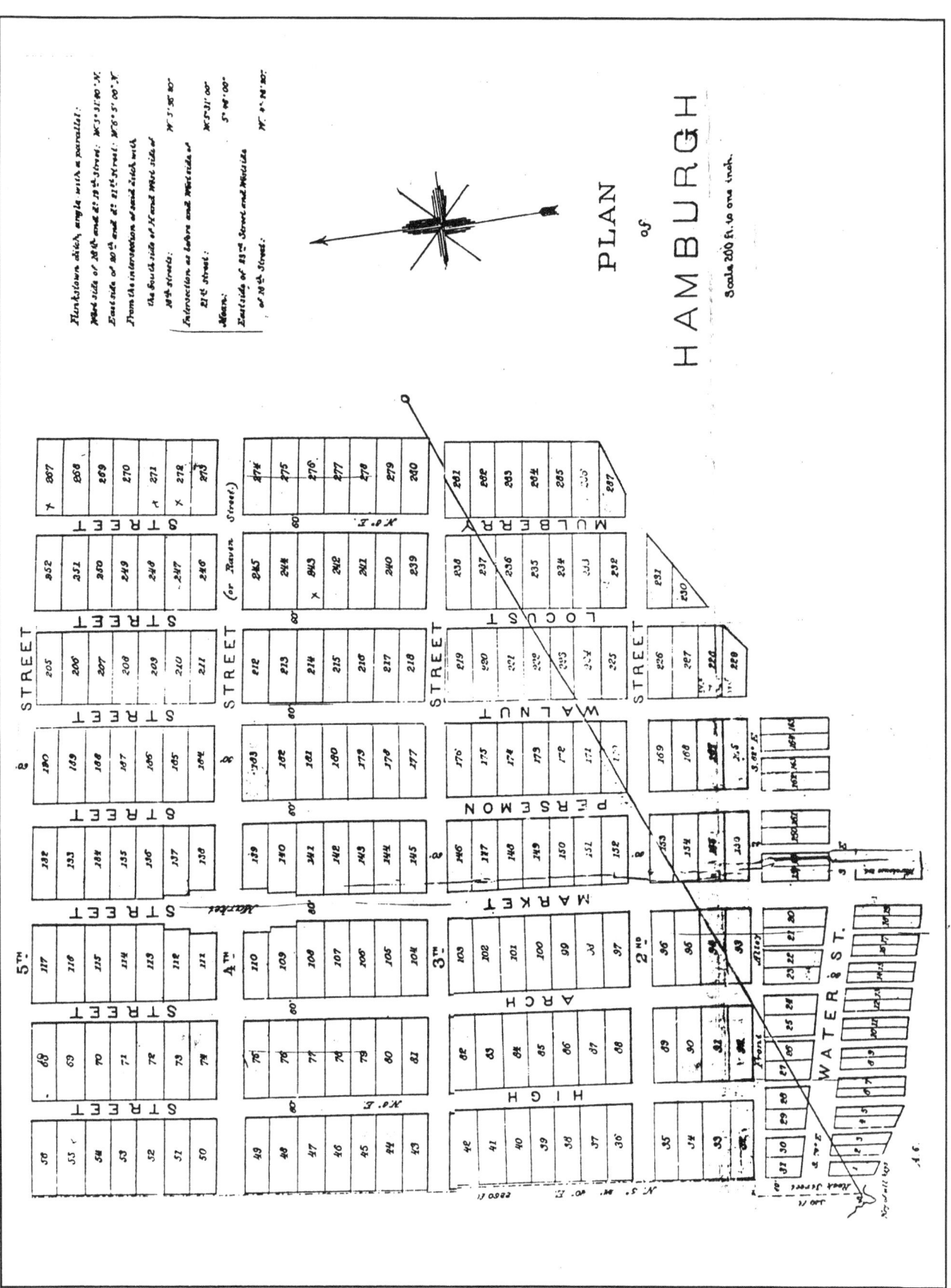

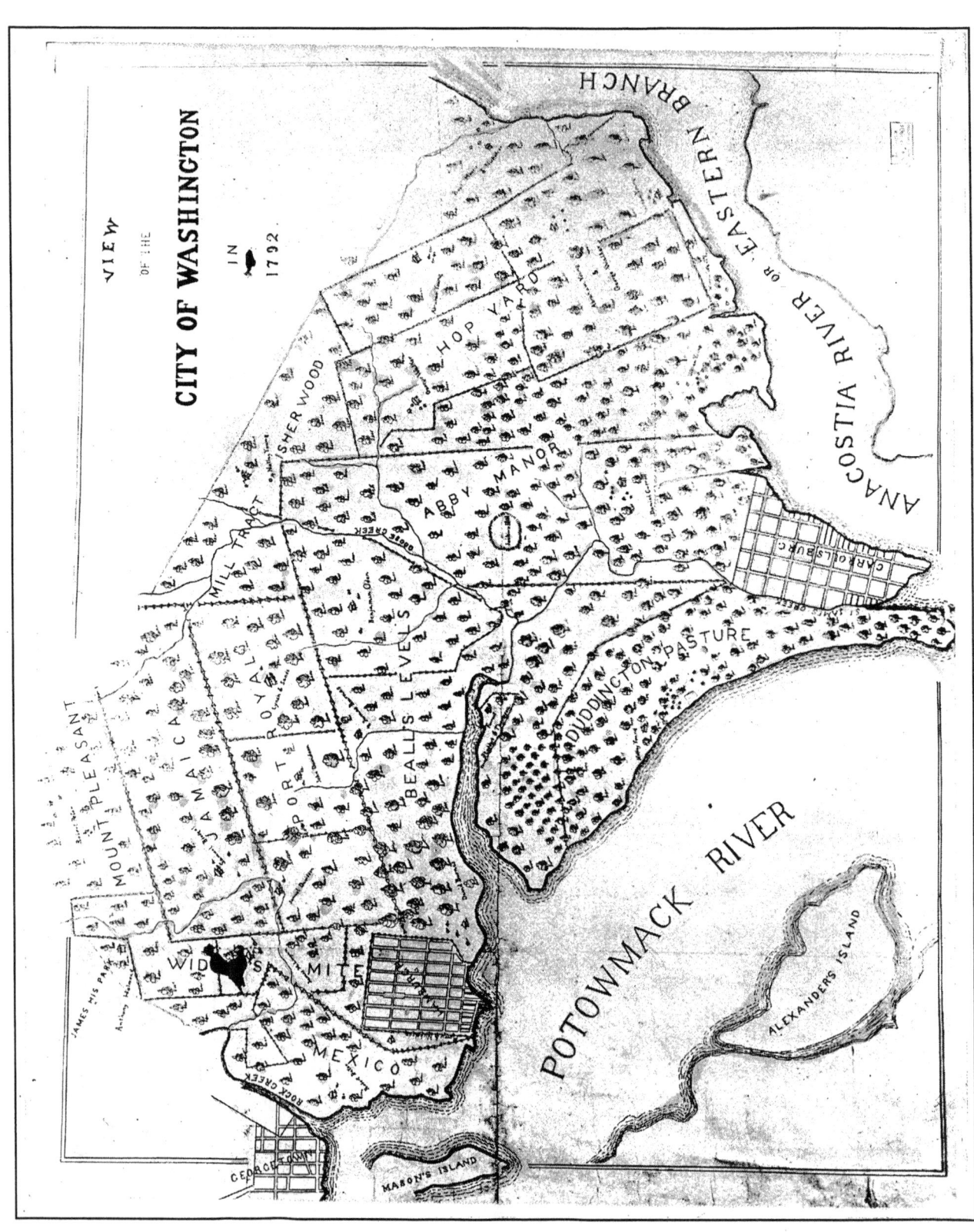

PART FIRST

♦

HAMBURGH

I. — TABULAR STATEMENT

Showing each lot situated in Hamburgh, and when, to whom and for what lot in Washington it was conveyed.

HAMBURGH LOT	TO WHOM CONVEYED	WASHINGTON SQUARE	WASHINGTON LOT(s)	DATE OF CERTIFICATE* OR CONVEYANCE BY COMMISSIONERS	LIBER	OLD PAGE	NEW PAGE
1	John Mountz	63	11	June 24, 1794			
2	Thomas Johns	63	9	June 20, 1793			
3	Wm. French & John Marr heirs[8]	81	14	Sept. 23, 1793	B2A	321	451
4	Baltis Font	63	3	April 19, 1794			
5	Thomas Johns (see 2)	63	9	June 20, 1793			
6	James Beall[9] of James	63	8	June 24, 1794			
7	Robert Allison	63	7	June 24, 1794			
8	James M. Lingan	63	5	June 20, 1793			
9	Charles Shell	123	1	Mar. 24, 1794			
10	James M. Lingan (see 8)	63	5	June 20, 1793			
11	Christian Kemp	63	6	June 24, 1794			
12	Anthony Holmead	62	1	Aug. 2, 1793			
13	Thomas Beatty, Sr.	63	2	June 20, 1793			
14	Michael Nichols	63	4	June 24, 1794			
15	Henry Yoel	89	12	June 24, 1794			
16	Henry Klinger	124	4	Sept. 7, 1793	B2A		446
17	John Kephart	89	11	June 24, 1794			
18	W. Regan, devisee of Joshua	89	13	June 20, 1794			
19	Christian Orindorf	89	14	June 24, 1794			
20	William M. Beall	88	14	July 2, 1793			
21	Michael Gross	88	13	May 3, 1794			
22	Wm. M. Beall (see 20)	88	14	July 2, 1793			
23	Anthony Holmead (see 12)	62	1	Aug. 2, 1793			
24	John J. Leroy	88	12	June 24, 1794			
25	James M. Lingan	62	4	June 19, 1793			
26	Thomas O. Williams (see 222)	121	2	Aug. 7, 1793			
27	James M. Lingan (see 25)	62	4	June 19, 1793			
28	Margaret Beard	62	6	Sept. 12, 1793			
29	Michael Gangaware	62	2	June 24, 1794			
30	Jacob Tomton	62	3				
31	Francis Cost	62	5	Feb. 20, 1794			
32	Benjamin Stoddert (see 91)	62	7,8&9	Feb. 20, 1794			
33	John J. Leroy	88	22	June 24, 1794			
34	Mathias Bucke, assignee of Michael Ramer	61	3	June 28, 1793			
35	Aaron Ritenover	61	2	June 18, 1793			
36	James Wells	60	2	June 24, 1794			
37	John Hackett	88	24	June 24, 1794			
38	Philip H. Mires	61	11	June 24, 1794			

---

[7] The original work by Faehtz and Pratt did not include this data.
[8] Of Henry County, Virginia.
[9] Assigned by Jacob Funk to Patrick Law who purchased a lottery ticket [see D.C. Deeds, Liber A1, p. 421 new].

HAMBURGH LOT	TO WHOM CONVEYED	WASHINGTON SQUARE	WASHINGTON LOT(s)	DATE OF CERTIFICATE* OR CONVEYANCE BY COMMISSIONERS	RECORD OF CONVEYANCE LIBER	RECORD OF CONVEYANCE OLD PAGE	RECORD OF CONVEYANCE NEW PAGE
39	Benjamin Spiker	61	12	June 24, 1794			
40	James Kirk	61	6				
41	Conrad Merkle	61	10				
42	Joakim Streeves	61	9				
43	Dr. P. Thomas	44	1	June 18, 1793			
44	Benjamin Stoddert	56	4,5,6,7	Feb. 20, 1794			
45	Benjamin Stoddert	56	4,5,6,7	Feb. 20, 1794			
46	Jacob Boyer	57	2	June 18, 1793			
47	John McDade	81	9	June 24, 1794			
48	Christian Orindorf	59	3	June 24, 1794			
49	John Spoor	60	4	June 24, 1794			
50	Lodowick Kemp	56	3	June 24, 1794			
51	Samuel Porter and James Sterrett	79	3	Sept. 20, 1793	B2A	316	444
52	Conrad Merkle	79	5	June 24, 1794			
53	William Gerrard	79	4	June 24, 1794			
54	John and A. Rench	79	10	June 24, 1794			
55	Benjamin Stoddert	56	4,5,6,7	Feb. 20, 1794			
56	Jonathan Hagar	56	8	Mar. 20, 1794			
68[10]	Conrad Doll and J. Hoof	56	9	June 18, 1793			
69	Casper Mantz	56	10	June 18, 1793			
70	Andrew Kesler	79	12	June 24, 1794			
71	Frederick Maley	79	11	June 24, 1794			
72	William Murdock Beall	56	11	July 2, 1793			
73	Charles Shell	57	8	June 18, 1793			
74	Wm. and Eliza Waugh, heirs of B. Wigell, one-half; and A. Fishers' heirs, one-half	57	1	June 24, 1794			
75	D. Reintzel, for Calvinist Society	80	9	June 28, 1793			
76	Marsham Warring	57	3	June 18, 1793			
77	George Holstine	81	16	June 24, 1794			
78	John Rhorer	56	4,5,6,7	Feb. 20, 1794			
79	Henry Pauling	81	4	July 25, 1793			
80	Walter Baker	81	5	June 5, 1794			
81	Evan Thomas	59	2	June 24, 1794			
82	Thomas Beatty, Sr.	60	5	June 18, 1793			
83	Casper Youst	81	3	June 24, 1794			
84	Robert Peter	60	6				
85	Frederick Hocandofer	61	5	June 20, 1793			
86	Frederick Hocandofer	61	4	Feb. 20, 1794			
87	George Murdock	143	6	April 19, 1794			
88	William Magrath	61	1	June 10, 1793			
89	Henry Coontz	61	8	June 18, 1793			
90	Nicholas Kinsor	88	19	June 24, 1794			
91	Benjamin Stoddert (see 32)	62	7,8,9	Feb. 20, 1794			

[10] Hamburgh Lots Nos. 57 to 67 are not accounted for.

HAM-BURGH LOT	TO WHOM CONVEYED	WASHINGTON		DATE OF CERTIFICATE* OR CONVEYANCE BY COMMISSIONERS	RECORD OF CONVEYANCE		
		SQUARE	LOT(s)		LIBER	OLD PAGE	NEW PAGE
92	Benjamin Stoddert (92,97,98)	84	5,6,7,8	Feb. 20, 1794			
93	John Walgamot	62	11	June 18, 1793			
94	Adam Ott	87	3	June 18, 1793			
95	John Hamell	88	25	June 24, 1794			
96	Andrew Link	84	11	June 20, 1794			
97	Christian Lower (see 92)	84	5,6,7,8	Feb. 20, 1794			
98	Christian Lower (see 92)	84	5,6,7,8	Feb. 20, 1794			
99	Joseph Garlick, P. McMahon	84	9	July 31, 1793			
100	Samuel Blodget[11]	84	10	Aug. 3, 1793			
101	Elias Youhman	s./104	3	June 24, 1794			
102	Henry Hilleary, Jr.	83	2	July 29, 1793			
103	Joseph Garlick	83	4	Feb. 20, 1794			
104	John Rover, Benj. Stoddert	81	1,2,21	Feb. 20, 1794			
105	Joseph Garlick	104	6	June 24, 1794			
106	William Buddicomb	81	13	June 24, 1794			
107	Valentine Hoof	81	15	June 28, 1794			
108	William Deakins	80	10	July 2, 1793			
109	Gilbert Kemp	81	10	June 24, 1794			
110	Daniel Hester	81	11	June 24, 1794			
111	John J. Leroy	80	8	June 24, 1794			
112	Valentine Hoof	80	7	June 28, 1793			
113	Henry Klinger	80	6	June 28, 1793	B2A	316½	445
114	Frederick Golden's heirs	79	6	June 18, 1793			
115	Charles Beatty	79	7	June 24, 1794			
116	Mathias Ritenover	79	8	June 24, 1794			
117	Benjamin Stoddert and James Lingan (see 251)	102	7,8,9	Feb. 20, 1794			
132[12]	Elias Davison	80	16	June 24, 1794			
133	Casper Youst	79	2	June 24, 1794			
134	Henry McClary	79	1	June 18, 1793			
135	A. Fleak and S. Miller	80	5				
136	Frederick Kemp	80	11				
137	Peter and F. Curts	80	2				
138	Rev. Mr. Golden	80	1				
139	George Holstine	81	17				
140	Henry Warman	81	18				
141	W. Hellen	81	19				
142	Martin Casner	104	9				
143	Hezakiah Clagot	81	20				
144	French & Marr, of Va. (see 3)	81	14	Sept. 25, 1793	B2A		452
145	Henry Sneberly[13]	83	1		B2B		151
146	Frederick Mann	15	84				
147	Michael Stoker	84	14				

[11] Certificate to William French and the heirs of John Marr of Henry Co., Va., 25 SEP 1793 [see D.C. Deeds, Liber B2A, fol. 452 new].
[12] Hamburgh Lots Nos. 118 to 131 are not accounted for.
[13] Commissioners' certificate issued to Dr. Henry Schenebely.

HAM-BURGH LOT	TO WHOM CONVEYED	WASHINGTON SQUARE	WASHINGTON LOT(s)	DATE OF CERTIFICATE* OR CONVEYANCE BY COMMISSIONERS	RECORD OF CONVEYANCE LIBER	RECORD OF CONVEYANCE OLD PAGE	RECORD OF CONVEYANCE NEW PAGE
148		121	1				
149	John Hass, devisee	84	13				
150	Thomas Cramphin	84	3				
151	[blank] Hatfield	84	2				
152	Dr. Philip Thomas	87	8				
153	Philip Sybert	88	23				
154	Benjamin Spiker	88	20				
155	William Sidebottom	88	21				
156	Joshua Johnson	87	1				
157	William Deakins, Jr.	88	15				
158	Daniel Ragan	88	16				
159	Stoddert & Deakins	88, 89	5, 5	Feb. 20, 1794			
160	John Mantz	88	17	June 18, 1793			
161	George Swingle	88, 89	7, 7	June 24, 1794			
162	Michael Ramer	88, 89	6, 6				
163	Amos Smith	88, 89	3, 3	June 24, 1794			
164	Frederick Curts	88, 89	4, 4	June 24, 1794			
165	John Comp	88, 89	1, 1	June 24, 1794			
166	John Wilmore, Jr.	e./88	9	June 24, 1794			
167	Benjamin Stoddert	e./87	3,4,5				
168	Christian Lower	e./87	3,4,5	Feb. 20, 1794			
169	Samuel Craiger	e./87	7	June 24, 1794			
170	Robert Peter	e./87	8	June 20, 1793			
171	Joseph Doll	e./87	6	June 18, 1793			
172	Thomas Price	102	4	June 24, 1794			
173	Jacob Meddart and Samuel Liday	s./104	4	June 28, 1793			
174	Geo. F. Hawkins	122	8				
175	Christian Lower	s./104	5,6,7	Feb. 20, 1794			
176	Joseph N. Chiswell	104, 122	2, 8	Sept. 14, 1793			
177	Stoddert & Deakins	104	5	Feb. 20, 1794			
178	Christian Kemp	104	17	June 24, 1794			
179	John Beall	104	7	July 11, 1793			
180	Stoddert & Deakins	104	4	Feb. 20, 1794			
181	Jacob Zetter	104	8	June 18, 1793			
182	Charles Worthington	104	10	July 8, 1793			
183	Lutheran Congregation	121	5	June 28, 1793			
184	John Sholman	103	8	July 29, 1793			
185	John Sayle	103	5	July 2, 1793			

HAMBURGH LOT	TO WHOM CONVEYED	WASHINGTON SQUARE	LOT(s)	DATE OF CERTIFICATE* OR CONVEYANCE BY COMMISSIONERS	RECORD OF CONVEYANCE LIBER	OLD PAGE	NEW PAGE
186	Appelona Whitehair, heirs of George	103	10	June 18, 1793			
187	James M. Lingan	103	9	June 19, 1793			
188	John Mantz and Charles Shell heirs of Caspar Mantz	102	10	June 19, 1793			
189	Jacob Young	102	3	June 24, 1793			
190	John Tilley and Mrs. Johnson	102	1				
205[14]	Jacob Hess	120	2	June 24, 1794			
206	George Winters	120	3	June 24, 1794			
207	Henry Umhults	120	5	June 24, 1794			
208	William McGrath	103	11	June 18, 1793			
209	John & A. Rench	120	4	June 24, 1794			
210	George Linginfetter	103	2	June 24, 1794			
211	James M. Lingan	103	1	June 19, 1793			
212	James M. Lingan	104	12	June 19, 1793			
213	William King	104	13	Oct. 2, 1793			
214	James Terrell	104	16	June 19, 1793			
215	William and Eliza Waugh, heirs of B. Wigill, one-half; and A. Fisher's heirs, one-half	112	6	June 24, 1794			
216	Martin Hoofman	s./104	5,6,7	Feb. 20, 1794			
217	Edw. Skinner	122	12	June 24, 1794			
218	Christian Edelin	122	4	June 24, 1794			
219	George Striker	s./104	8	June 24, 1794			
220	Patrick Manual and wife[15]	122	5	Aug. 29, 1793	B2A	325	455
221	Gilbert Kemp	142	8	June 24, 1794			
222	Thomas O. Williams	121	2	Aug. 7, 1793			
223	Samuel Snowden	e./87	2	April 19, 1794			
224	Thomas Johnson	87	2	June 18, 1794			
225	Robert Peter	e./87	10	June 20, 1793			
226	Col. William Deakins	e./87	1	June 19, 1793			
227	Michael Raymer	84	12	June 19, 1793			
228	Stoddert & Deakins	e./88	13	Feb. 20, 1794			
229	Stoddert & Deakins	125	All	Feb. 20, 1794			
230	Stoddert & Deakins	124	3	Feb. 20, 1794			
231	Stoddert & Deakins	n./128	All	Feb. 20, 1794			
232	Stoddert & Deakins						
233	T. Beall and Levi Deakins	124	2	Aug. 5, 1793			
234	Peter Kemp	124	1	June 24, 1794			
235	Christ. Schell's heirs	124	6	June 18, 1793			
236	Henry Klinger	124	4	Sept. 7, 1793	B2A	317½	446
237	Chas. Schell	123	1	Mar. 24, 1794			
238	John Winter	123	4	June 24, 1794			
239	Thos. Cramphin	123	3	June 18, 1793			

[14] Hamburgh Lots Nos. 191 to 204 are not accounted for.
[15] Deed typescript record gives Patrick Maniville, husband of Mary Maniville.

HAM-BURGH LOT	TO WHOM CONVEYED	WASHINGTON SQUARE	LOT(s)	DATE OF CERTIFICATE* OR CONVEYANCE BY COMMISSIONERS	RECORD OF CONVEYANCE LIBER	OLD PAGE	NEW PAGE
240	John Shillman	124	7	Feb. 20, 1794			
241	Richard Snowden	81	1,2,21	Feb. 20, 1794			
242	David Harry	122	13	June 19, 1793			
243	Charles Beatty	141	7	June 24, 1794			
244	John and A. Rench	122	11	June 24, 1794			
245	Peter Ham	122	10	June 19, 1793			
246	Anthony Bitting	121	9	June 24, 1794			
247	James M. Lingan	121	3	June 19, 1793			
248	Thomas Johns	120	14	June 24, 1794			
249	Joshua Johnson	121	8	June 20, 1793			
250	Valentine Reintzell	120	13	Feb. 20, 1794			
251	Christian Lower	102	7,8,9	Feb. 20, 1794			
252	Thomas Johns	120	1	June 19, 1793			
267[16]	Dr. Philip Thomas	141	8	June 18, 1793			
268	Conrad Merkle	120	12	June 24, 1794			
269	James M. Lingan	142	5	June 19, 1793			
270	P. and J. Mantz, David Isaac	143	8	July 2, 1794			
271	John J. Leroy	141	5	June 24, 1794			
272	John J. Leroy	141	4	June 24, 1794			
273	Leonard Reed	142	6	June 24, 1794			
274	Lawrence O'Neal	143	11	June 24, 1794			
275	Henry Walter	143	9	July 24, 1794			
276	Dr. Philip Thomas	104	14	June 18, 1793			
277	Richard Snowden	142	9	July 24, 1794			
278	John Mantz	143	7	July 2, 1793			
279	Dr. Philip Thomas	104	15	June 18, 1793			
280	Brook Beall	143	5	July 2, 1793			
281	Jacob Zetter	144	9	June 28, 1794			
282	Samuel Miller	144	8	June 28, 1793			
283	Wm. French & John Marr heirs	122	7	Sept. 23, 1793[17]	B2A	322	452
284	Henry Stall	144	7	June 24, 1794			
285	Dr. Philip Thomas	122	14	June 18, 1793			
286	Charles Beatty	141	6	June 24, 1794			
287	Stoddert & Deakins (see 229)	125	All	Feb. 20, 1794			

[16] Hamburgh Lots Nos. 253 to 266 are not accounted for.
[17] Certificate granted French on September 25, 1793.

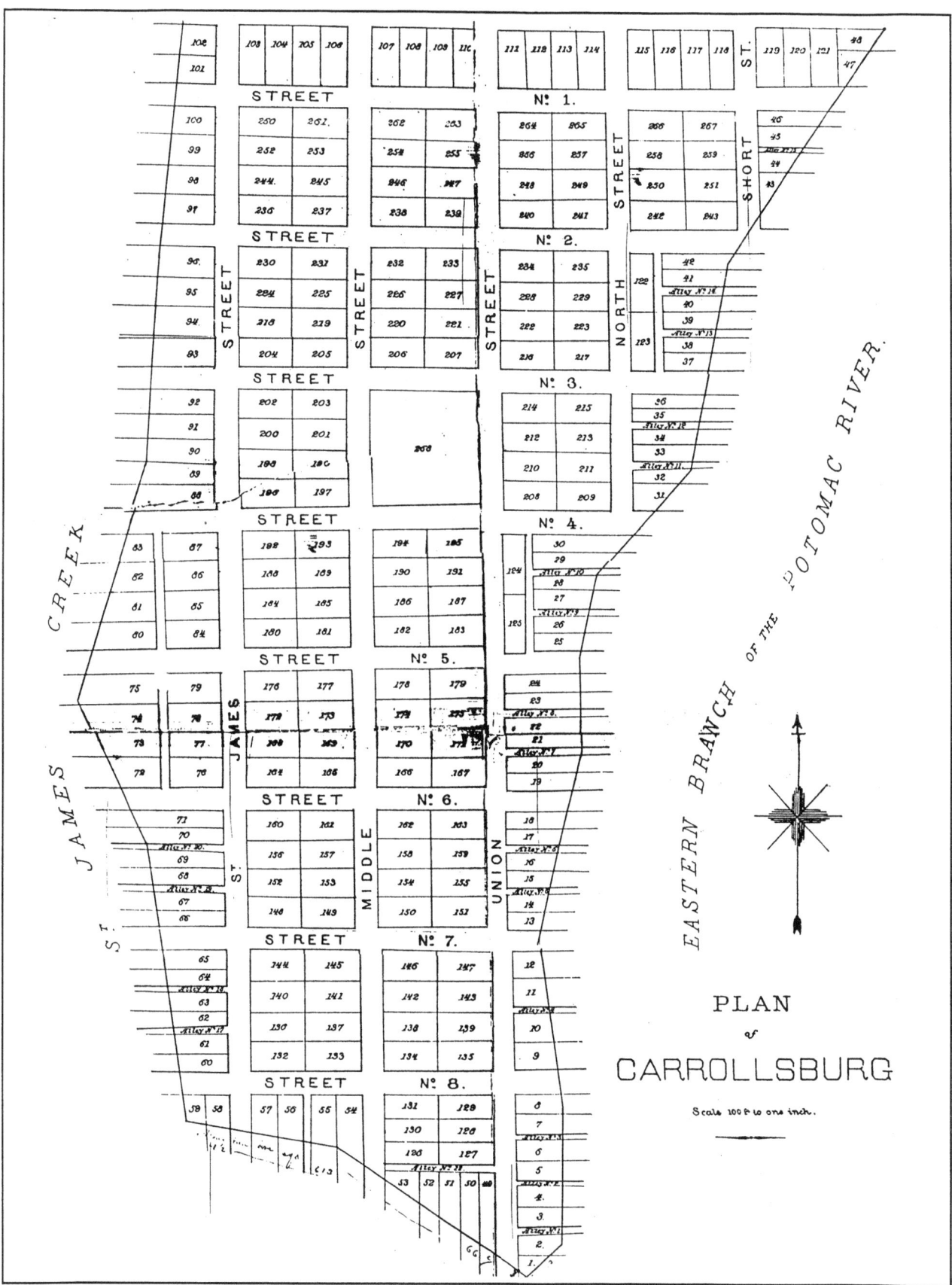

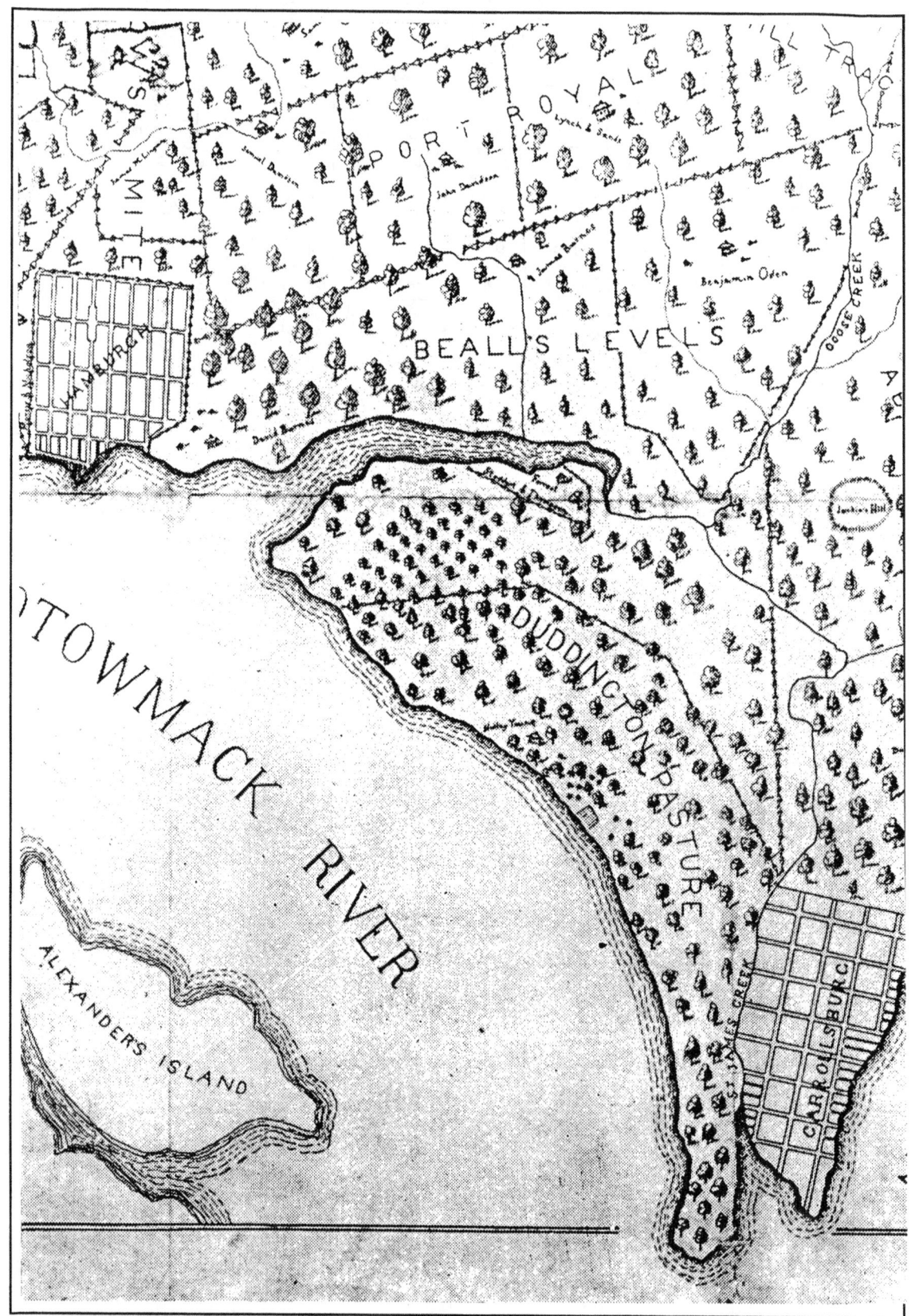

Expanded Section from "View of the City of Washington in 1792"

PART SECOND

♦

CARROLLSBURG

II. — TABULAR STATEMENT

Showing each lot situated in Carrollsburg, and when, to whom and for what lot in Washington it was conveyed.

CARROLLSBURG LOT	TO WHOM CONVEYED	WASHINGTON SQUARE	LOT(s)	DATE OF CERTIFICATE* OR CONVEYANCE BY COMMISSIONERS	RECORD OF CONVEYANCE[18] LIBER	OLD PAGE	NEW PAGE
1	James Williams	s. of s./667	2	Mar. 24, 1794			
2	Col. William Fitzhugh	s. of s./667	1	Feb. 7, 1794			
		e. of 667	1				
3	Henry Hill, of Pennsylvania	s. of 667	14	Mar. 24, 1794			
		e. of s./667	3				
4	John R. Magruder (see No. 39)	e. of 708	7	Oct. 17, 1793			
5	Job Fowler	s. of 667	15	Mar. 24, 1794			
		e. of s./667	2				
6	Jas. Neill, devisee of Bennet	s. of 667	10	Nov. 18, 1793			
		e. of s./667	7				
7	Darby Lux (Wm. Russell)	s. of 667	11	Mar. 24, 1794			
		e. of s./667	6				
8	S. Galloway	s. of 667	6	Mar. 24, 1794			
		e. of s./667	11				
9	William Lux (Matthew Ridley)	667	1	Mar. 24, 1794			
		e. of 667	1				
10	Uriah Forrest (Geo. Plater)	667	16	Mar. 24, 1794			
		e. of 667	2				
11	William Hemersley	667	10	July 30, 1793			
		e. of 667	8				
12	Jas. Wharton	667	9	Aug. 28, 1793			
		e. of 667	9				
13	Charles Carroll of Carrollton	665	1	Sept. [ ], 1793			
		666	1				
14	John Campbell	665	21	Mar. 24, 1794			
		666	3				
15	Barnes & Redgate	665	20	Mar. 24, 1794			
		666	4				
16	John Craig	665	19	Mar. 24, 1794			
		666	5				
17	Dr. James Craig, of Alexandria	665	13	July 8, 1793			
		666	11				
18	Thomas Jennings	665	11	Mar. 24, 1794			
		666	13				
19	James Brown	664	1	Mar. 24, 1794			
		e. of 664	1				
20	William Augustine Washington	664	3	Aug. 3, 1793	B2A	319	449
		e. of 664	3				

---

[18] The original work by Faehtz and Pratt did not include this data.

CARROL LSBURG LOT	TO WHOM CONVEYED	WASHINGTON		DATE OF CERTIFICATE* OR CONVEYANCE BY COMMISSIONERS	RECORD OF CONVEYANCE		
		SQUARE	LOT(s)		LIBER	OLD PAGE	NEW PAGE
21	Thomas Johnson	664	6	Oct. 16, 1793			
		e. of 664	6	Mar. 20, 1794			
22	David Ross	664	8	July 30, 1793			
		e. of 664	8				
23	James Earle	664	7	Mar. 24, 1794			
		e. of 664	7				
24	Samuel Collidge (see No. 28)	s. of 708	3	Aug. 28, 1793			
25	Capt. Wm. Macgakin	664	2	Mar. 24, 1794			
		e. of 664	2				
26	Richard Tilghman	665	12	Mar. 24, 1794			
		e. of 666	12				
27	Notley Young	s. of 708	2	Mar. 22, 1794			
28	Samuel Collidge (see No. 24)	s. of 708	3				
29	Henry Rozer	665	15	Mar. 24, 1794			
		666	9				
30	Jonathan (David) Slater	708	13	Mar. 24, 1794			
		e. of 708	2				
31	Ignatius Fenwick (Ralph Forster)	708	1	Oct. 17, 1793			
		e. of 708	1				
32	Dr. James Craig, of Alexandria	708	12	July 8, 1793			
		e. of 708	3				
33	Matthew Tilghman	708	9	Mar. 24, 1794			
		e. of 708	6				
34	Samuel Collard	e. of 708	9	June 20, 1793			
35	Daniel Carroll of Duddington	e. of 708	10	Mar. 24, 1794			
36	Daniel Carroll of Duddington	e. of 708	11	Mar. 24, 1794			
37	Frederick Grammar (John Smith)	707	1	Aug. 28, 1793			
38	William Sidebottom	705	13	Mar. 24, 1794			
39	John R. Magruder (see No. 4)	e. of 708	7	Oct. 17, 1793			
40	William Clagett (James Williams)	705	12	Mar. 24, 1794			
41	John Traverse	705	11	Mar. 24, 1794			
42	James Johnson, Jr.	705	8	Aug. 1, 1793			
43	William Digges	705	1	Mar. 24, 1794			
44	Ann Lick	705	14	Mar. 24, 1794			
45	James Wharton	705	10	Mar. 24, 1794			
46	Rignold Hillary	705	9	Mar. 24, 1794			
47	Charles Stuart	667	11	Mar. 24, 1794	B2A	327	458
		e. of 667	7				
48	Daniel Jennifer, Jr.	s. of 744	8				
49	Mary Carroll of Daniel	613	1	July 29, 1793			
50	Mary Young and Elizabeth Carroll	613	2	July 29, 1793			
51	Dr. John Stuart	611	2	July 1, 1793			
		613	4				
52	Daniel Carroll, Commissioner	611	3	June 23, 1793			
		613	5				

CARROLLSBURG LOT	TO WHOM CONVEYED	WASHINGTON SQUARE	LOT(s)	DATE OF CERTIFICATE* OR CONVEYANCE BY COMMISSIONERS	LIBER	OLD PAGE	NEW PAGE
53	I. Penrose	611	4	April 17, 1794			
		613	6				
54		611	7	April 17, 1794			
		613	9				
55	Charles Carroll, Jr.	611	5	Mar. 7, 1794			
		613	7				
56	Francis Leek	611	6	April 17, 1794			
		613	8				
57	Samuel Snowden (water lot)	610	1	Mar. 26, 1794			
		612	1				
58	Roger Johnson (water lot)	610	6	Aug. 1, 1793			
		612	6				
59	Dr. Upton Scott (water lot)	610	4	April 16, 1794			
		612	4				
60	Samuel Snowden	608	2	Mar. 26, 1794			
61	Charles Carroll, Jr.	610	9	April 17, 1794			
62	Benedict Calvert, dec.	610	13	July 30, 1793[19]	B2A	328	460
63	William Augustine Washington	606	2	Aug. 3, 1793	B2A	318	448
64	Samuel Coolidge	608	4	Aug. 28, 1793	B2A	325	456
65	Raphael Boarman	608	14	June 20, 1793			
66	Stephen Moylan	608	12	June 23, 1793			
67	Benjamin Brooke	608	6	Jan. 14, 1794			
68	George Slye	608	8	April 7, 1794			
69	Thomas Buchanan	608	10	Aug. 28, 1793			
70	Thomas Richardson	606	3	April 17, 1794			
71	Ann Gay	606	5	April 17, 1794			
72	Dr. John Stuart	606	7	July 1, 1793			
73	Samuel Davidson	604	2	Aug. [ ], 1793			
74	Josias W. King	604	3	Oct. [ ], 1793[20]	B2A	327	458
75	John Craig	604	5	April 17, 1794			
76	Stephen Moyland, of Pennsylvania	606	1	Aug. 28, 1793			
77	Ignatius Fenwick	657	12	Feb. 26, 1794			
78	Christopher Richmond	606	10	June 28, 1793			
79	Daniel Carroll, son of Charles, Jr.	604	6	April 17, 1794			
80	Henry Hill, of Pennsylvania	602	3	April 17, 1794			
81	Matthew Ridley	602	4	April 17, 1794			
82	Notley Young	602	6	Mar. 22, 1794			
83	Thomas Richardson & Co.	602	7	April 17, 1794			
84	Thomas Johnson	603	2	April 17, 1794[21]	B2A	328	460
85	Matthew Ridley	603	4	April 17, 1794			
86	Joseph Young	603	5	April 17, 1794			
87	Dr. John Stuart	603	8	July 1, 1793			

---

[19] Certificate granted March 20, 1794.
[20] Certificate granted March 20, 1794.
[21] Certificate granted March 20, 1794.

CARROLLSBURG LOT	TO WHOM CONVEYED	WASHINGTON SQUARE	WASHINGTON LOT(s)	DATE OF CERTIFICATE* OR CONVEYANCE BY COMMISSIONERS	RECORD OF CONVEYANCE LIBER	RECORD OF CONVEYANCE OLD PAGE	RECORD OF CONVEYANCE NEW PAGE
88	Wm. A. Washington (Thomas Ringold, Jr.) (see No. 63)	606	2	Sept. 20, 1793	B2A	318	448
89	Benedict Calvert (see No. 62)	610	12	Mar. 22, 1794*	B2A	328	460
90	Samuel Galloway	601	9	April 17, 1794			
91	Barnes & Redgate	601	10	April 17, 1794			
92	Matthew (Redgate) Tilghman	601	11	April 17, 1794			
93	Charles Carroll, Jr., of Charles	593	3	April 17, 1794			
94	William Wooten	599	4	April 17, 1794			
95	Basil Warring, 3d	599	5	April 17, 1794			
96	Sarah Slater	599	6	Mar. 21, 1794[22]	B2A	326	457
97	Robert Brown	598	3	April 17, 1794			
98	John Davidson	598	4	Mar. 21, 1794[23]	B2A	327	459
99	Daniel and Thomas Jennifer	598	7	April 17, 1794			
100	Richard Tilghman	598	9	April 17, 1794			
101	Dick & Stuart	598	10	Mar. 21, 1794[24]	B2A	327	459
102	Ignatius Diggs	598	8	Mar. 22, 1794	B2A	329	461
103	Henry Hill, of Pennsylvania	650	4	July 30, 1793			
104	Henry Bradford	650	3	April 17, 1794			
105	Peregrine Tilghman	650	2	April 17, 1794			
106	Mary (Young) and Elizabeth Carroll	650	1	Oct. 17, 1794			
107	John Smith, Sr., of Baltimore	706	5	April 17, 1794			
108	Elizabeth Laidler	653	15	April 17, 1794			
109	James Brown	661	14	April 17, 1794			
110	Daniel Carroll, Commissioner	702	11	June 23, 1793			
111	William Claggett and John Watson	703	9	April 17, 1794			
112	Stephen Moylan, of Pennsylvania	702	10	June 23, 1793			
113	William Russell	703	16	April 17, 1794			
114	Thomas Jennings	703	14	April 20, 1794			
115	Ignatius Fenwick	657	1	Feb. 26, 1794			
116	Stephen Moyland, of Pennsylvania	703	18	Aug. 28, 1793			
117	James Tilghman	703	15	April 17, 1794			
118	John Eden	s. of 744	5	April 17, 1794			
119	Samuel Collard	703	1	June 20, 1793			
120	Notley Young	653	12	Mar. 22, 1794			
121	William Russell	703	17	April 17, 1794			
122	A. Lawson	708	6	April 17, 1794			
123	Alex. Buchan	708	7	July 13, 1793			
124	Thomas Johnson, Jr.	660	1	June 20, 1793	B2A	328	460
125	Dick & Stuart	662	6	Mar. 21, 1794	B2A	327	459
126	Barnes & Redgate	611	1	April 17, 1794			
127	Charles Carroll, Jr.	s. of 667	2	Mar. 7, 1794			
128	Notley Young	s. of 667	3	Oct. 17, 1793			

[22] Certificate granted March 20, 1794.
[23] Certificate granted March 20, 1794.
[24] Certificate granted March 20, 1794.

CARROLLSBURG LOT	TO WHOM CONVEYED	WASHINGTON		DATE OF CERTIFICATE* OR CONVEYANCE BY COMMISSIONERS	RECORD OF CONVEYANCE		
		SQUARE	LOT(s)		LIBER	OLD PAGE	NEW PAGE
129	John B. Bordley, of Pennsylvania	s. of 667	5	April 17, 1794			
130	Thomas Buchanan	611	9	Aug. 28, 1793			
131	Martha Hall	606	8	April 17, 1794			
132	Edward Parkinson	609	2	April 17, 1794			
133	Thomas Turner[25]	611	12	July 11, 1793			
134	William Russell	609	1	April 17, 1794			
135	John Brice	667	2	July 8, 1793			
136	William Wootten	610	16	April 17, 1794			
137	Frederick Garner	611	10	Aug. 28, 1793			
138	Wm. Macgakin	611	16	April 17, 1794			
139	John Smith, Sr., of Baltimore	706	4	April 17, 1794			
140	Henry Addison	611	11	June 20, 1793			
141	Samuel Galloway	611	14	April 17, 1794			
142	Ignatius Diggs	611	15	Mar. 22, 1794[26]	B2A	329	461
143	Daniel Carroll, Commissioner	667	7	June 28, 1793			
144	Richard Henderson	610	14	July 8, 1793			
145		611	13	April 17, 1794			
146	William Augustine Washington	609	9	Aug. 3, 1793	B2A	317½	446
147	Cyrus Copper	667	8	April 17, 1794			
148	William Brogden	608	1	April 17, 1794			
149	A. Lawson	608	15	April 17, 1794			
150	John Craig	607	5	April 17, 1794			
151	(James Miller,) Alex. Buchan	665	3	July 13, 1793			
152	Jonathan Slater	608	17	April 17, 1794			
153	Joseph Wharton	609	6	Aug. 28, 1793			
154	Henry Rozer	663	4	April 17, 1794			
155	Francis Leek	665	5	April 17, 1794			
156	Richard Graham	608	8	Aug. 28, 1793			
157	William Diggs	609	7	Mar. 22, 1794			
158	Reuben Meriwhether	609	10	April 17, 1794			
159	Ignatius Diggs (see No. 208)	660	6	Mar. 22, 1794	B2A	329	461
160	David Ross	609	8	Aug. 1, 1793			
161	Notley Young	607	10	June 20, 1793			
162	Henry Rozer	663	1	April 17, 1794			
163	William Hindman	665	9	April 17, 1794			
164	James Holliday	605	4	April 17, 1794			
165	Daniel Jennifer, Jr.	607	1	July 30, 1793			
166	Henry Rozer	663	2	April 17, 1794			
167	James Brown	661	1	April 17, 1794			
168	William A. Washington	607	7	Aug. 3, 1793	B2A	315	443
169	John Casey, Jr.	605	3	July 30, 1793			
170	Thomas Addison	667	3	April 17, 1794			
171	Henry Rozer	663	9	April 17, 1794			

[25] Lot 133 was first the property of Daniel Cook (a British subject), confiscated from him by the state of Maryland, and then purchased by Thomas Turner for 30 pounds current money [see D.C. Deeds, Liber B2, p. 285 new].
[26] Certificate granted March 20, 1794.

CARROLLSBURG LOT	TO WHOM CONVEYED	WASHINGTON		DATE OF CERTIFICATE* OR CONVEYANCE BY COMMISSIONERS	RECORD OF CONVEYANCE		
		SQUARE	LOT(s)		LIBER	OLD PAGE	NEW PAGE
172	William Sidebottom	607	8	April 17, 1794			
173		605	2	April 17, 1794			
174	Dr. James Craig	661	3	July 8, 1793			
175	Matthew Tilghman	663	8	April 17, 1794			
176	Joseph Diggs	699	1	April 17, 1794			
177	Eleanor Laidler	605	1	April 17, 1794			
178	James Tilghman	663	6	April 17, 1794			
179	William Augustine Washington (Thomas Ringold, Jr.)	663	7	Aug. 3, 1793	B2A	320	450
180	Robert Brown	602	1	April 17, 1794			
181	Ignatius Fenwick	655	1	Feb. 26, 1794			
182	Samuel Chase	661	2	April 17, 1794			
183	A. Leitch	660	4	April 17, 1794			
184		603	6	April 17, 1794			
185	Henry Warring	603	13	Jan. 8, 1794			
186	Barnes & Redgate	661	6	April 17, 1794			
187	David Crawford	661	11	April 17, 1794			
188	John B. Bordley, of Pennsylvania	603	12	April 17, 1794			
189	Fielder Bowie	603	11	April 17, 1794			
190	Daniel Carroll, Commissioner	661	7	June 23, 1793			
191	Evan Thomas	662	5	April 17, 1794			
192	Thomas Johnson, Jr.	603	1	June 20, 1793[27]	B2A	328	460
193	Samuel Hepburn	658	5	July 14, 1793			
194	Darby Lux (Sarah Stewart)	661	8	April 17, 1794			
195	Richard Conway	658	6	Aug. 5, 1793			
196	Thomas Richardson & Co.	601	6	April 17, 1794			
197	John Smith, Sr., of Baltimore	706	3	April 17, 1794			
198	Peregrine Tilghman	601	3	April 17, 1794			
199	Samuel Galloway	601	4	April 17, 1794			
200	Ebenezer Mackie	656	7	July 30, 1793			
201	David Crawford	656	10	Aug. 28, 1793			
202	Peter Casanave	656	8	April 17, 1794			
203	Thomas Johnson	656	9	Oct. 16, 1793[28]			
204	John Campbell	654	2	April 17, 1794			
205	Col. William Fitzhugh	654	1	Feb. 7, 1794			
206	Robert T. Hooe	655	2	July 8, 1793	B2A	322	453
207	Edward Tilghman	657	2	April 17, 1794			
208	Ignatius Diggs (see No. 159)	660	6	April 17, 1794	B2A	329	461
209	David Crawford	662	2	Aug. 28, 1793			
210	Richard Tilghman, of Richard	660	3	Aug. 28, 1793			
211	Matthew Ridley	660	2	April 17, 1794			
212	Daniel Carroll of Duddington	662	9	Aug. 24, 1793			
213	Daniel Carroll of Duddington	708	8	Aug. 24, 1793			

---

[27] Certificate granted March 20, 1794.
[28] Certificate granted March 20, 1794.

CARROLLSBURG LOT	TO WHOM CONVEYED	WASHINGTON SQUARE	LOT(s)	DATE OF CERTIFICATE* OR CONVEYANCE BY COMMISSIONERS	RECORD OF CONVEYANCE LIBER	OLD PAGE	NEW PAGE
214	Daniel Carroll of Duddington (see No. 212)	662	9	Aug. 24, 1793			
215	Daniel Carroll of Duddington	708	2	Aug. 24, 1793			
216	William Hemersley	657	10	July 30, 1793			
217	Henry Hill, of Pennsylvania	704	2	Aug. 28, 1793			
218	James Neill, of Bennet	599	2	Nov. 18, 1798			
219	John Eden	656	18	April 17, 1794			
220	Jonathan Hall	656	4	April 17, 1794			
221	Mary Young and Elizabeth Carroll	655	9	Feb. 26, 1794			
222	Mary Young and Elizabeth Carroll	653	18	Mar. 22, 1794			
223	Richard Henderson	704	10	July 8, 1793			
224	Charles Carroll, Jr.	657	13	April 17, 1794			
225	Thomas Buchanan	654	8	Aug. 28, 1793			
226	Matthew Tilghman	654	5	April 17, 1794			
227	Alex. Buchan	655	8	July 13, 1793			
228	John Casey, Jr.	657	14	July 30, 1793			
229	William Augustine Washington	704	8	Aug. 3, 1793	B2A	318	447
230	William Diggs	599	8	Mar. 22, 1794			
231	Thomas Morton, Jr.	654	7	Sept. 7, 1793			
232	Richard Graham	655	6	April 17, 1794			
233	Notley Young	655	7	June 20, 1793			
234	Col. Uriah Forrest (George Plater) (see No. 267)	706	2	April 17, 1794			
235	Thomas Dick	704	7	July 14, 1793			
236	Charles Carroll, Jr.	652	2	April 17, 1794			
237	Samuel Coolidge	652	1	Aug. 28, 1793[29]	B2A	325	456
238	Daniel Carroll, Commissioner	653	2	June 23, 1793			
239	Dr. U. Scott	653	1	April 16, 1794			
240	Anne Torrin	702	2	April 17, 1794			
241	Barnes & Redgate	702	1	April 17, 1794			
242	John Mason	705	3	Aug. 2, 1793			
243	Dick & Stuart	703	2	Mar. 21, 1794[30]	B2A	327	459
244	Notley Young	652	3	June 20, 1793			
245	David Crawford	652	20	Aug. 28, 1793			
246	Dr. John Stuart	653	3	July 1, 1793			
247	Thomas Johnson (Denton Jaques)	653	19	April 17, 1794[31]			
248	Thomas Addison	705	4	April 17, 1794			
249	Jas. Mawburn (Cyrus Copper)	702	20	Aug. 28, 1793			
250	Thomas Addison	705	5	April 17, 1794			
251	J. Hepburn, Jr. and E. Spriggs, Jr.	703	19	April 17, 1794			
252	Wm. Bayley	652	5	April 17, 1794			

---

[29] Certificate granted March 20, 1794.
[30] Certificate granted March 20, 1794.
[31] Certificate granted March 20, 1794.

CARROLLSBURG LOT	TO WHOM CONVEYED	WASHINGTON SQUARE	WASHINGTON LOT(s)	DATE OF CERTIFICATE* OR CONVEYANCE BY COMMISSIONERS	RECORD OF CONVEYANCE LIBER	RECORD OF CONVEYANCE OLD PAGE	RECORD OF CONVEYANCE NEW PAGE
253	Joseph Diggs	652	18	April 17, 1794			
254	Ignatius Fenwick	657	11	Feb. 26, 1794			
255	Ralph Foster	653	17	Mar. 22, 1794			
256	Thomas Richardson & Co.	702	3	April 17, 1794			
257	James Hollyday	702	19	April 17, 1794			
258	Edward Tilghman	703	4	April 17, 1794			
259	Dick & Stuart	703	3	Mar. 21, 1794[32]	B2A	327	459
260	William Russell	652	11	April 17, 1794			
261	William Beanes	652	12	April 17, 1794			
262	William A. Washington	653	10	Aug. 3, 1793	B2A	315	442
263	Notley Young	653	11	June 20, 1793			
264	Charles Carroll of Carrollton	704	6	April 17, 1794			
265	Thomas Johnson, Jr.	603	3,14	Aug. 1, 1793[33]	B2A	328	460
266	Thomas Addison	705	6	April 17, 1794			
267	Col. Uriah Forrest (George Plater) (see No. 234)	706	2	April 17, 1794			

As already stated, after the subdivision of "Duddington Manor" and "Duddington Pasture" into lots, and calling the new settlement "Carrollsburg," the lots were disposed of by a lottery, the drawing of which is exhibited in the following Statement III, which is introduced here in explanation of the manner by which some of the subsequent lot-holders in Washington city had first become lot-holders in Carrollsburg.

---

[32] Certificate granted March 20, 1794.
[33] Certificate granted March 20, 1794.

III. — TABULAR STATEMENT

Exhibiting the drawing of lots in Carrollsburg.

No. of Ticket	No. of Lot	To Whom Conveyed	No. of Ticket	No. of Lot	To Whom Conveyed
1	13	Charles Carroll of Carrollton	53	84	Samuel Jacques
2	264	Charles Carroll of Carrollton	54	124	Thomas Johnson, Jr.
3	216	William Hemersley	55	158	R. Merewhether
4	11	William Hemersley	56	204	John Campbell
5	164	James Holliday	57	182	S. Chase, Jr.
6	92	Matthew Tilghman	58	259	Dick & Stuart
7	175	Matthew Tilghman	59	243	Dick & Stuart
8	226	Matthew Tilghman	60	239	Dr. Scott
9	33	Matthew Tilghman	61	192	Thomas Johnson, Jr.
10	257	James Holliday	62	42	James Johnson
11	163	William Hindman	63	58	Roger Johnson
12	63	Thomas Ringold	64	265	Thomas Johnson, Jr.
13	179	Thomas Ringold	65	21	Jacques & Johnson
14	20	Thomas Ringold	66	5	Job Fowler
15	229	Thomas Ringold	67	47	Charles Stewart
16	207	Ed. Tilghman	68	101	Dick & Stuart
17	258	Ed. Tilghman	69	125	Dick & Stuart
18	145		70	59	Dr. Scott
19	180	Robert Brown	71	105	Perry Tilghman
20	97	Robert Brown	72	198	Perry Tilghman
21	100	Richard Tilghman	73	178	James Tilghman
22	26	Richard Tilghman	74	117	James Tilghman
23	23	James Earle	75	14	John Campbell
24	210	Richard Tilghman, Jr.	76	113	Daniel Cock
25	131	Martha Hall	77	120	Notley Young
26	177	E.W. Laidlew	78	189	F. Bowie and W. Deakins
27	108	E.W. Laidlew	79	252	Collin Dunlap & Son
28	86	Joseph Young	80	41	Collin Dunlap & Son
29	219	John Eden	81	70	Thomas Richardson
30	118	John Eden	82	45	J. Wharton
31	68	George Slye	83	249	James Mawburn (Cyrus Copper)
32	248	Thomas Addison	84	153	J. Wharton
33	250	Thomas Addison	85	142	Joseph Diggs
34	170	Thomas Addison	86	254	Robert Buchanan
35	266	Thomas Addison	87	77	Robert Buchanan
36	171	H.T. Rozer	88	32	Dr. Craig
37	162	H.T. Rozer	89	17	Dr. Craig
38	154	H.T. Rozer	90	174	Dr. Craig
39	228	John Casey, Jr.	91	30	Jonathan Slater
40	169	John Casey, Jr.	92	152	Jonathan Slater
41	197	Thomas Ewing	93	115	Capt. Jordan
42	189	Thomas Ewing	94	183	A. Leitch
43	107	Thomas Ewing	95	144	Richard Henderson
44	139	John Brice, Jr.	96	263	Notley Young
45	78	Samuel Davidson	97		Notley Young
46	114	Thomas Jennings	98	244	Notley Young
47	18	Thomas Jennings	99	83	Thomas Richardson
48	99	Daniel of St. Thomas Jennifer	100	126	Barnes & Redgate
49	165	Daniel of St. Thomas Jennifer	101	91	Barnes & Redgate
50	48	Daniel of St. Thomas Jennifer	102	241	Barnes & Redgate
51	247	Samuel Chase, Jr.	103	78	Charles Richmond
52	203	Samuel Jacques	104	246	Dr. Stewart

No. of Ticket	No. of Lot	To Whom Conveyed	No. of Ticket	No. of Lot	To Whom Conveyed
105	49	M.J. Carroll, daughter of Daniel	161	231	Thomas Morton, Jr.
106	191	Evan Thomas	162	90	S. Galloway
107	172	William Sidebottom	163	141	S. Galloway
108	89	Benjamin Calvert	164	38	William Sidebottom
109	74	Joseph Digges	165	132	Ed. Parkinson
110	106	M. and E. Carroll	166	223	Richard Henderson
111	237	Judson Coolidge	167	222	M. and E. Carroll
112	201	N. Offutt	168	102	Ignatius Diggs
113	28	Judson Coolidge	169	69	Ralph [Boarman]
114	64	Judson Coolidge	170	111	Peter Campbell, William Clagett
115	24	Judson Coolidge	171	137	A. Leitch
116	173	Thomas Governor	172	72	Dr. Stewart
117	206	Robert T. Hooe	173	164	H.J. Bradford
118	103	H. Hill	174	40	P. Campbell and Clagett
119	37	Secretary Smith	175	256	T. Richardson & Co.
120	80	H. Hill	176	220	Jonathan Hall
121	116	S. Moylan	177	166	H. Rozer
122	66	S. Moylan	178	29	H. Rozer
123	236	C. Carroll, Jr.	179	181	George Buchanan
124	31	Ralph Foster	180	176	Joseph Digges
125	98	John Davidson	181	211	M. Ridley
126	208	Joseph Digges	182	81	M. Ridley
127	155	F. Leak	183	188	John Beall Bordley
128	56	F. Leak	184	129	John Beall Bordley
129	76	S. Moylan	185	134	Wm. Magackin
130	112	S. Moylan	186	95	Basil Warring
131	44	Ann Hepburn	187	46	R. Hillary
132	209	N. Offutt	188	119	S. Collard
133	193	S. Hepburn	189	34	S. Collard
134	51	Walter Dulany	190	242	Burton Clack
135	37	Walter Dulany	191	113	William Rapell
136	69	Thomas Buchanan	192	85	William Lux
137	130	Thomas Buchanan	193	9	William Lux
138	137	David Crawford	194	7	Darby Lux
139	15	Barnes & Redgate	195	194	Darby Lux
140	245	David Crawford	196	121	William Rapell
141	225	Thomas Buchanan	197	75	John Creigh
142	4	J.R. Magruder	198	151	John Miller
143	39	J.R. Magruder	199	123	John Miller
144	262	Thomas Ringold	200	227	John Miller
145	168	Thomas Ringold	201	67	Benjamin Brooke
146	156	Charles Grahame	202	261	William Beanes
147	62	Benedict Calvert	203	230	William Digges
148	232	Charles Grahame	204	157	William Digges
149	88	Thomas Ringold	205	43	William Digges
150	146	Thomas Ringold	206	202	J. Evans
151	8	S. Galloway	207	53	James Pennack
152	255	Ralph Foster	208	196	Thomas Richardson & Co.
153	217	H. Hill	209	12	J. Wharton
154	3	H. Hill	210	147	Cyrus Copper
155	159	Joseph Digges	211	150	John Creigh
156	257	J. Hepburn	212	16	John Creigh
157	221	M. and E. Carroll	213	167	James Brown
158	253	Joseph Digges	214	109	James Brown
159	50	M. and E. Carroll	215	19	James Brown
160	199	S. Galloway	216	186	Barnes & Redgate
217	267	George Plater	240	60	S. Snowden
218	234	George Plater	241	224	C. Carroll, Jr.

No. of Ticket	No. of Lot	To Whom Conveyed	No. of Ticket	No. of Lot	To Whom Conveyed
219	10	George Plater	242	25	Capt. Macquaken
220	235	Robert Dick	243	138	Capt. Macquaken
221	27	Notley Young	244	149	A. Lawson
222	233	Notley Young	245	122	A. Lawson
223	128	Notley Young	246	195	Richard Conway
224	61	C. Carroll, Jr.	247	140	Henry Addison
225	1	Benath Ragh	248	185	Bazil Warring
226	96	Sarah Slater	249	2	Col. William Fitzhugh
227	93	Charles Carroll, Jr.	250	205	Col. William Fitzhugh
228	79	Charles Carroll, Jr.	251	218	B. Neal
229	55	Charles Carroll, Jr.	252	6	B. Neal
230	127	Charles Carroll, Jr.	253	260	William Russell
231	148	William Brogden, Jr.	254	71	Ann Gay
232	184		255	240	A. Torrin
233	196	William Wharton	256	190	Daniel Carroll
234	95	William Wharton	257	238	Daniel Carroll
235	54		258	52	Daniel Carroll
236	200	El. Mackie	259	110	Daniel Carroll
237	22	Dr. Rap	260	143	Daniel Carroll
238	160	Dr. Rap	261	161	Notley Young
239	57	S. Snowden			

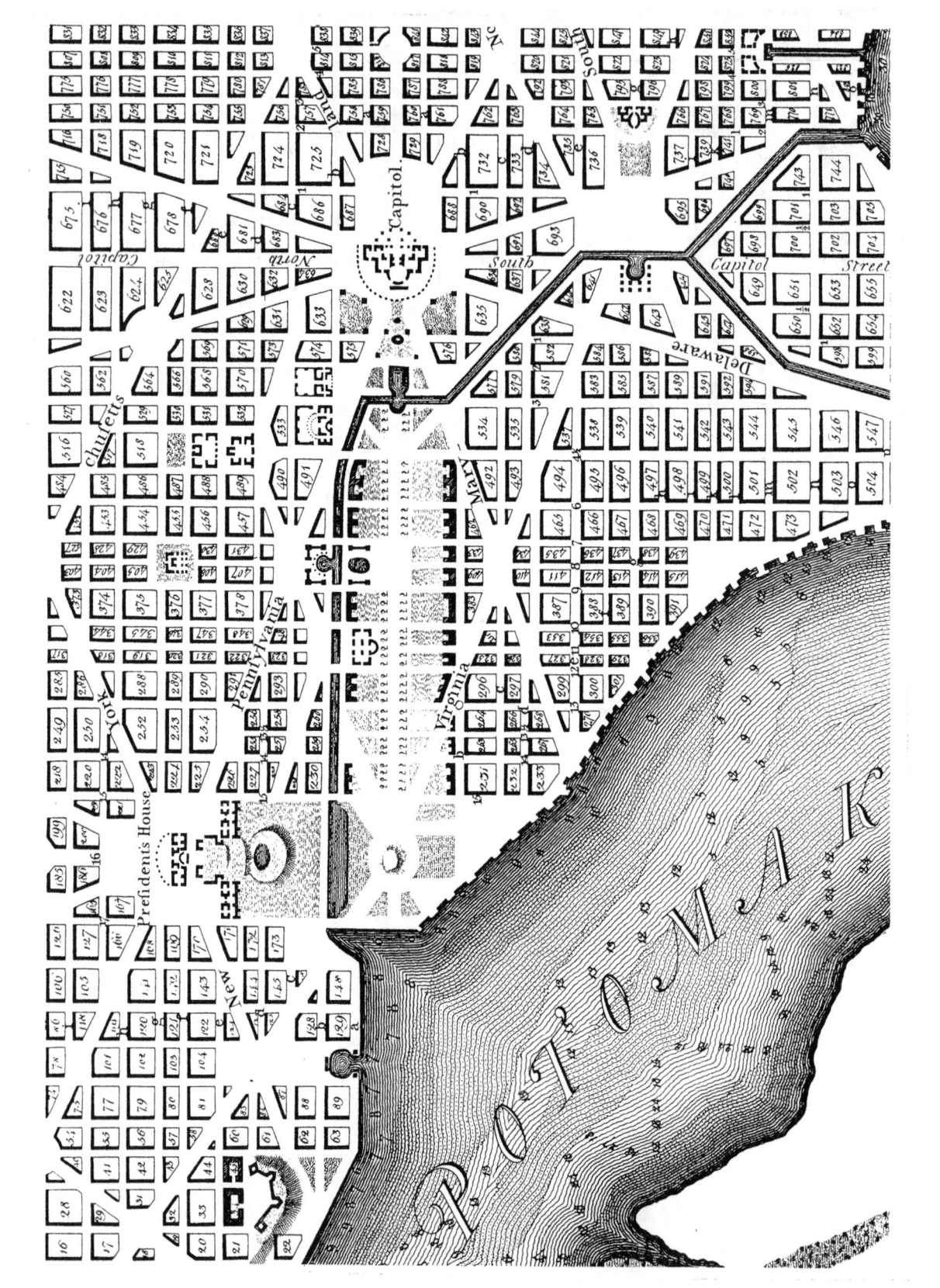

PART THIRD

✦

CITY OF WASHINGTON

This part contains a tabular arrangement of the conveyance of every single lot within the precincts of Washington city at the time when it was laid out, and hence embraces again the property of Hamburgh and Carrollsburg, besides all those estates and parcels which were not subdivided into lots previous to that event, but were owned in different bulks by private parties, generally designated as original proprietors.

This repetition of accounting for the lots in the two settlements enumerated in the preceding pages could not well be avoided without destroying the regularity and completeness of this exceedingly valuable part; moreover, this repetition has the great advantage of adding material evidence of its accuracy since the facts rendered in each account emanate from different sources of record, and, as they exactly correspond with each other, remove thereby all doubt of error.

Among the original proprietors, of course the nineteen signers of the Agreement of March 29, 1791, are most prominent, and their names are given in the foregoing pages, yet there were others also, most of whom added subsequently their signatures to the said instrument; and, again, some are who original owners, because they had very early acquired property, and hence they are mentioned in some of the original conveyances. Among the latter two classes the following are the most conspicuous, viz: Samuel Blodget, William Bailey, Samuel Davidson, William Deakins, Jr., James Greenleaf, Thomas Johnson, Robert Lingan, James M. Lingan, Dominick Lynch, Robert Morris, John Nicholson, Benjamin Oden, John H. Stone, Comfort Sands, John P. Van Ness, George Walker, and others.

IV. — TABULAR STATEMENT

Showing when and how each Square was divided by the Trustees between the Original Owners and the United States.[34]

Square — No. of Lots	Date of Division	Original Owners, Lots Retained by Them, and Conveyed to the United States
1 — 22 lots	Jan. 4, 1793	Robert Peter: 1-3, 8-10, 12, 13, 16, 17, 20 United States: 4-7, 11, 14, 15, 18, 19, 21, 22
2 — 2 lots	June 27, 1795	Robert Peter: 1 United States: 2
3		No division of this Square
4 — 20 lots	Oct. 8, 1792	Robert Peter: 5-14 United States: 1-4, 15-20
W of 4, 11 lots	Jan. 5, 1795	Robert Peter: None United States: 1-4[35]
N of 4, 5 lots	July 27, 1796	Robert Peter: 1, 2, 5 United States: 3, 4
5 — 26 lots	Oct. 8, 1792	Robert Peter: 1, 3, 5, 7, 9, 10, 13-16, 19, 20, 25 United States: 2, 4, 6, 8, 11, 12, 17, 18, 21-24, 26
6 — 8 lots	Jan. 13, 1797†	Robert Peter: 2-6 United States: 1, 7, 8
7 — 3 lots	June 27, 1795	Robert Peter: 2 United States: 1, 3
8 — 18 lots	Oct. 8, 1792	Robert Peter: 8-16 United States: 1-7, 17, 18
9 — 4 lots	June 22, 1793	Robert Peter: 2, 4 United States: 1, 3
10 — 3 lots	June 27, 1795	Robert Peter: 2 United States: 1, 3
11 — 3 lots	Jan. 13, 1797	Robert Peter: 2 United States: 1, 3
12 — 12 lots	Oct. 11, 1792	Robert Peter: 4, 6, 7, 9-11 United States: 1-3, 5, 8, 12
S of 12, 6 lots	May 19, 1800	Robert Peter: 3-6 United States: 1, 2
13 — 14 lots	Mar. 22, 1797	Robert Peter and William Bailey: 1, 2, 6, 7, 9, 11, 14 United States: 3-5, 8, 10, 12, 13
14 — 18 lots	May 15, 1795	Robert Peter: All

---

[34] Whenever it occurs, (†) for "C.R." means Capitol Record, and (‡) for "S.O." means Surveyor's office where the plats are located.
[35] According to the records in the Capitol. The records in the Surveyor's office show that Lots 7 and 8 went to the United States, and the balance of the Square to Thomas Johnson by decision of court of chancery, June 18, 1796.

Square — No. of Lots	Date of Division	Original Owners, Lots Retained by Them, and Conveyed to the United States
W of 14, 3 lots	July 27, 1796	Robert Peter: 2 United States: 1, 3
15 — 16 lots	Nov. 1, 1794	Robert Peter: 4-12 United States: 1-3, 13-16
16 — 28 lots	Oct. 8, 1792	Robert Peter: 1, 2, 6-8, 12-14, 18-20, 24, 25, 28 United States: 3-5, 9-11, 15-17, 21-23, 26-27
17 — 17 lots	July 27, 1796	Robert Peter: 4-11 United States: 1-3, 12-17
S of 17, 2 lots	Oct. 22, 1799	Robert Peter: All
18 — 3 lots	July 27, 1796	Robert Peter: All
19 — 10 lots	July 27, 1796	Robert Peter: 1-5 United States: 6-10
20 — 20 lots	July 27, 1796	Robert Peter: 9-18 United States: 1-8, 19, 20
21 — 4 lots	April 19, 1794	Robert Peter: 2, 3 United States: 1, 4
22 — 6 lots	July 27, 1796	Robert Peter: 3-5 United States: 1, 4
S of 22 - water		Robert Peter: Not Divided
23 — 12 lots	Nov. 3, 1795	Peter, Holmead, and Butler: 1, 3, 5, 7, 9, 11 United States: 2, 4, 6, 8, 10, 12
W of 23, 3 lots	Mar. 22, 1797	Robert Peter and Wm. Bailey: 1, 3 United States: 2
24 — 34 lots	Oct. 22, 1796	Robert Peter and John H. Stone: 1-4, 13-21, 31-34 United States: 5-12, 19-25
25 — 28 lots	Oct. 22, 1796	John H. Stone and Robert Peter: 1-4, 12-18, 26-28 United States: 5-11, 19-25
26 — 2 lots	Sept. 19, 1797	Robert Peter: 1 United States: 2
27 — 11 lots	Nov. 1, 1794	Robert Peter: 1-3, 10, 11 United States: 4-9
28 — 29 lots	Jan. 4, 1793	Robert Peter: 2-4, 8, 9, 12-14, 18-22, 26, 27 United States: 1, 5-7, 10, 11, 15-17, 23-25, 28, 29
29 — 6 lots	July 27, 1796	Robert Peter: 4-6 United States: 1-3
30 — 6 lots	July 27, 1796	Robert Peter: 3-5 United States: 1, 2, 6
31 — 15 lots	July 27, 1796	Robert Peter: 3, 9, 11-13 United States: 1, 2, 4-8, 10, 14, 15

Square — No. of Lots	Date of Division	Original Owners, Lots Retained by Them, and Conveyed to the United States
32 — 18 lots	Oct. 1, 1796	Robert Peter, John Nicholson and Robert Morris: Morris and Nicholson: 4 Robert Peter: 1-3, 14-18 United States: 5-13
33 — 26 lots	Sept. 13, 1796[36]	Robert Peter, Robert Morris and John Nicholson Robert Peter: 12-17 Morris and Nicholson: 18-24 United States: 1-11, 25, 26
34		No such Square (Naval Observatory)
35 — 8 lots	Mar. 16, 1812	Robert Peter and Anthony Holmead: 1, 3, 5, 7 United States: 2, 4, 6, 8
36 — 28 lots	Oct. 22, 1796	John H. Stone, Robert Peter and Anthony Holmead: 1-3, 10-16, 25-28 United States: 4-9, 17-24
37 — 22 lots	Oct. 22, 1796	John H. Stone, Robert Peter and Anthony Holmead: 1, 2, 9-14, 20-22 United States: 3-8, 15-19
38 — 5 lots	July 27, 1796	Robert Peter All to the United States
39 — 3 lots	July 27, 1796	Robert Peter: 1, 3 United States: 2
40 — 13 lots	July 27, 1796	Robert Peter: 2-7 United States: 1, 8-13
41 — 16 lots	Oct. 8, 1792	Robert Peter: 6-13 United States: 1-5, 14-16
42 — 16 lots	Oct. 8, 1792	Robert Peter: 1-6, 15, 16 United States: 7-14
re-division	Sept. 27, 1796	Robert Peter: 3-6 Robert Morris and John Nicholson: 7-10 United States: 1, 2, 11-16
43 — 5 lots	Sept. 7, 1796	Robert Morris and John Nicholson: 3-5 United States: 1, 2
44 — 15 lots	Sept. 7, 1796	Robert Morris and John Nicholson: 2, 3, 6-8 United States: 4, 5, 9, 10, 11, and parts of 12-15[37]
45		No such Square
46		No such Square
47 — 2 lots	Sept. 14, 1796	Robert Morris, John Nicholson and Anthony Holmead Morris and Holmead: 1 United States: 2

[36] This is a re-division, the first one of October 8, 1792 was declared void.
[37] The part lying in Hamburgh disposed of as follows: 1 for 43 in Hamburgh; also, United States: parts of 12, 13, 14 and 15.

Square — No. of Lots	Date of Division	Original Owners, Lots Retained by Them, and Conveyed to the United States
48 — 6 lots	Sept. 14, 1796	Robert Morris, John Nicholson and Anthony Holmead Morris and Nicholson: 1, 6 Anthony Holmead: 2 United States: 3-5
49 — 13 lots	Sept. 14, 1796	Robert Morris, John Nicholson and Anthony Holmead Morris and Nicholson: 1-3 Anthony Holmead: 4, 7, 9 United States: 5, 6, 10-13
50 — 28 lots	Sept. 23, 1796	Robert Morris, John Nicholson, John H. Stone, Anthony Holmead and Robert Peter John H. Stone: 3-7, 18-24 Morris and Nicholson: 8, 9 United States: 1, 2, 10-17, 25-28
51 — 21 lots	July 27, 1796	Robert Peter: 1, 6, 8-13, 19-21 United States: 2-5, 7, 14-18
52 — 1 lot	July 27, 1796	Robert Peter All to the United States
53 — 1 lot	July 27, 1796	Robert Peter: All
54 — 16 lots	June 27, 1795	Robert Peter: 1, 2, 10-16 United States: 3-9
55 — 16 lots	Oct. 8, 1792	Robert Peter: 6-13 United States: 1-5, 14-16
re-division	Sept. 27, 1796	Robert Peter: 3-6 Robert Morris and John Nicholson: 7-10 United States: 1, 2, 11-16
56 — 12 lots	June 26, 1794	Assigned by the government No. 3 for No. 50 in Hamburgh Assigned 4-7 for No. 55, 45, 44, 78 in Hamburgh Assigned 8 for No. 56 in Hamburgh Assigned 9 for No. 68 in Hamburgh Assigned 10 for No. 69 in Hamburgh Assigned 11 for No. 72 in Hamburgh United States retained 1, 2, 12
57 — 8 lots	June 26, 1794	Assigned 1 for No. 74 in Hamburgh Assigned 2 for No. 46 in Hamburgh Assigned 3 for No. 76 in Hamburgh Assigned 8 for No. 73 in Hamburgh United States retained 4-7
58 — 1 lot	June 26, 1794	All to the United States
59 — 4 lots	June 26, 1794	Assigned 2 for No. 81 in Hamburgh Assigned 3 for No. 48 in Hamburgh United States retained 1, 4
60 — 6 lots	June 26, 1794	Assigned 2 for No. 36 in Hamburgh Assigned 4 for No. 49 in Hamburgh Assigned 5 for No. 82 in Hamburgh Assigned 6 for No. 84 in Hamburgh United States retained 1, 3

Square — No. of Lots	Date of Division	Original Owners, Lots Retained by Them, and Conveyed to the United States
61 — 13 lots	June 26, 1794	Assigned 1 for No. 88 in Hamburgh Assigned 2 for No. 35 in Hamburgh Assigned 3 for No. 34 in Hamburgh Assigned 4 for No. 86 in Hamburgh Assigned 5 for No. 85 in Hamburgh Assigned 6 for No. 40 in Hamburgh Assigned 8 for No. 89 in Hamburgh Assigned 9 for No. 42 in Hamburgh Assigned 10 for No. 41 in Hamburgh Assigned 11 for No. 38 in Hamburgh Assigned 12 for No. 39 in Hamburgh United States retained 7, 13
62 — 11 lots	June 26, 1794	Assigned 1 for Nos. 12 and 23 in Hamburgh Assigned 2 for No. 29 in Hamburgh Assigned 3 for No. 30 in Hamburgh Assigned 4 for Nos. 25 and 27 in Hamburgh Assigned 5 for No. 31 in Hamburgh Assigned 6 for No. 28 in Hamburgh Assigned 7-9 for Nos. 32 and 91 in Hamburgh Assigned 11 for No. 93 in Hamburgh United States retained 10
63 — lots	June 26, 1794	Assigned 2 for No. 13 in Hamburgh Assigned 3 for No. 4 in Hamburgh Assigned 4 for No. 14 in Hamburgh Assigned 5 for Nos. 8 and 10 in Hamburgh Assigned 6 for No. 11 in Hamburgh Assigned 7 for No. 7 in Hamburgh Assigned 8 for No. 6 in Hamburgh Assigned 9 for Nos. 2 and 5 in Hamburgh Assigned 11 for No. 1 in Hamburgh United States retained 1, 10
64		No such Square
65 — 2 lots	Aug. 9, 1797	Anthony Holmead: All
66 — 8 lots	Aug. 31, 1796	Anthony Holmead, Robert Morris, and John Nicholson: All to Anthony Holmead
67 — 19 lots	1796	Robert Morris, John Nicholson and Anthony Holmead. Morris and Nicholson: 6-12, 16-18 United States: 1-5, 13-15, 19
68 — 20 lots	Sept. 7, 1796	Robert Morris and John Nicholson: 5-14 United States: 1-4, 15-20
69 — 22 lots	Sept. 7, 1796	Robert Morris and John Nicholson: 1-4, 16-22 United States: 5-15
70 — 23 lots	Oct. 1, 1796	Robert Peter, Robert Morris and John Nicholson Robert Peter: 4, 10-13 Morris and Nicholson: 2, 3, 5, 6, 19-21 United States: 1, 7-9, 14-18, 22, 23
71 — 3 lots	July 27, 1796	Robert Peter: 1 United States: 2, 3

Square — No. of Lots	Date of Division	Original Owners, Lots Retained by Them, and Conveyed to the United States
72 — 18 lots	July 27, 1796	Robert Peter: 1, 3, 5, 6, 7, 9, 11, 16, 17 United States: 2, 4, 8, 10, 12-15, 18
73 — 24 lots	Oct. 22, 1799	Robert Peter, Uriah Forrest and Benjamin Stoddert Robert Peter: 3-23 Forrest and Stoddert: 1 United States: 2, 24
74 — 18 lots	Oct. 31, 1795 Dec. 8, 1795	James Greenleaf and Robert Peter James Greenleaf: 1-4, 14-18, also part of 5 United States: 9, 6, and part of 5, 12, part of 13, 10 Robert Peter: 7, 8, 11
75 — 20 lots	June 27, 1795	Robert Peter and James Greenleaf James Greenleaf: 1-5, 16-20 United States: 6-15
76 — 30 lots	Oct. 1, 1796[38]	Benjamin Stoddert, Uriah Forrest, James M. Lingan and Robert Peter James M. Lingan: 4-7, 13-18, 23-27 United States: 1-3, 8-12, 19-22, 28-30
77 — 26 lots	Oct. 9, 1792	Benjamin Stoddert: 1-3, 6, 7, 12-16, 19, 20, 26 United States: 4, 5, 8-11, 17, 18, 21-25
78 — 30 lots	Oct. 17, 1791	Uriah Forrest, Benjamin Stoddert and James M. Lingan: 4-7, 13-18, 23-27 United States: 1-3, 8-12, 19-22, 28-30
79 — 21 lots	Sept. 7, 1796	Robert Morris and John Nicholson: parts of 13-20 not included in Hamburgh Assigned 1 for No. 134 in Hamburgh Assigned 2 for No. 133 in Hamburgh Assigned 3 for No. 51 in Hamburgh Assigned 4 for No. 53 in Hamburgh Assigned 5 for No. 52 in Hamburgh Assigned 6 for No. 114 in Hamburgh Assigned 7 for No. 115 in Hamburgh Assigned 8 for No. 116 in Hamburgh Assigned 10 for No. 54 in Hamburgh Assigned 11 for No. 71 in Hamburgh Assigned 12 for No. 70 in Hamburgh United States retained 9, 21 and the parts of lots 13-20 included in Hamburgh

---

[38] One-half of this square, to wit No. 76, having been divided by the government on October 17, 1791, as No. 77 by mistake, with Benjamin Stoddert, Uriah Forrest and James M. Lingan, under an idea that they were the original proprietors thereof, and it since appearing that Robert Peter was joint proprietor, and Forrest and Stoddert having since sold their part of the said Square 76 to James Greenleaf, who sold the same to Robert Morris and John Nicholson, to Commissioners James M. Lingan, Robert Peter, Robert Morris and John Nicholson agreed this day to divide the same as above.

Square — No. of Lots	Date of Division	Original Owners, Lots Retained by Them, and Conveyed to the United States
80 — 16 lots	June 26, 1794	Assigned 1 for No. 138 in Hamburgh Assigned 2 for No. 137 in Hamburgh Assigned 5 for No. 135 in Hamburgh Assigned 6 for No. 113 in Hamburgh Assigned 7 for No. 112 in Hamburgh Assigned 8 for No. 111 in Hamburgh Assigned 9 for No. 75 in Hamburgh Assigned 10 for No. 108 in Hamburgh Assigned 11 for No. 136 in Hamburgh Assigned 16 for No. 132 in Hamburgh United States retained 3, 4, 12-15
81 — 21 lots	June 26, 1794	Assigned 1, 2 and 21 for Nos. 104 and 241 in Hamburgh Assigned 3 for No. 83 in Hamburgh Assigned 4 for No. 79 in Hamburgh Assigned 5 for No. 80 in Hamburgh Assigned 9 for No. 47 in Hamburgh Assigned 10 for No. 109 in Hamburgh Assigned 11 for No. 110 in Hamburgh Assigned 13 for No. 106 in Hamburgh Assigned 14 for Nos. 3 and 144 in Hamburgh Assigned 15 for No. 107 in Hamburgh Assigned 16 for No. 77 in Hamburgh Assigned 17 for No. 139 in Hamburgh Assigned 18 for No. 140 in Hamburgh Assigned 19 for No. 141 in Hamburgh Assigned 20 for No. 143 in Hamburgh United States retained 6-8, 12
82 — 1 lot	June 26, 1794	Assigned all to the United States
83 — 5 lots	June 26, 1794	Assigned 1 for No. 145 in Hamburgh Assigned 2 for No. 102 in Hamburgh Assigned 4 for No. 103 in Hamburgh United States retained 3, 5
84 — 15 lots	June 26, 1794	Assigned 2 for No. 151 in Hamburgh Assigned 3 for No. 150 in Hamburgh Assigned 5, 6, 7, 8 for Nos. 92, 97, 98 in Hamburgh Assigned 9 for No. 99 in Hamburgh Assigned 10 for No. 100 in Hamburgh Assigned 11 for No. 96 in Hamburgh Assigned 12 for No. 227 in Hamburgh Assigned 13 for No. 149 in Hamburgh Assigned 14 for No. 147 in Hamburgh Assigned 15 for No. 146 in Hamburgh United States retained 1, 4
85 — 22 lots	Oct. 17, 1791	James M. Lingan: 3, 4 United States: 1, 2, 5-8, 21, 22
re-division	Nov. 3, 1796	James M. Lingan: 14 United States: 1-3, 15-22
86 — 22 lots	Oct. 17, 1791	James M. Lingan: 3, 4, 9-13, 16-19 United States: 1, 2, 5-8, 14, 15, 20, 22

Square — No. of Lots	Date of Division	Original Owners, Lots Retained by Them, and Conveyed to the United States
87 — 8 lots	June 26, 1794	Assigned 1 for No. 156 in Hamburgh Assigned 2 for No. 224 in Hamburgh Assigned 3 for No. 94 in Hamburgh Assigned 8 for No. [252?] in Hamburgh United States: 4-7
E of 87, 10 lots	June 26, 1794	Assigned 1 for No. 226 in Hamburgh Assigned 2 for No. 223 in Hamburgh Assigned 3-5 for Nos. 167, 168 in Hamburgh Assigned 6 for No. 171 in Hamburgh Assigned 7 for No. 169 in Hamburgh Assigned 8 for No. 170 in Hamburgh Assigned 10 for No. 225 in Hamburgh United States: 9
88 — 25 lots	June 26, 1794	Assigned 1 for No. 165 in Hamburgh Assigned 3 for No. 163 in Hamburgh Assigned 4 for No. 164 in Hamburgh Assigned 5 for No. 159 in Hamburgh Assigned 6 for No. 162 in Hamburgh Assigned 7 for No. 161 in Hamburgh Assigned 12 for No. 24 in Hamburgh Assigned 13 for No. 21 in Hamburgh Assigned 14 for Nos. 20 and 22 in Hamburgh Assigned 15 for No. 157 in Hamburgh Assigned 16 for No. 158 in Hamburgh Assigned 17 for No. 160 in Hamburgh Assigned 19 for No. 90 in Hamburgh Assigned 20 for No. 154 in Hamburgh Assigned 21 for No. 155 in Hamburgh Assigned 22 for No. 33 in Hamburgh Assigned 23 for No. 153 in Hamburgh Assigned 24 for No. 37 in Hamburgh Assigned 25 for No. 95 in Hamburgh United States: 2, 8-11, 18
E of 88, 16 lots	June 26, 1794	Assigned 9 for No. 166 in Hamburgh Assigned 13 for No. 288 in Hamburgh United States: 1-8, 10-12, 14-16
89 — 14 lots	June 26, 1794	Assigned 1 for No. 165 in Hamburgh Assigned 3 for No. 163 in Hamburgh Assigned 4 for No. 164 in Hamburgh Assigned 5 for No. 159 in Hamburgh Assigned 6 for No. 162 in Hamburgh Assigned 7 for No. 161 in Hamburgh Assigned 11 for No. 17 in Hamburgh Assigned 12 for No. 15 in Hamburgh Assigned 13 for No. 18 in Hamburgh Assigned 14 for No. 19 in Hamburgh United States: 2, 8-10
90 — 3 lots	Aug. 9, 1979	Anthony Holmead United States: All
91 — 5 lots	Aug. 9, 1797	Anthony Holmead and James M. Lingan United States: All

Square — No. of Lots	Date of Division	Original Owners, Lots Retained by Them, and Conveyed to the United States
92 — 7 lots	Aug. 9, 1797	Anthony Holmead and James M. Lingan United States: All
93 — 17 lots	Aug. 9, 1797	Anthony Holmead and James M. Lingan United States: All
94 — 6 lots	Jan. 17, 1797	James M. Lingan United States: All
95 — 6 lots	Jan. 17, 1797	James M. Lingan United States: All
96 — 16 lots	Jan. 17, 1797	James M. Lingan: All
97 — 12 lots	Jan. 17, 1797	James M. Lingan United States: All
98 — 1 lot	Nov. 3, 1796	James M. Lingan: All
99 — 11 lots	Nov. 3, 1796	James M. Lingan: 6-10 United States: 1-5, 11
N of 99	Jan. 17, 1797	James M. Lingan: All
100 — 36 lots	Oct. 5, 1792[39]	James M. Lingan: 1, 5-7, 11-13, 18-19, 23-25, 28-31, 35-36 United States: 2-4, 8-10, 14-17, 20-22, 26, 27, 32-34
101 — 30 lots	Oct. 17, 1791	Uriah Forrest and Benjamin Stoddert: 1-4, 13, 14, 20-27, 30 United States: 5-12, 15-19, 28, 29
102 — 19 lots	Sept. 7, 1796	Assigned Robert Morris and John Nicholson: That part not included in Hamburgh, of 11-15, and 16, 17 and 18 Assigned 1 for No. 190 in Hamburgh Assigned 3 for No. 189 in Hamburgh Assigned 4 for No. 172 in Hamburgh Assigned 7-9 for Nos. 117 and 251 in Hamburgh Assigned 10 for No. 188 in Hamburgh United States: 2, 5, 6, 19, together with parts of 11, 12, 13, 14, 15, included in Hamburgh
103 — 12 lots	Aug. 28, 1799	Assigned 1 for No. 211 in Hamburgh Assigned 2 for No. 210 in Hamburgh Assigned 5 for No. 185 in Hamburgh Assigned 6 for No. 184 in Hamburgh Assigned 9 for No. 187 in Hamburgh Assigned 10 for No. 186 in Hamburgh Assigned 11 for No. 208 in Hamburgh United States: 3, 4, 7, 8, 12

---

[39] This Square No. 100, heretofore divided as the sole property of James M. Lingan, and it appearing that Robert Peter was partly interested, James M. Lingan hereby assigned all [continue].

Square — No. of Lots	Date of Division	Original Owners, Lots Retained by Them, and Conveyed to the United States
104 — 17 lots	Aug. 28, 1799	Assigned 4 for No. 180 in Hamburgh Assigned 5 for No. 177 in Hamburgh Assigned 6 for No. 105 in Hamburgh Assigned 7 for No. 179 in Hamburgh Assigned 8 for No. 181 in Hamburgh Assigned 9 for No. 142 in Hamburgh Assigned 10 for No. 182 in Hamburgh Assigned 12 for No. 212 in Hamburgh Assigned 13 for No. 213 in Hamburgh Assigned 14 for No. 276 in Hamburgh Assigned 15 for No. 279 in Hamburgh Assigned 16 for No. 214 in Hamburgh Assigned 17 for No. 178 in Hamburgh United States: 1, 2, 3, 11
S of 104, 8 lots	Aug. 28, 1799	Assigned 2 for No. 176 in Hamburgh Assigned 3 for No. 101 in Hamburgh Assigned 4 for No. 178 in Hamburgh Assigned 5-7 for Nos. 216 and 175 in Hamburgh Assigned 8 for No. 219 in Hamburgh United States: 1
105 — 30 lots	Oct. 17, 1791	Uriah Forrest, Benjamin Stoddert and James M. Lingan: 1, 2, 5, 8, 9-13, 18, 19, 22, 23, 29, 30 United States: 3, 4, 7, 8, 14-17, 20, 21, 24-28
106 — 30 lots		James M. Lingan: 6-13, 21-27 United States: 1-5, 14-20, 28-30
107 — 30 lots	Oct. 17, 1791	James M. Lingan: 6-12 United States: 1-5, 29, 30
re-division	Nov. 8, 1796	James M. Lingan: 18-20 United States: 21-28
108		No such Square
109 — 1 lot	Aug. 31, 1796	Anthony Holmead All to the United States
110 — 16 lots	Aug. 9, 1797	Anthony Holmead and James M. Lingan James M. Lingan: All
111 — 12 lots	Jan. 17, 1797	James M. Lingan: All
112 — 1 lot	Jan. 17, 1797	James M. Lingan All to the United States
113 — 2 lots	Jan. 17, 1797	James M. Lingan: All
114 — 3 lots	Jan. 17, 1797	James M. Lingan: All
115 — 14 lots	Jan. 17, 1797	James M. Lingan: All
116 — 24 lots	Jan. 17, 1797	James M. Lingan: 4-9, 16-21 United States: 1-3, 10-15, 20-24
117 — 32 lots	Oct. 5, 1792	James M. Lingan: 1, 4, 5, 9-11, 16, 17, 20, 21, 24-27, 31, 32 United States: 2, 3, 6-8, 12-15, 18, 19, 22, 23, 28-30

Square — No. of Lots	Date of Division	Original Owners, Lots Retained by Them, and Conveyed to the United States
re-division 30 lots	Sept. 12, 1797	James M. Lingan and Robert Peter James M. Lingan: 4-11, 19-25 United States: 1-3, 12-18, 26-30
118 — 13 lots	June 27, 1795	James M. Lingan and James Greenleaf James M. Lingan: 6-8; United States: 1-5, 9-13
119 — 13 lots	June 29, 1795	James Greenleaf: 1-3, 7-10 United States: 4-6, 11-13
120 — 14 lots	Sept. 7, 1796	Assigned that part not included in the town of Hamburgh, Robert Morris and John Nicholson: 9-11 Assigned 1 for No. 252 in Hamburgh Assigned 2 for No. 205 in Hamburgh Assigned 3 for No. 206 in Hamburgh Assigned 4 for No. 209 in Hamburgh Assigned 5 for No. 207 in Hamburgh Assigned 12 for No. 268 in Hamburgh Assigned 13 for No. 250 in Hamburgh Assigned 14 for No. 248 in Hamburgh United States: parts of 6, 7, 8
121 — 9 lots	Aug. 28, 1799	Assigned 1 for No. 148 in Hamburgh Assigned 2 for Nos. 26 and 222 in Hamburgh Assigned 3 for No. 247 in Hamburgh Assigned 5 for No. 188 in Hamburgh Assigned 8 for No. 249 in Hamburgh Assigned 9 for No. 246 in Hamburgh United States: 4, 6, 7
122 — 14 lots	June 26, 1794	Assigned 4 for No. 218 in Hamburgh Assigned 5 for No. 220 in Hamburgh Assigned 6 for No. 215 in Hamburgh Assigned 7 for No. 283 in Hamburgh Assigned 8 for No. 176 in Hamburgh Assigned 10 for No. 245 in Hamburgh Assigned 11 for No. 244 in Hamburgh Assigned 12 for No. 217 in Hamburgh Assigned 13 for No. 242 in Hamburgh Assigned 14 for No. 285 in Hamburgh United States: 1, 2, 3, 9
123 — 4 lots	Aug. 28, 1799	Assigned 1 for Nos. 9 and 237 in Hamburgh Assigned 3 for No. 239 in Hamburgh Assigned 4 for No. 238 in Hamburgh United States: 2
124 — 7 lots	Aug. 28, 1799	Assigned 1 for No. 234 in Hamburgh Assigned 2 for No. 233 in Hamburgh Assigned 3 for No. 230 in Hamburgh Assigned 4 for Nos. 16 and 236 in Hamburgh Assigned 6 for No. 235 in Hamburgh Assigned 7 for No. 240 in Hamburgh United States: 5
125 — 1 lot	Jan. 12, 1797	Assigned for Nos. 229 and 287 in Hamburgh
126 — 33 lots	Oct. 7, 1791	Samuel Davidson: 1-3, 8-14, 20, 21, 32, 33 United States: 4, 5, 15-19, 22-24, 25-31

Square — No. of Lots	Date of Division	Original Owners, Lots Retained by Them, and Conveyed to the United States
127 — 33 lots	Oct. 17, 1791	Samuel Davidson: 1-6, 9-13, 24, 25, 31-33 United States: 7, 8, 14-23, 27-30
128 — 14 lots	Dec. 26, 1796	David Burnes: 1, 9-14 United States: 2-8
N of 128, 1 lot	June 26, 1794	Assigned all for Nos. 231 and 232 in Hamburgh
129 — 2 lots	Dec. 26, 1796	David Burnes: 1 United States: 2
130		No such Square
131 — 9 lots	Aug. 9, 1797	Anthony Holmead and James M. Lingan All to the United States
132 — 20 lots	Aug. 9, 1797	Anthony Holmead and James M. Lingan Anthony Holmead: All
133 — 20 lots	Jan. 17, 1797	James M. Lingan and Anthony Holmead James M. Lingan: All
134 — 15 lots	Jan. 17, 1797	James M. Lingan and Samuel Blodget All to the United States
135 — 3 lots	Jan. 17, 1797	James M. Lingan All to the United States
136 — 6 lots	Aug. 16, 1799	James M. Lingan and Samuel Blodget James M. Lingan: 1-3 United States: 4-6
137 — 4 lots	Jan. 17, 1797	James M. Lingan and Samuel Blodget All to the United States
N of 137, 1 lot	Aug. 16, 1799	James M. Lingan and Samuel Blodget All to Samuel Blodget
138 — 4 lots	Jan. 17, 1797	James M. Lingan: All
139 — 25 lots	Jan. 17, 1797	James M. Lingan (for improvements, 13-16): 5-12, 17-22 United States: 1-4, 23-25
re-division	Jan. 1, 1808	James M. Lingan: All
140 — 36 lots	Oct. 5, 1792	James M. Lingan: 1, 4-7, 11-13, 18, 19, 24, 25, 28-31, 35, 36 United States: 2, 3, 8-10, 14-17, 20-23, 26, 27, 32-34
re-division	Sept. 12, 1797	James M. Lingan: 1-4, 13-21, 31-34 United States: 5-12, 22-30
141 — 20 lots	Sept. 2, 1796	Robert Morris, John Nicholson and David Burnes Morris and Nicholson: 14-18 United States: parts of 8, 9, 18, 19, and all of 1, 2, 10, 11, 12 and 20 Assigned 4 for No. 272 in Hamburgh Assigned 5 for No. 271 in Hamburgh Assigned 6 for No. 286 in Hamburgh Assigned 7 for No. 243 in Hamburgh Assigned 8 for No. 267 in Hamburgh

Square — No. of Lots	Date of Division	Original Owners, Lots Retained by Them, and Conveyed to the United States
142 — 15 lots	Sept. 6, 1796	David Burnes: 1, 2, 15 United States: 3, 4, 7, 10-14 Assigned 5 for No. 269 in Hamburgh Assigned 6 for No. 273 in Hamburgh Assigned 8 for No. 221 in Hamburgh Assigned 9 for No. 277 in Hamburgh
143 — 20 lots	Aug. 23, 1796	David Burnes: 13-17, and one-half of the front of 18 lying next and adjoining 176, and running the length of 18 United States: 1, 2, 3, and half of front of 18 adjoining 19, and running the length of 18, and lots 19 and 20 Assigned 5 for No. 280 in Hamburgh Assigned 7 for No. 278 in Hamburgh Assigned 8 for No. 280 in Hamburgh Assigned 11 for No. 274 in Hamburgh Assigned 6 for No. 87 in Hamburgh Assigned 9 for No. 275 in Hamburgh Also to the United States: 4, 10, 12
144 — 16 lots	Oct. 24, 1799	David Burnes (heirs): 1-4, 10-16 United States: 5, 6 Assigned 7 for No. 284 in Hamburgh Assigned 8 for No. 282 in Hamburgh Assigned 9 for No. 281 in Hamburgh
145 — 8 lots	Oct. 24, 1799	David Burnes (heirs): 3-6 United States: 1, 2, 7, 8
146 — 3 lots	Oct. 24, 1799	David Burnes (heirs) All to the United States
147 — 4 lots		David Burnes (heirs): 1, 3 United States: 2, 4
148 — 2 lots	Oct. 24, 1799	David Burnes (heirs): 1 United States: 2
149 — 1 lot	Sept. 19, 1797	Robert Peter: All
150 — 13 lots	Jan. 17, 1797	Robert Peter and James M. Lingan Robert Peter: 7, 8 James M. Lingan: 4, 5, 6 United States: 1, 2, 3, 9, 10, 11, 12, 13
151 — 26 lots	Jan. 17, 1797	James M. Lingan: All
152 — 21 lots	Jan. 17, 1797	James M. Lingan All to the United States
153 — 16 lots	Jan. 17, 1797	James M. Lingan All to the United States
S of 153, 1 lot	Aug. 16, 1799	James M. Lingan and Samuel Blodget All to Samuel Blodget
154 — 14 lots	Jan. 17, 1797	James M. Lingan and Samuel Blodget All to James M. Lingan
155 — 22 lots	June 18, 1798	Samuel Blodget and James M. Lingan All to the United States

Square — No. of Lots	Date of Division	Original Owners, Lots Retained by Them, and Conveyed to the United States
156 — 32 lots	June 18, 1798	Samuel Blodget: All
157 — 22 lots	June 18, 1798	Samuel Blodget: All
158 — 22 lots	June 18, 1798	Samuel Blodget All to the United States
159 — 16 lots	June 27, 1795	Samuel Blodget: 6-12 United States: 1-5, 13-16
160 — 4 lots	Oct. 4, 1796	Samuel Blodget All to the United States
161 — 10 lots	Oct. 4, 1796	Samuel Davidson and Samuel Blodget Samuel Davidson: 2, 9, 10 Samuel Blodget: 8 United States: 1, 3-7
162 — 21 lots	May 31, 1797	Samuel Davidson and Samuel Blodget All to the United States
163 — 14 lots	Sept. 27, 1796	Samuel Davidson: 1-4, 8-11 United States: 5-7, 12-14
164 — 9 lots	Dec. 23, 1796	Samuel Davidson All to the United States
165 — 13 lots	Sept. 27, 1796	Samuel Davidson: All
166 — 27 lots	Oct. 13, 1792	Samuel Davidson: 1, 4-7, 11-13, 17-19, 25-27 United States: 2, 3, 8-10, 14-16, 20-24
167 — 24 lots	Oct. 12, 1792	Samuel Davidson: All
168 — 21 lots	Aug. 29, 1796	Samuel Davidson and David Burnes Samuel Davidson, with consent of David Burnes: 1-3, 5-7, 12-14, 19, 20 United States: 4, 8-11, 15-18, 21
169 — 22 lots	Aug. 29, 1796	Samuel Davidson and David Burnes Samuel Davidson, with consent of David Burnes: 1-5, 11-13, 17, 18, 22 United States: 6-10, 14-16, 19-21
170 — 16 lots	Nov. 19, 1796	Samuel Davidson and David Burnes Samuel Davidson: 9, 10, 13 David Burnes: 1, 2, 5, 6, 14 United States: 3, 4, 7, 8, 11, 12, 15, 16
171 — 1 lot	Oct. 8, 1792	David Burnes: All
172 — 28 lots	Oct. 8, 1792	David Burnes All to the United States
173 — 22 lots	Oct. 8, 1792	David Burnes: All
S of 173, 1 lot	July 16, 1793	David Burnes: All for improvements.
174 — 6 lots	Sept. 19, 1797	Robert Peter: All

Square — No. of Lots	Date of Division	Original Owners, Lots Retained by Them, and Conveyed to the United States
175 — 16 lots	Sept. 19, 1797	Robert Peter All to the United States
176 — 7 lots	Sept. 19, 1797	Robert Peter: All
177 — 16 lots	Jan. 17, 1797	Robert Peter and James M. Lingan Robert Peter: 1-3, 10-16 United States: 4-9
N of 177, 3 lots	Sept. 19, 1797	Robert Peter All to the United States
178 — 20 lots	Nov. 6, 1798	Robert Peter and Samuel Blodget Samuel Blodget: 9-18 United States: 1-8, 19, 20
179 — 20 lots	June 18, 1798	Samuel Blodget All to the United States
180 — 20 lots	June 18, 1798	Samuel Blodget: All
181 — 30 lots	June 22, 1795	Samuel Blodget All to the United States
S of 181, 1 lot	Aug. 19, 1799	Samuel Blodget All to the United States
182 — 17 lots	June 22, 1795	Samuel Blodget: All
N of 182, 1 lot	Aug. 19, 1799	Samuel Blodget All to the United States
183 — 32 lots	May 31, 1797	Samuel Davidson and Samuel Blodget Samuel Davidson: 1-4, 13, 16, 19, 20, 29-32 Samuel Blodget: 18 United States: 5-12, 17, 21-28 Samuel Davidson, for improvements: 14, 15
184 — 21 lots re-division	Oct. 8, 1792 Nov. 7, 1797	Samuel Davidson: 2, 3, 6-9, 13, 14, 17-19 United States: 1, 4, 5, 10-12, 15, 16, 20, 21
185 — 21 lots	Oct. 8, 1792	Samuel Davidson: 3, 4, 7-9, 14, 15, 18-20 United States: 1, 2, 5, 6, 10-13, 16, 17, 21
186 — 1 lot	Oct. 11, 1792	Samuel Davidson: All
187		No such Square
188 — 1 lot	Sept. 14, 1796	Robert Peter: All
S of 188, 1 lot	Sept. 14, 1796	Robert Peter All to the United States
189 — 10 lots	Sept. 14, 1796	Robert Peter All to the United States
N of 189, 1 lot	Sept. 14, 1796	Robert Peter: All
190 — 20 lots	Sept. 14, 1796	Robert Peter All to the United States

Square — No. of Lots	Date of Division	Original Owners, Lots Retained by Them, and Conveyed to the United States
191 — 20 lots	Sept. 14, 1796	Robert Peter: All
192 — 20 lots	Nov. 6, 1798	Samuel Blodget and Robert Peter Samuel Blodget: 1-8, 19, 20 United States: 9-18
193 — 20 lots	June 18, 1798	Samuel Blodget: All
194 — 20 lots	June 18, 1798	Samuel Blodget All to the United States
195 — 30 lots	June 22, 1795	Samuel Blodget: All
S of 195, 1 lot	Aug. 19, 1799	Samuel Blodget: All
196 — 17 lots	July 22, 1795	Samuel Blodget All to the United States
re-division	Dec. 24, 1799	Samuel Davidson: 1, 2, 7 United States: 3-6, 8-17
N of 196, 1 lot	Aug. 19, 1799	Samuel Blodget: All
197 — 32 lots	Sept. 27, 1796	Samuel Davidson: 5-12, 21-28 United States: 1-4, 13-20, 29-32
198 — 21 lots re-divided	Oct. 8, 1792 Nov. 7, 1797	Samuel Davidson: 3, 4, 7-9, 13, 14, 17-19 United States: 1, 2, 5, 6, 10-12, 15, 16, 20, 21
199 — 21 lots	Oct. 8, 1792	Samuel Davidson: 3, 4, 7-9, 13, 14, 17-20 United States: 1, 2, 5, 6, 10-12, 15, 16, 21
200 — 18 lots	Oct. 11, 1792	Samuel Davidson All to the United States
201		No such Square
202 — 1 lot	Sept. 14, 1796	Robert Peter: All
203 — 20 lots	Sept. 14, 1796	Robert Peter: All
204 — 20 lots	Sept. 14, 1796	Robert Peter All to the United States
205 — 24 lots	Sept. 14, 1796	Robert Peter: 1-4, 17-24 United States: 5-16
206 — 24 lots	Nov. 6, 1798	Robert Peter and Samuel Blodget Robert Peter: 3-24 United States: 1, 2
207 — 24 lots	Nov. 6, 1798	Robert Peter and Samuel Blodget Samuel Blodget: 1-4, 17-24 United States: 5-16
208 — 26 lots	Oct. 4, 1796	Samuel Blodget: All
209 — 26 lots	Oct. 4, 1796	Samuel Blodget All to the United States
210 — 20 lots	Oct. 4, 1796	Samuel Blodget: All

Square — No. of Lots	Date of Division	Original Owners, Lots Retained by Them, and Conveyed to the United States
211 — 19 lots	Oct. 4, 1796	Samuel Blodget All to the United States
212 — 16 lots	Nov. 29, 1798	John Davidson's heirs and Samuel Blodget John Davidson's heirs: 3, 4 Samuel Blodget: 5-10 United States: 1, 2, 11-16
213 — 2 lots	Oct. 4, 1796	John Davidson's heirs: All
214 — 20 lots	May 8, 1797	Samuel Davidson and John Davidson's heirs John Davidson's heirs: 1, 8-11, 19, 20 Samuel Davidson, trustee: 2-7, 12-18
215 — 2 lots	Nov. 1, 1796	John Davidson's heirs: All
216 — 7 lots	Dec. 28, 1796	Samuel Davidson and heirs of John Davidson All to Samuel Davidson
217 — 10 lots	Nov. 1, 1796	Samuel Davidson and heirs of John Davidson All to Samuel Davidson
218 — 22 lots	Mar. 23, 1797	Samuel Davidson and heirs of John Davidson All to the United States
219 — 13 lots	Sept. 27, 1796	Samuel Davidson All to the United States
220 — 22 lots	Mar. 23, 1797	Samuel Davidson and heirs of John Davidson All to John Davidson's heirs
221 — 24 lots	Oct. 11, 1792	Samuel Davidson All to the United States
222 — 15 lots	Mar. 23, 1797	Samuel Davidson and heirs of John Davidson John Davidson's heirs: 4-8, 13, 14 United States: 1-3, 9-12, 15
223 — 7 lots	Sept. 20, 1797	David Burnes, heirs of John Davidson, and Samuel Davidson. David Burnes: 2, 5 John Davidson's heirs: 3, 4, 6 United States: 1, 7
224 — 16 lots	Oct. 4, 1792	David Burnes: 2, 3, 6, 7, 10, 11, 14, 15 United States: 1, 4, 5, 8, 9, 12, 13, 16
225 — 16 lots	Oct. 8, 1792	David Burnes All to the United States
226 — 14 lots	Oct. 8, 1792	David Burnes: All
227 — 16 lots	Oct. 4, 1792	David Burnes: 2, 3, 6, 7, 10, 11, 14, 15 United States: 1, 4, 5, 8, 9, 12, 13, 16
228	Oct. 8, 1792‡ Oct. 18, 1792†	David Burnes All to the United States
229 — 5 lots	Oct. 4, 1799	David Burnes' heirs Marcia Burnes: 1, 5 United States: 2, 3, 4

Square — No. of Lots	Date of Division	Original Owners, Lots Retained by Them, and Conveyed to the United States
230 — 12 lots	Sept. 10, 1796	Uriah Forrest, Benjamin Stoddert and David Burnes: 1, 3, 5, 7, 9, 11 United States: 2, 4, 6, 8, 10, 12
231 — 28 lots	Dec. 26, 1796	Notley Young and Daniel Carroll of Duddington Notley Young: 1-10, 24, 26-28 Daniel Carroll of Duddington: 14-18, 23, 25 United States: 11-13, 19-22
232 — 22 lots	Jan. 12, 1797	Notley Young: All
233 — 1 lot	Jan. 12, 1797	Notley Young: All
234 — 1 lot		Robert Peter: All for improvements.
235 — 20 lots	Sept. 14, 1796	Robert Peter: All
236 — 20 lots	Sept. 14, 1796	Robert Peter All to the United States
237 — 24 lots	Sept. 14, 1796	Robert Peter All to the United States
238 — 24 lots Lot 16 not recorded‡	Nov. 6, 1798	Robert Peter and Samuel Blodget Robert Peter: 10-16 Samuel Blodget: 2-9 United States: 1, 17-24
239 — 24 lots	Oct. 4, 1796	Samuel Blodget: All
240 — 24 lots	Oct. 4, 1796	Samuel Blodget All to the United States
241 — 1 lot	June 18, 1798	Samuel Blodget: All
242 — 17 lots	June 18, 1798	Samuel Blodget All to the United States
N of 242, 2 lots	Oct. 4, 1796	Samuel Blodget: All
243 — 6 lots	Oct. 4, 1796	Samuel Blodget All to the United States
244 — 2 lots	Nov. 29, 1798‡ Nov. 29, 1796†	Heirs of John Davidson and Samuel Blodget All to the United States
245 — 16 lots	Nov. 1, 1796	Samuel Blodget and heirs of John Davidson All to the United States
246 — 2 lots	Nov. 1, 1796	Heirs of John Davidson All to the United States
247 — 18 lots	Nov. 1, 1796	Heirs of John Davidson All to the United States
248 — 20 lots	Nov. 1, 1796	Heirs of John Davidson: All
249 — 30 lots	Nov. 1, 1796	Heirs of John Davidson All to the United States

Square — No. of Lots	Date of Division	Original Owners, Lots Retained by Them, and Conveyed to the United States
250 — 30 lots	Nov. 1, 1796	Heirs of John Davidson All to the United States
251 — 2 lots	Nov. 1, 1796	Heirs of John Davidson: All
252 — 27 lots	Jan. 30, 1797	Heirs of John Davidson and David Burnes John Davidson's heirs: 13-17 David Burnes: 5-12 United States: 1-4, 18-27
253 — 26 lots	Oct. 4, 1792	David Burnes: 2-5, 10, 11, 15-18, 22-25 United States: 1, 6-9, 12-14, 19-21, 26
254 — 27 lots	Oct. 5, 1792	David Burnes: 3, 4, 6, 8, 9, 12, 13, 16, 17, 18, 22, 23, 26, 27 United States: 1, 2, 5, 7, 10, 11, 14, 15, 19, 20, 21, 24, 25
255 — 14 lots	Oct. 4, 1792	David Burnes: 1, 2, 6, 7, 10-12 United States: 3-5, 8, 9, 13, 14
256 — 14 lots	Oct. 4, 1792	David Burnes: 1, 2, 3, 6, 7, 11, 12 United States: 4, 5, 8-10, 13, 14
257 — 10 lots	July 19, 1796	David Burnes: 1, 7-10 United States: 2-6
258 — 18 lots	Oct. 5, 1792	David Burnes: 3-5, 8, 9, 13, 14, 17, 18 United States: 1, 2, 6, 7, 10, 12, 15, 16
259 — 8 lots	Sept. 10, 1796	Uriah Forrest, Benjamin Stoddert and David Burnes: 1, 3, 5, 7 United States: 2, 4, 6, 8
260 — 8 lots	Sept. 10, 1796	Uriah Forrest, Benjamin Stoddert and David Burnes: 2, 4, 6, 8 United States: 1, 3, 5, 7
261		No such Square
262		No such Square
263 — 24 lots	Nov. 5, 1796	Notley Young and Daniel Carroll of Duddington Daniel Carroll of Duddington: 4-15 United States: 1-3, 16-24
264 — 24 lots	Nov. 5, 1796	Notley Young and Daniel Carroll of Duddington Daniel Carroll of Duddington: 4-15 United States: 3-14
265 — 16 lots	Jan. 12, 1797	Notley Young: All
266 — 20 lots	Mar. 24, 1797	Notley Young All to the United States
267 — 16 lots	Jan. 12, 1797	Notley Young: All
SE of 267, 1 lot	Mar. 24, 1797	Notley Young: All
268 — 11 lots	Mar. 24, 1797	Notley Young All to the United States
269 — 9 lots	Mar. 23, 1797‡ Mar. 4, 1797†	Notley Young All to the United States

Square — No. of Lots	Date of Division	Original Owners, Lots Retained by Them, and Conveyed to the United States
270 — 1 lot	Mar. 24, 1797	Notley Young All to the United States
271 — 1 lot	Sept. 14, 1796	Robert Peter: All
272 — 14 lots	Sept. 14, 1796	Robert Peter: All
273 — 14 lots	Sept. 14, 1796	Robert Peter All to the United States
274 — 18 lots	Sept. 14, 1796	Robert Peter All to the United States
275 — 18 lots	Nov. 6, 1798	Robert Peter and Samuel Blodget Robert Peter: 9-14 Samuel Blodget: 3-7 United States: 1, 2, 8, 15-18
276 — 18 lots	Oct. 4, 1796	Samuel Blodget All to the United States
277 — 9 lots	Oct. 4, 1796	Samuel Blodget: All
S of 177, 1 lot	June 18, 1798	Samuel Blodget All to the United States
278 — 2 lots	June 18, 1798	Samuel Blodget All to the United States
N of 278, 1 lot	June 18, 1798	Samuel Blodget: All
279 — 1 lot	June 18, 1798	Samuel Blodget: All
280 — 18 lots	Nov. 29, 1798	Samuel Blodget and John Davidson's heirs Samuel Blodget: 3-11 United States: 1, 2, 12-18
281 — 16 lots	Nov. 1, 1796	Heirs of John Davidson: 3-10 United States: 1, 2, 11-16
282 — 9 lots	Nov. 1, 1796	Heirs of John Davidson: 1, 2, 8, 9 United States: 3-7
283 — 5 lots	Nov. 1, 1796	Heirs of John Davidson: All
284 — 1 lot† (24 lots‡)	May 20, 1800	Heirs of John Davidson: All for improvements.
285 — 20 lots	Nov. 1, 1796	Heirs of John Davidson: All
286 — 13 lots	Nov. 1, 1796	Heirs of John Davidson All to the United States
287 — 10 lots	Nov. 1, 1796	Heirs of John Davidson: All
288 — 26 lots	Jan. 30, 1797	Heirs of John Davidson and David Burnes David Burnes: 1-3, 17-26 United States: 4-16
289 — 20 lots	Oct. 4, 1792	David Burnes: 2, 3, 6-8, 12-14, 17, 18 United States: [1†], 4, 5, 9-11, 15, 16, 19, 20

Square — No. of Lots	Date of Division	Original Owners, Lots Retained by Them, and Conveyed to the United States
290 — 20 lots	Oct. 5, 1792	David Burnes: 4-6, 9, 10, 14-16, 19, 20 United States: 1-3, 7, 8, 11-13, 17, 18
291 — 12 lots	July 19, 1796	David Burnes: 3-5, 9-11 United States: 1, 2, 6-8, 12
292 — 4 lots	July 19, 1796	David Burnes: 3, 4 United States: 1, 2
293 — 20 lots	Oct. 5, 1792	David Burnes: 4-6, 9, 10, 14-16, 19, 20 United States: 1-3, 7, 8, 11-13, 17, 18
294 — 5 lots	July 19, 1796	David Burnes: 2, 4, 5 United States: 1, 3
295 — 6 lots	Sept. 10, 1796	Uriah Forrest, Benjamin Stoddert and David Burnes: 2, 4, 6 United States: 1, 3, 5
296 — 24 lots	Jan. 12, 1797	Notley Young and Daniel Carroll of Duddington All to Notley Young
297 — 26 lots	Mar. 24, 1797	Notley Young All to the United States
298 — 1 lot	Sept. 26, 1797	Notley Young All to the United States
299 — 18 lots	Mar. 24, 1797	Notley Young All to the United States
300 — 1 lot	Oct. 18, 1794†	Notley Young All to the United States All to James Greenleaf
301		No such Square
302 — 14 lots	Sept. 14, 1796	Robert Peter: All
303 — 8 lots	Sept. 14, 1796	Robert Peter: All
304 — 8 lots	Sept. 14, 1796	Robert Peter All to the United States
305 — 12 lots	Sept. 14, 1796	Robert Peter All to the United States
306 — 12 lots	Nov. 5, 1798† Nov. 6, 1798‡	Robert Peter and Samuel Blodget Samuel Blodget: 1-4, 11, 12 United States: 5-10
307 — 2 lots	Oct. 4, 1796	Samuel Blodget All to the United States
308 — 1 lot	Oct. 4, 1796	Samuel Blodget: All
309 — 10 lots	Oct. 4, 1796	Samuel Blodget All to the United States
310 — 2 lots	Oct. 4, 1796	Samuel Blodget: All

Square — No. of Lots	Date of Division	Original Owners, Lots Retained by Them, and Conveyed to the United States
311 — 2 lots	Oct. 4, 1796	Samuel Blodget All to the United States
312 — 8 lots	Oct. 4, 1796	Samuel Blodget All to the United States
313 — 10 lots	Nov. 29, 1798‡ Aug. 18, 1797†	Samuel Blodget and heirs of John Davidson John Davidson's heirs: 1, 10 Samuel Blodget: 7-9 United States: 2-6
314 — 14 lots	Nov. 1, 1796	Heirs of John Davidson All to the United States
315 — 11 lots	Nov. 1, 1796	Heirs of John Davidson: 2-6 United States: 1, 7-11
316 — 8 lots	Nov. 1, 1796	Heirs of John Davidson: All
317 — 14 lots	Nov. 1, 1796	Heirs of John Davidson All to the United States
318 — 12 lots	Jan. 30, 1797	Heirs of John Davidson and David Burnes John Davidson's heirs: 3-6, 7, 9 United States: 1, 2, 8, 10-12
319 — 16 lots	July 20, 1796	David Burnes: 3, 4, 6, 9, 11-13, 15 United States: 1, 2, 5, 7, 8, 10, 14, 16
320 — 12 lots	Oct. 5, 1792	David Burnes: 3-5, 9-11 United States: 1, 2, 6-8, 12
321 — 16 lots	Oct. 5, 1792	David Burnes: 3, 4, 7, 8, 11, 12, 15, 16 United States: 1, 2, 5, 6, 9, 10, 13, 14
322 — 12 lots	July 19, 1796	David Burnes: 2, 4, 7, 10-12 United States: 1, 3, 5, 6, 8, 9
323 — 14 lots	Oct. 5, 1792	David Burnes: 3, 4, 7, 10, 11, 13, 14 United States: 1, 2, 5, 6, 8, 9, 12
324 — 12 lots	Oct. 5, 1792	David Burnes: 3-5, 9-11 United States: 1, 2, 6-8, 12
325 — 9 lots	Mar. 24, 1797	Notley Young: All
326 — 10 lots	Mar. 24, 1797	Notley Young: All
327 — 11 lots	Mar. 24, 1797	Notley Young: All
328 — 4 lots	Mar. 24, 1797	Notley Young: All
329 — 1 lot		Notley Young: All for improvements.
330 — 1 lot	Sept. 14, 1796	Robert Peter: All
331 — 8 lots	Sept. 14, 1796	Robert Peter: All
332 — 8 lots	Sept. 14, 1796	Robert Peter All to the United States

Square — No. of Lots	Date of Division	Original Owners, Lots Retained by Them, and Conveyed to the United States
333 — 12 lots	Sept. 14, 1796	Robert Peter All to the United States
334 — 2 lots	Oct. 4, 1796	Samuel Blodget: All
N of 334, 1 lot	Aug. 16, 1799	Samuel Blodget All to the United States
335 — 12 lots	Oct. 4, 1796	Samuel Blodget All to the United States
336 — 12 lots	Oct. 4, 1796	Samuel Blodget: All
337 — 5 lots	Oct. 4, 1796	Samuel Blodget: All
N of 337, 1 lot	June 18, 1798	Samuel Blodget: All
338 — 8 lots	Oct. 4, 1796	Samuel Blodget: All
339 — 10 lots	Nov. 29, 1798	Heirs of John Davidson and Samuel Blodget Samuel Blodget: 1, 7-10 United States: 2-6
340 — 14 lots	Nov. 1, 1796	Heirs of John Davidson: All
341 — 12 lots	Nov. 1, 1796	John Davidson's heirs: 1, 8-12 United States: 2-7
342 — 7 lots	Nov. 1, 1796	John Davidson's heirs: All
343 — 7 lots	Nov. 1, 1796	John Davidson's heirs All to the United States
344 — 10 lots	Jan. 30, 1797	David Burnes and John Davidson's heirs John Davidson's heirs: 1, 7-10 United States: 2-6
345 — 16 lots	July 20, 1796	David Burnes: 1, 5, 6, 8, 9, 13-15 United States: 2-4, 7, 10-12, 16
346 — 12 lots	Oct. 7, 1792	David Burnes: 3-5, 9-11 United States: 1, 2, 6-8, 12
347 — 16 lots	Oct. 5, 1792	David Burnes: 3, 4, 7, 8, 11, 12, 15, 16 United States: 1, 2, 5, 6, 9, 10, 13, 14
348 — 18 lots	Oct. 5, 1792	David Burnes: 3, 4, 7-9, 12, 13, 17, 18 United States: 1, 2, 5, 6, 10, 11, 14-16
349 — 8 lots	July 19, 1796	David Burnes: 3-5, 7 United States: 1, 2, 6, 8
350 — 12 lots	Oct. 5, 1792	David Burnes: 3-5, 9-11 United States: 1, 2, 6-8, 12
351 — 16 lots	Sept. 26, 1797	Notley Young All to the United States
N of 351, 2 lots	Nov. 5, 1796	Notley Young and Daniel Carroll of Duddington Daniel Carroll of Duddington: 1 United States: 2

Square — No. of Lots	Date of Division	Original Owners, Lots Retained by Them, and Conveyed to the United States
352 — 5 lots	Mar. 24, 1797	Notley Young All to the United States
353 — 14 lots	Mar. 24, 1797	Notley Young: All
354 — 16 lots	Mar. 24, 1797	Notley Young All to the United States
355 — 4 lots		Notley Young: All for improvements.
356 — 1 lot		Notley Young: All for improvements.
357 — 1 lot	Sept. 14, 1796	Robert Peter: All
358 — 1 lot	Sept. 14, 1796	Robert Peter: All
359 — 5 lots	Sept. 14, 1796	Robert Peter All to the United States
360 — 4 lots	Sept. 14, 1796	Robert Peter All to the United States
361 — 14 lots	Nov. 6, 1798	Robert Peter and Samuel Blodget Robert Peter: 6-11 Samuel Blodget: 1, 12-14 United States: 2-5
362 — 20 lots	Oct. 4, 1796	Samuel Blodget All to the United States
363 — 20 lots	Oct. 4, 1796	Samuel Blodget: All
364 — 15 lots	Oct. 4, 1796	Samuel Blodget All to the United States
365 — 17 lots	Oct. 4, 1796	Samuel Blodget: All
366 — 16 lots	Oct. 4, 1796	Samuel Blodget: All
367 — 18 lots	Dec. 26, 1796	Heirs of John Davidson, Dominick Lynch, Comfort Sands and Samuel Blodget All to John Davidson's heirs
368 — 22 lots	Sept. 26, 1796† Dec. 26, 1796‡	John Davidson's heirs, Dominick Lynch and Comfort Sands: 1-4, 11-22 John Davidson's heirs: 5-10
369 — 20 lots	Dec. 6, 1796†	John Davidson's heirs, Comfort Sands and Dominick Lynch All to the United States
370 — 10 lots	Nov. 28, 1796	John Davidson's heirs, Comfort Sands and Dominick Lynch All to Lynch and Sands
371 — 5 lots	Dec. 26, 1796	John Davidson's heirs, Dominick Lynch and Comfort Sands All to the United States
372 — 5 lots	Dec. 26, 1796	John Davidson's heirs, Dominick Lynch and Comfort Sands All to John Davidson's heirs

Square — No. of Lots	Date of Division	Original Owners, Lots Retained by Them, and Conveyed to the United States
373 — 12 lots	Dec. 26, 1796	John Davidson's heirs, Dominick Lynch and Comfort Sands Lynch and Sands: 1, 2, 10-12 John Davidson's heirs: 3-9
374 — 20 lots	Jan. 12, 1797	Dominick Lynch, Comfort Sands, David Burnes and John Davidson's heirs David Burnes: 5-9, 13, 14 John Davidson's heirs: 10-12 United States: 1-4, 15-20
375		David Burnes: All for improvements.
376 — 22 lots	Oct. 4, 1792	David Burnes: 2-4, 8, 9, 13-15, 19-21 United States: 1, 5-7, 10-12, 16-18, 22
377 — 24 lots	Oct. 4, 1792	David Burnes: 2-4, 8-10, 14-16, 20-22 United States: 1, 5-7, 11-13, 17-19, 23, 24
378 — 26 lots	Oct. 5, 1792	David Burnes: 1, 2, 5, 6, 9-11, 14, 15, 18, 19, 22, 23 United States: 3, 4, 7, 8, 12, 13, 16, 17, 20, 21, 24-26
379 — 11 lots	July 19, 1796	David Burnes: 3, 5, 8, 10, 11 United States: 1, 2, 4, 6, 7, 9
380 — 6 lots	July 20, 1796	David Burnes: 1, 4, 5 United States: 2, 3, 6
381 — 6 lots	July 19, 1796	David Burnes: 1, 2, 6 United States: 3-5
382 — 9 lots	July 19, 1796	David Burnes: 1, 4, 6, 8, 9 United States: 2, 3, 5, 7
383 — 1 lot	Jan. 12, 1797	Notley Young: All
384 — 8 lots	Mar. 24, 1797‡ Mar. 4, 1797†	Notley Young All to the United States
385 — 8 lots	Mar. 24, 1797† Mar. 4, 1797†	Notley Young All to the United States
386 — 1 lot	Sept. 26, 1797	Notley Young All to the United States
387 — 76 lots	Mar. 24, 1797	Notley Young All to the United States
388 — 38 lots	Mar. 24, 1797	Notley Young All to the United States
389 — 1 lot		Notley Young: All for improvements.
390 — 1 lot		Notley Young: All for improvements.
391 — 4 lots		Notley Young: All for improvements.
392		No such Square

Square — No. of Lots	Date of Division	Original Owners, Lots Retained by Them, and Conveyed to the United States
393 — 10 lots	Nov. 6, 1798	Robert Peter and Samuel Blodget Robert Peter: 5-7 Samuel Blodget: 1-3, 10 United States: 4, 8, 9
394 — 12 lots	Oct. 4, 1796	Samuel Blodget All to the United States
395 — 12 lots	Oct. 4, 1796	Samuel Blodget: All
396 — 3 lots	Oct. 4, 1796	Samuel Blodget: All
N of 396, 5 lots	Oct. 4, 1796	Samuel Blodget: All
397 — 12 lots	Oct. 4, 1796	Samuel Blodget: All
398 — 8 lots	Aug. 16, 1799	Samuel Blodget: 1-3, 8 United States: 4-7
399 — 10 lots	Jan. 3, 1796	Dominick Lynch and Comfort Sands All to the United States
400 — 16 lots	June 3, 1796	Dominick Lynch and Comfort Sands All to the United States
401 — 14 lots	June 3, 1796	Dominick Lynch and Comfort Sands All to the Lynch and Sands
402 — 12 lots	June 3, 1796	Dominick Lynch and Comfort Sands All to the United States
403 — 12 lots	June 3, 1796	Dominick Lynch and Comfort Sands Lynch and Sands: 2, 3, 6, 7, 10, 11 United States: 1, 4, 5, 8, 9, 12
404 — 10 lots	July 20, 1796	David Burnes: 1, 2, 8-10 United States: 3-7
405 — 14 lots	July 20, 1796	David Burnes: 1, 5, 8, 10-13 United States: 2-4, 6, 7, 9, 14
406 — 14 lots	May 3, 1792	David Burnes: 2, 3, 8, 11-14 United States: 1, 4-7, 9, 10
407 — 18 lots	Oct. 5, 1792	David Burnes: 1, 2, 5, 6, 10, 11, 14-16 United States: 3, 4, 7-9, 12, 13, 17, 18
408 — 12 lots	Oct. 4, 1792	David Burnes: 3-5, 9-11 United States: 1, 2, 6-8, 12
409 — 8 lots	Nov. 5, 1796	Notley Young and Daniel Carroll of Duddington Daniel Carroll of Duddington: 2-5 United States: 1, 6-8
410 — 16 lots	Mar. 24, 1797	Notley Young: All
411 — 40 lots	Mar. 24, 1797	Notley Young: All
412 — 14 lots	Mar. 24, 1797	Notley Young: All
413 — 14 lots	Jan. 12, 1797	Notley Young: All

Square — No. of Lots	Date of Division	Original Owners, Lots Retained by Them, and Conveyed to the United States
414 — 6 lots	Jan. 12, 1797	Notley Young: All
415 — 1 lot		Notley Young: All for improvements.
S of 415, 1 lot		Notley Young: All for improvements.
416 — 5 lots	Nov. 6, 1798	Robert Peter and Samuel Blodget Samuel Blodget: 1, 2, 3 United States: 4, 5
417 — 12 lots	Oct. 4, 1796	Samuel Blodget: All
418		No such Square
419 — 12 lots	Oct. 4, 1796	Samuel Blodget All to the United States
420 — 5 lots	Oct. 4, 1796	Samuel Blodget All to the United States
N of 420, 1 lot	Oct. 4, 1796	Samuel Blodget All to the United States
421 — 12 lots	Oct. 4, 1796	Samuel Blodget All to the United States
422 — 8 lots	Dec. 15, 1796	Dominick Lynch, Comfort Sands and Samuel Blodget Samuel Blodget: 2-5 United States: 1, 6-8
423 — 12 lots	June 3, 1796	Dominick Lynch and Comfort Sands All to the United States
424 — 16 lots	June 3, 1796	Dominick Lynch and Comfort Sands All to Lynch and Sands
425 — 14 lots	June 3, 1796	Dominick Lynch and Comfort Sands All to the United Sands
426 — 12 lots	June 3, 1796	Dominick Lynch and Comfort Sands All to Lynch and Sands
427 — 12 lots	June 3, 1796	Dominick Lynch, Comfort Sands and David Burnes David Burnes: 1 United States: 2, 3, 6, 7, 10, 11 Lynch and Sands: 4, 5, 8, 9, 12
428 — 10 lots	July 20, 1796	David Burnes: 1, 7-10 United States: 2-6
429 — 14 lots	July 12, 1796† July 20, 1796‡	David Burnes: 3, 8-13 United States: 1, 2, 4-7, 14
430 — 14 lots	May 3, 1792	David Burnes: 1, 4, 9, 10, 12-14 United States: 2, 3, 6-8, 11
431 — 18 lots	Oct. 5, 1792	David Burnes: 1, 2, 5, 6, 10, 11, 14-16 United States: 3, 4, 7-9, 12, 13, 17, 18
432 — 12 lots	Oct. 4, 1792	David Burnes: 3-5, 9-11 United States: 1, 2, 6-8, 12

Square — No. of Lots	Date of Division	Original Owners, Lots Retained by Them, and Conveyed to the United States
433 — 8 lots	Nov. 5, 1796	Daniel Carroll of Duddington: 2-5 United States: 1, 6-8
434 — 12 lots	Mar. 24, 1797	Notley Young All to the United States
435 — 24 lots	Mar. 24, 1797	Notley Young All to the United States
436 — 16 lots	Mar. 24, 1797	Notley Young All to the United States
437 — 14 lots	Jan. 12, 1797	Notley Young: All
438 — 14 lots	Jan. 12, 1797	Notley Young: All
439 — 14 lots		Notley Young: All for improvements.
S of 439	Jan. 12, 1797	Notley Young: All
440 — 2 lots	Aug. 16, 1799	Samuel Blodget All to the United States
441 — 20 lots	Oct. 4, 1796	Samuel Blodget All to the United States
442 — 16 lots	Oct. 4, 1796	Samuel Blodget: All
443		No such Square
444 — 19 lots	Oct. 4, 1796	Samuel Blodget All to the United States
445 — 20 lots	Oct. 4, 1796	Samuel Blodget: All
446 — 16 lots	Dec. 15, 1796	Dominick Lynch, Comfort Sands and Samuel Blodget Lunch and Sands: 1-3, 16 Samuel Blodget: 8-11 United States: 407, 12-15
447 — 22 lots	June 3, 1796	Dominick Lynch and Comfort Sands All to the United States
448 — 24 lots	June 3, 1796	Dominick Lynch and Comfort Sands All to the United States
449 — 24 lots	June 3, 1796	Dominick Lynch and Comfort Sands: All
450 — 12 lots	June 3, 1796	Dominick Lynch and Comfort Sands: All
451 — 5 lots	June 3, 1796	Dominick Lynch and Comfort Sands All to the United States
452 — 11 lots	Nov. 16, 1796	Dominick Lynch, Comfort Sands and David Burnes David Burnes: 5-6 Lynch and Sands: 7-9 United States: 1-4, 10, 11
453 — 20 lots	Jan. 30, 1797	David Burnes: 1-4, 15-20 United States: 5-14

Square — No. of Lots	Date of Division	Original Owners, Lots Retained by Them, and Conveyed to the United States
454 — 26 lots	Jan. 30, 1797	David Burnes: 5-17 United States: 1-4, 18-26
455 — 22 lots	Oct. 4, 1792	David Burnes: 2-4, 8-10, 14-16, 20, 21 United States: 1, 5-7, 11-13, 17-19, 22
456 — 24 lots	Oct. 4, 1792	David Burnes: 2-4, 8-10, 14-16, 20-22 United States: 1, 5-7, 11-13, 17-19, 23, 24
457 — 26 lots	Oct. 4, 1792	David Burnes: 2-4, 8-11, 15-17, 21-23 United States: 1, 5-7, 12-14, 18-20, 24-26
458 — 7 lots	July 19, 1796	David Burnes: 4, 6, 7 United States: 1, 2, 3, 5
459 — 6 lots	July 19, 1796	David Burnes: 1, 3, 5 United States: 2, 4, 6
460 — 6 lots	July 19, 1796	David Burnes: 1, 3, 6 United States: 2, 4, 5
461 — 7 lots	April 20, 1796	David Burnes: 2, 3, 6, 7 United States: 1, 4, 5
462 — 6 lots	Nov. 5, 1796	Daniel Carroll of Duddington: 4-6 United States: 1-3
463 — 2 lots	Nov. 5, 1796	Daniel Carroll of Duddington: 2 United States: 1
S of 463, 2 lots	Nov. 5, 1796	Daniel Carroll of Duddington: 2 United States: 1
464 — 11 lots	Mar. 24, 1797	Daniel Carroll of Duddington and Notley Young All of the United States
465 — 56 lots	Mar. 24, 1797	Notley Young All to the United States
466 — 26 lots	Jan. 12, 1797	Notley Young: All
467 — 26 lots	Mar. 24, 1797	Notley Young: All
468 — 34 lots	Mar. 24, 1797	Notley Young All to the United States
469 — 34 lots	Mar. 24, 1797	Notley Young All to the United States
470 — 28 lots	Mar. 24, 1797	Notley Young All to the United States
471 — 24 lots	Mar. 24, 1797	Notley Young: All
W of 471, 6 lots	Oct. 28, 1800	Notley Young: All
472 — 1 lot	Jan. 12, 1797‡ Jan. 12, 1796†	Notley Young: All
473	Oct. 28, 1800	Notley Young All to the United States

Square — No. of Lots	Date of Division	Original Owners, Lots Retained by Them, and Conveyed to the United States
474		No such Square
475 — 7 lots	Oct. 4, 1796	Samuel Blodget All to the United States
E of 475	June 18, 1798‡ June 8, 1798†	Samuel Blodget: All
S of 475, 4 lots	Oct. 4, 1796	Samuel Blodget All to the United States
476 — 2 lots	Oct. 4, 1796	Samuel Blodget: All
477 — 12 lots	Oct. 4, 1796	Samuel Blodget All to the United States
478 — 12 lots	Oct. 4, 1796	Samuel Blodget: All
479 — 10 lots	April 7, 1797	Dominick Lynch, Comfort Sands, Samuel Blodget and William Deakins, Jr.: 1, 2, 8-10 United States: 3-7
480 — 12 lots	June 4, 1796	Dominick Lynch, Comfort Sands and William Deakins, Jr.: 2-4 Lynch and Sands: 507 United States: 1, 8-12
481 — 14 lots	June 4, 1796	Dominick Lynch, Comfort Sands and William Deakins, Jr. William Deakins, Jr.: 6-8 Lynch and Sands: 2-5 United States: 1, 9-14
482 — 12 lots	June 3, 1796	Dominick Lynch and Comfort Sands: All
S of 482, 1 lot	June 5, 1796	Dominick Lynch and Comfort Sands Al to the United States
483 — 7 lots	June 3, 1796	Dominick Lynch and Comfort Sands All to the United States
484 — 8 lots	June 7, 1796	Benjamin Oden, James Greenleaf, Dominick Lynch and Comfort Sands: 2, 4, 6, 8 United States: 1, 3, 5, 7
W of 484, 5 lots	June 3, 1796	Dominick Lynch and Comfort Sands: All
485 — 1 lot	Oct. 19, 1796	Benjamin Oden: All
486 — 34 lots	July 17, 1829	Benjamin Oden and John P. Van Ness Benjamin Oden: 1, 8, 9, 17, 18, 25, 28, 29, 34 John P. Van Ness: 6, 7, 10-12, 24, 26, 27 United States: 2-5, 13-16, 19-23, 30-33
487 — 10 lots	Oct. 5, 1792	David Burnes: 2-4, 8, 9 United States: 1, 5-7, 10
488 — 14 lots	Oct. 4, 1792	David Burnes: 1, 4-7, 10, 11 United States: 2, 3, 8, 9, 10, 11
489 — 16 lots	Oct. 5, 1792	David Burnes: 3, 4, 7, 8, 10, 11, 14, 15 United States: 1, 2, 5, 6, 9, 12, 13, 16

Square — No. of Lots	Date of Division	Original Owners, Lots Retained by Them, and Conveyed to the United States
490 — 25 lots	Oct. 19, 1792	David Burnes: 4-7, 9-11, 15, 16, 19-23 United States: 1-3, 8, 12-14, 17, 18, 22, 24, 25
491 — 24 lots	July 19, 1796	David Burnes: 3, 6, 8, 9, 13-15, 17, 18, 21-23 United States: 1, 2, 4, 5, 7, 10-12, 16, 19, 20, 24
492 — 14 lots	Nov. 5, 1796	Daniel Carroll of Duddington: 1, 2, 7, 12-14 United States: 3-6, 8-11
N of 492, 2 lots	Nov. 5, 1796	Daniel Carroll of Duddington: 2 United States: 1
NW of 492, 2 lots	Nov. 5, 1796	Daniel Carroll of Duddington: 2 United States: 1
493 — 15 lots	Nov. 5, 1796	Daniel Carroll of Duddington: 1-4, 11-15 United States: 5-10
494 — 15 lots	Nov. 5, 1796	Notley Young and Daniel Carroll of Duddington Daniel Carroll of Duddington: 1-3, 11-15 United States: 4-10
496 — 42 lots	Mar. 24, 1797	Notley Young All to the United States
497 — 28 lots	Jan. 12, 1797	Notley Young: All
498 — 42 lots	Mar. 24, 1797	Notley Young All to the United States
499 — 26 lots	Jan. 12, 1797	Notley Young: All
500 — 43 lots	Mar. 24, 1797‡ Mar. 4, 1797†	Notley Young All to the United States
501 — 28 lots	Jan. 12, 1797	Notley Young: All
502 — 74 lots	Mar. 24, 1797	Notley Young All to the United States
503 — 49 lots	Mar. 24, 1797	Notley Young All to the United States
504 — 28 lots	Oct. 18, 1794	Notley Young All to the United States
505 — 1 lot	Jan. 12, 1797	Notley Young: All
506 — 1 lot	Mar. 24, 1797	Notley Young: All
S of 506, 1 lot	Mar. 24, 1797	Notley Young: All
S of S of 506		No record.
507 — 8 lots	June 18, 1798	Samuel Blodget All to the United States
N of 507, 1 lot	June 18, 1798	Samuel Blodget All to the United States
508 — 4 lots	June 18, 1798	Samuel Blodget: All

Square — No. of Lots	Date of Division	Original Owners, Lots Retained by Them, and Conveyed to the United States
N of 508, 1 lot	June 17, 1798	Samuel Blodget: All
509 — 12 lots	June 18, 1798	Samuel Blodget: All
E of 509, 7 lots	June 18, 1798	Samuel Blodget All to the United States
510 — 19 lots	Aug. 28, 1799	Samuel Blodget, Robert Morris and John Nicholson Samuel Blodget: 4, 10-13, 15-18 United States: 1-3, 5-9, 14, 19[40]
E of 510, 1 lot	June 18, 1798	Samuel Blodget All to the United States
511 — 19 lots	Sept. 3, 1796	William Deakins, Jr.: 5, 6, 11-14, 17-19 United States: 1-4, 7-10, 15, 16
512 — 26 lots	Sept. 3, 1796	William Deakins, Jr.: 1-5, 19-26 United States: 6-18
513 — 48 lots	June 4, 1796	Dominick Lynch, Comfort Sands and William Deakins, Jr. William Deakins, Jr.: 8-13, 18-21, 33-36, 38-41 Lynch and Sands: 7, 14-17, 37 United States: 1-6, 22-32, 42-28
514 — 24 lots	June 3, 1796	Dominick Lynch and Comfort Sands United States: 2, 4, 6, 8, 10, 12, 14, 16, 18, 20, 22, 24 Lynch and Sands: 1, 3, 5, 7, 9, 11, 13, 15, 17, 19, 21, 23
515 — 28 lots	June 3, 1796	Dominick Lynch and Comfort Sands: All
N of 515, 9 lots		Dominick Lynch and Comfort Sands All to the United States
516 — 28 lots	June 7, 1796	Benjamin Oden, James Greenleaf, and Dominick Lynch and Comfort Sands Claimants: 2, 4, 6, 8, 10, 12, 14, 16, 18, 20, 22, 24, 26, 28 United States: 1, 3, 5, 7, 9, 11, 13, 15, 17, 19, 21, 23, 25, 27
S of 516, 22 lots	Oct. 19, 1796	Benjamin Oden All to the United States
517 — 36 lots	Oct. 19, 1796	Benjamin Oden All to the United States
518 — 8 lots	Oct. 24, 1796	David Burnes and Benjamin Oden: 1, 3, 5, 7 United States: 2, 4, 6, 8
519 — 3 lots	June 18, 1798	Samuel Blodget: All
520 — 12 lots	June 18, 1798	Samuel Blodget All to the United States
521 — 12 lots	Aug. 28, 1799	William Deakins, Jr. or Morris and Nicholson, and Samuel Blodget: 2, 4, 6, 7, 10, 11 United States: 1, 3, 5, 8, 9, 12[41]

---

[40] See proceedings of the Commissioners, 1798-1800, folio 204.
[41] See proceedings of the Commissioners, 1798-1800, folio 204.

Square — No. of Lots	Date of Division	Original Owners, Lots Retained by Them, and Conveyed to the United States
522 — 1 lot	Sept. 3, 1796	William Deakins, Jr.: All
523 — 10 lots	June 4, 1796	Lynch and Sands, and William Deakins, Jr. Lynch and Sands: 7-10 William Deakins, Jr.: 1 United States: 2-6
524 — 2 lots	June 3, 1796	Lynch and Sands: All
525 — 9 lots	June 3, 1796	Lynch and Sands: All
526 — 12 lots	June 3, 1796	Lynch and Sands: All
527 — 12 lots	Oct. 19, 1796	Benjamin Oden All to the United States
528 — 12 lots	Oct. 19, 1796	Benjamin Oden: All
529 — 20 lots	Oct. 19, 1796	Benjamin Oden All to the United States
530 — 20 lots	Oct. 19, 1796	Benjamin Oden All to the United States
531 — 14 lots	Oct. 4, 1792	David Burnes: 1, 2, 5-7, 9, 10 United States: 3, 4, 8, 11-14
532 — 16 lots	Oct. 5, 1792	David Burnes: 2-4, 7, 8, 11, 14, 15 United States: 1, 5, 6, 9, 10, 12, 13, 16
533 — 25 lots	Oct. 5, 1792	David Burnes: 3, 8-12, 14, 18, 19, 22-24 United States: 1, 2, 4-7, 13, 15-17, 20, 21, 25
534 — 34 lots	Sept. 14, 1796	Daniel Carroll of Duddington: 1-5, 22-34 United States: 6-21
535 — 18 lots	Nov. 5, 1796	Daniel Carroll of Duddington: 1-4, 14-18 United States: 5-13
536 — 7 lots	Nov. 5, 1796	Daniel Carroll of Duddington: All
537 — 7 lots	Nov. 5, 1796	Daniel Carroll of Duddington All to the United States
538 — 28 lots	Sept. 15, 1796	Daniel Carroll of Duddington All to the United States
539 — 28 lots	Jan. 12, 1797	Notley Young: All
540 — 28 lots	Mar. 24, 1797	Notley Young: All
541 — 28 lots	Mar. 24, 1797	Notley Young: All
542 — 26 lots	Mar. 24, 1797	Notley Young: All
543 — 26 lots	Mar. 24, 1797	Notley Young: All
544 — 28 lots	Jan. 12, 1797	Notley Young: All
545 — 78 lots	Mar. 24, 1797	Notley Young All to the United States

Square — No. of Lots	Date of Division	Original Owners, Lots Retained by Them, and Conveyed to the United States
546 — 37 lots	Mar. 24, 1797	Notley Young All to the United States
E of 546, 17 lots	Oct. 28, 1800	Notley Young All to the United States
547 — 22 lots	Mar. 24, 1797	Notley Young All to the United States
E of 547	Oct. 28, 1800	Notley Young All to the United States
548 — 23 lots	Jan. 12, 1797	Notley Young: All
E of 548	Jan. 12, 1797	Notley Young: All
E of E of 548, 1 lot	Oct. 18, 1794	Notley Young: All
549 — 18 lots	Mar. 24, 1797	Notley Young All to the United States
E of 549, 1 lot	Jan. 12, 1797	Notley Young: All
S of 549, 1 lot	Oct. 28, 1800	Notley Young: All
550 — 2 lots	Aug. 28, 1799	Notley Young, Robert Morris, John Nicholson and Samuel Blodget All to the United States[42]
551 — 24 lots	Aug. 28, 1799	Notley Young, Robert Morris, John Nicholson and Samuel Blodget Morris and Nicholson: 6, 7, 10-12, 19 United States: 1-5, 8, 9, 13-18, 24 Not accounted for: 20-23[43]
552 — 32 lots	Aug. 28, 1799	Notley Young, Robert Morris, John Nicholson and Samuel Blodget Notley Young: 1-6, 31, 32 Morris and Nicholson: 25-30 United States: 7-24
553 — 28 lots[44]		Notley Young: 7-20 United States: 1-6, 21-28
W of 553, 5 lots	Sept. 3, 1796	William Deakins, Jr.: 1, 2 United States: 3-5
554 — 30 lots[45]		Notley Young: 7-21 United States: 1-6, 22-30
W of 554, 1 lot	Sept. 3, 1796	William Deakins, Jr. All to the United States

---

[42] See proceedings of the Commissioners, 1798-1800, folio 204.
[43] See proceedings of the Commissioners, 1798-1800, folio 204.
[44] See Book of Division and Sales, no date.
[45] See Book of Division and Sales, no date.

Square — No. of Lots	Date of Division	Original Owners, Lots Retained by Them, and Conveyed to the United States
555 — 26 lots	Dec. 26, 1796	Notley Young, William Deakins, Jr., Dominick Lynch and Comfort Sands Notley Young: 23-26 William Deakins, Jr.: 3 Lynch and Sands: 4-7, 17, 20-22 United States: 1, 2, 8-19
556 — 2 lots	June 3, 1796	Lynch and Sands All to the United States
557 — 35 lots	Dec. 26, 1796	William Deakins, Jr., Notley Young, Dominick Lynch and Comfort Sands William Deakins, Jr.: 1, 2, 31-35 Notley Young: 16-23 Lynch and Sands: 7, 10, 11 United States: 3-6, 8, 9, 12-15, 24-30
558 — 10 lots	June 7, 1796	Benjamin Oden, James Greenleaf, Dominick Lynch and Comfort Sands: 1, 3, 5, 7, 9 United States: 2, 4, 6, 8, 10
559 — 14 lots	Dec. 26, 1796	William Deakins, Jr., Benjamin Oden, Notley Young, Dominick Lynch and Comfort Sands Benjamin Oden: 6, 8-12 Lynch and Sands: 7 United States: 1-5, 13, 14
560 — 1 lot	Oct. 19, 1796	Benjamin Oden: All
561 — 8 lots	Oct. 19, 1796	Benjamin Oden All to the United States
562 — 22 lots	Oct. 19, 1796	Benjamin Oden: All
S of 562, 19 lots	Oct. 19, 1796	Benjamin Oden All to the United States
563 — 1 lot	Oct. 19, 1796	Benjamin Oden: All
564 — 1 lot	Oct. 19, 1796	Benjamin Oden: All
565 — 8 lots	April 17, 1797	Benjamin Oden All to the United States
566 — 1 lot	Oct. 19, 1796	Benjamin Oden: All
567 — 21 lots	Oct. 19, 1796	Benjamin Oden All to the United States
568 — 33 lots	Oct. 19, 1796	Benjamin Oden All to the United States
569 — 44 lots	Oct. 19, 1796	Benjamin Oden All to the United States
570 — 6 lots	Oct. 24, 1796	Benjamin Oden and David Burnes: 1, 3, 5 United States: 2, 4, 6
571 — 1 lot	Oct. 19, 1796	Benjamin Oden: All

Square — No. of Lots	Date of Division	Original Owners, Lots Retained by Them, and Conveyed to the United States
572 — 2 lots	Oct. 24, 1796	Benjamin Oden and David Burnes: 1 United States: 2
S of 572, 2 lots	Jan. 30, 1797	David Burnes: 2 United States: 1
573 — 6 lots	Dec. 28, 1796	Benjamin Oden and David Burnes: 2, 4, 6 United States: 1, 3, 5
574 — 4 lots	April 13, 1835‡	Daniel Carroll of Duddington, Benjamin Oden and John P. Van Ness: 1, 3 United States: 2, 4
575 — 11 lots	Sept. 22, 1796	Daniel Carroll of Duddington and David Burnes Daniel Carroll of Duddington: 1, 2, 6, 7, 11 United States: 3-5, 8-10
576 — 11 lots	Oct. 2, 1799	Daniel Carroll of Duddington: 1, 3, 5, 8-10 United States: 2, 4, 6, 7, 11
577 — 6 lots	Nov. 5, 1796	Daniel Carroll of Duddington: 1, 4, 5 United States: 2, 3, 6
578 — 3 lots	Nov. 5, 1796	Daniel Carroll of Duddington: 1, 3 United States: 2
579 — 4 lots	Nov. 5, 1796	Daniel Carroll of Duddington: 1, 4 United States: 2, 3
580 — 14 lots	Sept. 14, 1796	Daniel Carroll of Duddington: 7-13 United States: 1-6, 14
N of 580, 1 lot	Nov. 5, 1796	Daniel Carroll of Duddington All to the United States
581 — 6 lots	Nov. 5, 1796	Daniel Carroll of Duddington All to the United States
582 — 12 lots	Nov. 5, 1796	Daniel Carroll of Duddington: All
583 — 20 lots	Sept. 14, 1796	Daniel Carroll of Duddington: 4-13 United States: 1-3, 14-20
N of 533	Nov. 5, 1796	Daniel Carroll of Duddington All to the United States
584 — 24 lots	Sept. 15, 1796	Daniel Carroll of Duddington All to the United States
585 — 20 lots	Sept. 14, 1796	Daniel Carroll of Duddington All to the United States
586 — 1 lot	Sept. 15, 1796	Daniel Carroll of Duddington: All
587 — 20 lots	Sept. 14, 1796	Daniel Carroll of Duddington All to the United States
588 — 11 lots	Sept. 14, 1796	Daniel Carroll of Duddington All to the United States

Square — No. of Lots	Date of Division	Original Owners, Lots Retained by Them, and Conveyed to the United States
589 — 20 lots	Nov. 5, 1796	Notley Young and Daniel Carroll of Duddington Daniel Carroll of Duddington: 4-13 United States: 1-3, 14-20
590 — 7 lots	Sept. 14, 1796	Daniel Carroll of Duddington: All
E of 590, 1 lot	Sept. 15, 1796	Daniel Carroll of Duddington All to the United States
591 — 1 lot	Oct. 18, 1794	Notley Young All to the United States[46]
592 — 18 lots	Mar. 24, 1797	Notley Young: All
593 — 4 lots	Jan. 12, 1797	Notley Young: All
594 — 1 lot	Jan. 12, 1797	Notley Young: All
595 — 1 lot	Jan. 12, 1797	Notley Young: All
596 — 17 lots	Oct. 18, 1800	Notley Young All to the United States
597 — 21 lots	Oct. 28, 1800	Notley Young All to the United States
W of 597, 1 lot	Mar. 24, 1797	Notley Young All to the United States
598 — 12 lots	June 26, 1794	Assigned 3 for No. 97 in Carrollsburg Assigned 4 for No. 98 in Carrollsburg Assigned 7 for No. 99 in Carrollsburg Assigned 8 for No. 102 in Carrollsburg Assigned 9 for No. 100 in Carrollsburg Assigned 10 for No. 101 in Carrollsburg United States: 1, 2, 5, 6, 11, 12
599 — 9 lots	June 26, 1794	Assigned 1 for No. 176 in Carrollsburg Assigned 3 for No. 93 in Carrollsburg Assigned 4 for No. 94 in Carrollsburg Assigned 5 for No. 95 in Carrollsburg Assigned 6 for No. 96 in Carrollsburg Assigned 8 for No. 230 in Carrollsburg United States: 2, 7, 9
600 — 1 lot	June 26, 1794	All to the United States
601 — 15 lots	June 26, 1794	Assigned 3 for No. 198 in Carrollsburg Assigned 4 for No. 199 in Carrollsburg Assigned 6 for No. 196 in Carrollsburg Assigned 9 for No. 90 in Carrollsburg Assigned 10 for No. 91 in Carrollsburg Assigned 11 for No. 92 in Carrollsburg United States: 1, 2, 5, 7, 8, 12-15

---

[46] See proceedings of the Commissioners, 1791-1795, folio 284.

Square — No. of Lots	Date of Division	Original Owners, Lots Retained by Them, and Conveyed to the United States
602 — 10 lots	June 26, 1794	Assigned 1 for No. 180 in Carrollsburg Assigned 3 for No. 80 in Carrollsburg Assigned 4 for No. 81 in Carrollsburg Assigned 6 for No. 82 in Carrollsburg Assigned 7 for No. 83 in Carrollsburg
603 — 14 lots	June 26, 1794	Assigned 1 for No. 192 in Carrollsburg Assigned 2 for No. 84 in Carrollsburg Assigned 3 in No. 265 in Carrollsburg Assigned 4 for No. 85 in Carrollsburg Assigned 5 for No. 86 in Carrollsburg Assigned 6 for No. 184 in Carrollsburg Assigned 8 for No. 87 in Carrollsburg Assigned 11 for No. 189 in Carrollsburg Assigned 12 for No. 188 in Carrollsburg Assigned 13 for No. 185 in Carrollsburg Assigned 14 for No. 265 in Carrollsburg United States: 7, 9, 10
604 — 6 lots	June 26, 1794	Assigned 2 for No. 73 in Carrollsburg Assigned 3 for No. 74 in Carrollsburg Assigned 5 for No. 75 in Carrollsburg Assigned 6 for No. 79 in Carrollsburg United States: 1, 4
W of 605, 1 lot	Oct. 28, 1800	Notley Young: All
605 — 6 lots	June 26, 1794	Assigned 1 for No. 177 in Carrollsburg Assigned 2 for No. 173 in Carrollsburg Assigned 3 for No. 169 in Carrollsburg Assigned 4 for No. 164 in Carrollsburg United States: 5, 6
606 — 10 lots	June 26, 1794	Assigned 1 for No. 76 in Carrollsburg Assigned 2 for Nos. 63 and 88 in Carrollsburg Assigned 3 for No. 70 in Carrollsburg Assigned 5 for No. 71 in Carrollsburg Assigned 7 for No. 72 in Carrollsburg Assigned 8 for No. 131 in Carrollsburg Assigned 10 for No. 78 in Carrollsburg United States: 4, 6, 9
NW of 606, 1 lot		Notley Young All to the United States[47]
W of 606, 2 lots	Oct. 28, 1800	Notley Young: All
607 — 10 lots	June 26, 1794	Assigned 1 for No. 165 in Carrollsburg Assigned 5 for No. 150 in Carrollsburg Assigned 7 for No. 168 in Carrollsburg Assigned 8 for No. 172 in Carrollsburg Assigned 10 for No. 161 in Carrollsburg United States: 2-4, 6, 9

---

[47] See proceedings of the Commissioners, 1791-1795, folio 284.

Square — No. of Lots	Date of Division	Original Owners, Lots Retained by Them, and Conveyed to the United States
608 — 19 lots	June 26, 1794	Assigned 1 for No. 148 in Carrollsburg Assigned 2 for No. 60 in Carrollsburg Assigned 4 for No. 64 in Carrollsburg Assigned 6 for No. 67 in Carrollsburg Assigned 8 for No. 68 in Carrollsburg Assigned 10 for No. 69 in Carrollsburg Assigned 12 for No. 66 in Carrollsburg Assigned 14 for No. 65 in Carrollsburg Assigned 15 for No. 149 in Carrollsburg Assigned 16 for No. 156 in Carrollsburg Assigned 17 for No. 152 in Carrollsburg United States: 3, 5, 7, 9, 11, 13, 18, 19
609 — 14 lots	June 26, 1794	Assigned 1 for No. 134 in Carrollsburg Assigned 2 for No. 132 in Carrollsburg Assigned 6 for No. 153 in Carrollsburg Assigned 7 for No. 157 in Carrollsburg Assigned 8 for No. 160 in Carrollsburg Assigned 9 for No. 146 in Carrollsburg Assigned 10 for No. 158 in Carrollsburg United States: 3-5, 11-14
610 — 17 lots	June 26, 1794	Assigned 1 for No. 57 in Carrollsburg Assigned 4 for No. 59 in Carrollsburg Assigned 6 for No. 58 in Carrollsburg Assigned 9 for No. 61 in Carrollsburg Assigned 13 for Nos. 62 and 89 in Carrollsburg Assigned 14 for No. 144 in Carrollsburg Assigned 16 for No. 136 in Carrollsburg United States: 2, 3, 5, 7, 8, 10-12, 15, 17
611 — 17 lots	June 26, 1794	Assigned 1 for No. 126 in Carrollsburg Assigned 2 for No. 51 in Carrollsburg Assigned 3 for No. 52 in Carrollsburg Assigned 4 for No. 53 in Carrollsburg Assigned 5 for No. 55 in Carrollsburg Assigned 6 for No. 56 in Carrollsburg Assigned 7 for No. 54 in Carrollsburg Assigned 9 for No. 130 in Carrollsburg Assigned 10 for No. 137 in Carrollsburg Assigned 11 for No. 140 in Carrollsburg Assigned 12 for No. 133 in Carrollsburg Assigned 13 for No. 145 in Carrollsburg Assigned 14 for No. 141 in Carrollsburg Assigned 15 for No. 142 in Carrollsburg
612		Water lots
613 — 9 lots	June 26, 1794	Assigned 1 for No. 49 in Carrollsburg Assigned 2 for No. 50 in Carrollsburg Assigned 4 for No. 51 in Carrollsburg Assigned 5 for No. 52 in Carrollsburg Assigned 6 for No. 53 in Carrollsburg Assigned 7 for No. 55 in Carrollsburg Assigned 8 for No. 56 in Carrollsburg Assigned 9 for No. 54 in Carrollsburg United States: 3

Square — No. of Lots	Date of Division	Original Owners, Lots Retained by Them, and Conveyed to the United States
614 — 3 lots	July 28, 1796	Notley Young All to the United States
615 — 33 lots	July 28, 1796	Notley Young: 1-5, 24-33 United States: 6-23
616 — 26 lots	Aug. 9, 1796	Notley Young: 1-6, 19-26 United States: 7-18
617 — 27 lots	Aug. 9, 1796	Notley Young: 6-18 United States: 1-5, 19-27
618 — 8 lots	July 28, 1796	Notley Young All to the United States
619 — 18 lots	July 28, 1796	Notley Young All to the United States
620 — 24 lots	April 17, 1797	Notley Young and Benjamin Oden: 1-5, 12-17, 24 United States: 6-11, 18-23
621 — 24 lots	April 17, 1797	Notley Young and Benjamin Oden: 1-5, 12-17, 24 United States: 6-11, 18-23
622 — 52 lots	Oct. 19, 1796	Benjamin Oden: All
623 — 52 lots	Oct. 19, 1796	Benjamin Oden: All
W of 623, 1 lot	Oct. 19, 1796	Benjamin Oden All to the United States
624 — 78 lots	Oct. 19, 1796	Benjamin Oden: All
W of 624, 1 lot	Oct. 19, 1796	Benjamin Oden: All
625 — 1 lot	Oct. 19, 1796	Benjamin Oden: All
626 — 1 lot	Oct. 19, 1796	Benjamin Oden All to the United States
627 — 1 lot	Oct. 19, 1796	Benjamin Oden: All
628 — 8 lots	Oct. 24, 1796	Benjamin Oden and Daniel Carroll of Duddington: 2, 4, 6, 8 United States: 1, 3, 5, 7
629 — 2 lots	Dec. 28, 1796	Daniel Carroll of Duddington and Benjamin Oden: 1 United States: 2
630 — 6 lots	Oct. 24, 1796	Daniel Carroll of Duddington and Benjamin Oden: 2, 4, 6 United States: 1, 3, 5
631 — 8 lots	Dec. 28, 1796	Daniel Carroll of Duddington and Benjamin Oden: 1, 3, 5, 7 United States: 2, 4, 6, 8
632 — 11 lots	Sept. 27, 1797	Daniel Carroll of Duddington All to the United States
633 — 13 lots	Nov. 5, 1796	Daniel Carroll of Duddington: 1, 2, 7-10, 13 United States: 3-6, 11, 12
634 — 19 lots	June 26, 1794	Daniel Carroll of Duddington: 1, 5-7, 12-14, 18, 19 United States: 2-4, 8-11, 15-17

Square — No. of Lots	Date of Division	Original Owners, Lots Retained by Them, and Conveyed to the United States
635 — 21 lots	Sept. 14, 1796	Daniel Carroll of Duddington: 7, 8, 13-18, 20, 21 United States: 1-6, 9-12, 19
S of 635, 2 lots	Nov. 7, 1797	Daniel Carroll of Duddington All to the United States
636 — 14 lots	Oct. 10, 1792‡ Oct. 11, 1792†	Daniel Carroll of Duddington: 1-4, 11, 14 United States: 5-10, 12, 13
re-division 19 lots	Sept. 14, 1796	Re-divided on account of error Daniel Carroll of Duddington: 3-6, 10-12, 16-18 United States: 1, 2, 7-9, 13-15, 19
637 — 14 lots re-division	Oct. 14, 1792 Sept. 14, 1796	Daniel Carroll of Duddington: 4-6, 10-13 United States: 1-3, 7-9, 14
638 — 7 lots	Nov. 6, 1796	Daniel Carroll of Duddington: 4-7 United States: 1-3
639 — 3 lots	Nov. 5, 1796	Daniel Carroll of Duddington: 2, 3 United States: 1
640 — 26 lots	Sept. 15, 1796	Daniel Carroll of Duddington All to the United States
641 — 20 lots	Sept. 15, 1796	Daniel Carroll of Duddington All to the United States
642 — 22 lots	Sept. 15, 1796	Daniel Carroll of Duddington All to the United States
N of 642, 1 lot	Nov. 5, 1796	Daniel Carroll of Duddington: All
E of 642, 21 lots	Nov. 5, 1796	Daniel Carroll of Duddington All to the United States
643 — 20 lots	Sept. 14, 1796	Daniel Carroll of Duddington All to the United States
E of 643, 2 lots	Nov. 5, 1796	Daniel Carroll of Duddington: 1 United States: 2
S of 643, 28 lots	Sept. 15, 1796	Daniel Carroll of Duddington All to the United States
644 — 7 lots	Sept. 15, 1796	Daniel Carroll of Duddington All to the United States
645 — 28 lots	Sept. 15, 1796	Daniel Carroll of Duddington All to the United States
W of 645, 5 lots	Sept. 15, 1796	Daniel Carroll of Duddington All to the United States
646 — 4 lots	Sept. 15, 1796	Daniel Carroll of Duddington: All
647 — 9 lots	Sept. 15, 1796	Daniel Carroll of Duddington: All
648 — 18 lots	Sept. 15, 1796	Daniel Carroll of Duddington: All
649 — 20 lots	Sept. 14, 1796	Daniel Carroll of Duddington: All

Square — No. of Lots	Date of Division	Original Owners, Lots Retained by Them, and Conveyed to the United States
650 — 25 lots	Mar. 24, 1796† Mar. 24, 1797‡	Daniel Carroll of Duddington: 5-25 Assigned 1 for No. 106 in Carrollsburg Assigned 2 for No. 105 in Carrollsburg Assigned 3 for No. 104 in Carrollsburg Assigned 4 for No. 103 in Carrollsburg
N of 650, 5 lots	Sept. 15, 1796	Daniel Carroll of Duddington: All
651 — 32 lots	Sept. 14, 1796	Daniel Carroll of Duddington: All
652 — 20 lots	June 26, 1794	Assigned 1 for No. 237 in Carrollsburg Assigned 2 for No. 236 in Carrollsburg Assigned 3 for No. 244 in Carrollsburg Assigned 5 for No. 252 in Carrollsburg Assigned 11 for No. 260 in Carrollsburg Assigned 12 for No. 261 in Carrollsburg Assigned 18 for No. 253 in Carrollsburg Assigned 20 for No. 245 in Carrollsburg United States: 4, 6-10, 13-17, 19
653 — 19 lots	June 26, 1794	Assigned 1 for No. 239 in Carrollsburg Assigned 2 for No. 238 in Carrollsburg Assigned 3 for No. 246 in Carrollsburg Assigned 10 for No. 262 in Carrollsburg Assigned 11 for No. 263 in Carrollsburg Assigned 12 for No. 120 in Carrollsburg Assigned 15 for No. 108 in Carrollsburg Assigned 17 for No. 255 in Carrollsburg Assigned 18 for No. 222 in Carrollsburg Assigned 19 for No. 247 in Carrollsburg United States: 4-9, 13, 14, 16
654 — 10 lots	June 26, 1794	Assigned 1 for No. 205 in Carrollsburg Assigned 2 for No. 204 in Carrollsburg Assigned 7 for No. 231 in Carrollsburg Assigned 8 for No. 225 in Carrollsburg United States: 3, 4, 6, 9, 10
655 — 10 lots	June 26, 1794	Assigned 1 for No. 181 in Carrollsburg Assigned 2 for No. 206 in Carrollsburg Assigned 6 for No. 232 in Carrollsburg Assigned 7 for No. 233 in Carrollsburg Assigned 8 for No. 227 in Carrollsburg Assigned 9 for No. 221 in Carrollsburg United States: 3-5, 10
656 — 14 lots	June 26, 1794	Assigned 4 for No. 220 in Carrollsburg Assigned 7 for No. 200 in Carrollsburg Assigned 8 for No. 202 in Carrollsburg Assigned 9 for No. 203 in Carrollsburg Assigned 10 for No. 201 in Carrollsburg Assigned 13 for No. 219 in Carrollsburg United States: 1-3, 5, 6, 11, 12, 14

Square — No. of Lots	Date of Division	Original Owners, Lots Retained by Them, and Conveyed to the United States
657 — 14 lots	June 26, 1794	Assigned 1 for No. 115 in Carrollsburg Assigned 2 for No. 207 in Carrollsburg Assigned 10 for No. 216 in Carrollsburg Assigned 11 for No. 254 in Carrollsburg Assigned 12 for No. 77 in Carrollsburg Assigned 13 for No. 224 in Carrollsburg Assigned 14 for No. 228 in Carrollsburg
658 — 6 lots	June 26, 1794	Assigned 5 for No. 193 in Carrollsburg Assigned 6 for No. 195 in Carrollsburg United States: 1-4
659		No such Square
660 — 6 lots	June 26, 1794	Assigned 1 for No. 124 in Carrollsburg Assigned 2 for No. 211 in Carrollsburg Assigned 3 for No. 210 in Carrollsburg Assigned 4 for No. 183 in Carrollsburg Assigned 6 for Nos. 208 and 159 in Carrollsburg United States: 5
661 — 14 lots	June 26, 1794	Assigned 1 for No. 167 in Carrollsburg Assigned 2 for No. 182 in Carrollsburg Assigned 3 for No. 174 in Carrollsburg Assigned 6 for No. 186 in Carrollsburg Assigned 7 for No. 190 in Carrollsburg Assigned 8 for No. 194 in Carrollsburg Assigned 11 for No. 187 in Carrollsburg Assigned 14 for No. 109 in Carrollsburg United States: 4, 5, 9, 10, 12, 13
662 — 9 lots	June 26, 1794	Assigned 2 for No. 209 in Carrollsburg Assigned 5 for No. 191 in Carrollsburg Assigned 6 for No. 125 in Carrollsburg Assigned 9 for Nos. 214 and 212 in Carrollsburg United States: 1, 3, 4, 7, 8
E of 662, 1 lot	June 26, 1794	Assigned all to the United States
663 — 10 lots	June 26, 1794	Assigned 1 for No. 162 in Carrollsburg Assigned 2 for No. 166 in Carrollsburg Assigned 4 for No. 154 in Carrollsburg Assigned 6 for No. 178 in Carrollsburg Assigned 7 for No. 179 in Carrollsburg Assigned 8 for No. 175 in Carrollsburg Assigned 9 for No. 171 in Carrollsburg United States: 3, 5, 10
664 — 8 lots	June 26, 1794	Assigned 1 for No. 19 in Carrollsburg Assigned 2 for No. 25 in Carrollsburg Assigned 3 for No. 20 in Carrollsburg Assigned 6 for No. 21 in Carrollsburg Assigned 7 for No. 23 in Carrollsburg Assigned 8 for No. 22 in Carrollsburg United States: 4, 5

Square — No. of Lots	Date of Division	Original Owners, Lots Retained by Them, and Conveyed to the United States
E of 664, 8 lots	June 26, 1794	Assigned 1 for No. 19 in Carrollsburg Assigned 2 for No. 25 in Carrollsburg Assigned 3 for No. 20 in Carrollsburg Assigned 6 for No. 21 in Carrollsburg Assigned 7 for No. 23 in Carrollsburg Assigned 8 for No. 22 in Carrollsburg United States: 4, 5
665 — 22 lots	June 26, 1794	Assigned 1 for No. 13 in Carrollsburg Assigned 3 for No. 151 in Carrollsburg Assigned 5 for No. 155 in Carrollsburg Assigned 9 for No. 163 in Carrollsburg Assigned 11 for No. 18 in Carrollsburg Assigned 12 for No. 26 in Carrollsburg Assigned 13 for No. 17 in Carrollsburg Assigned 15 for No. 29 in Carrollsburg Assigned 19 for No. 16 in Carrollsburg Assigned 20 for No. 15 in Carrollsburg Assigned 21 for No. 14 in Carrollsburg United States: 2, 4, 6-8, 10, 14, 16-18, 22
666 — 13 lots	June 26, 1794	Assigned 1 for No. 13 in Carrollsburg Assigned 3 for No. 14 in Carrollsburg Assigned 4 for No. 15 in Carrollsburg Assigned 5 for No. 16 in Carrollsburg Assigned 9 for No. 29 in Carrollsburg Assigned 11 for No. 17 in Carrollsburg Assigned 12 for No. 26 in Carrollsburg Assigned 13 for No. 18 in Carrollsburg United States: 2, 6-8, 10
667 — 16 lots	June 26, 1794	Assigned 1 for No. 9 in Carrollsburg Assigned 2 for No. 135 in Carrollsburg Assigned 3 for No. 170 in Carrollsburg Assigned 7 for No. 143 in Carrollsburg Assigned 8 for No. 147 in Carrollsburg Assigned 9 for No. 12 in Carrollsburg Assigned 10 for No. 11 in Carrollsburg Assigned 11 for No. 47 in Carrollsburg Assigned 16 for No. 10 in Carrollsburg United States: 4-6, 12-15
E of 667, 9 lots	June 26, 1794	Assigned 1 for No. 9 in Carrollsburg Assigned 2 for No. 10 in Carrollsburg Assigned 7 for No. 47 in Carrollsburg Assigned 8 for No. 11 in Carrollsburg Assigned 9 for No. 12 in Carrollsburg United States: 3-6

Square — No. of Lots	Date of Division	Original Owners, Lots Retained by Them, and Conveyed to the United States
S of 667 15 lots	June 26, 1794	Assigned 1 for No. 2 in Carrollsburg Assigned 2 for No. 127 in Carrollsburg Assigned 3 for No. 128 in Carrollsburg Assigned 5 for No. 129 in Carrollsburg Assigned 6 for No. 8 in Carrollsburg Assigned 10 for No. 6 in Carrollsburg Assigned 11 for No. 7 in Carrollsburg Assigned 14 for No. 3 in Carrollsburg Assigned 15 for No. 5 in Carrollsburg United States: 4, 7-9, 12, 13
E of S 667 11 lots	June 26, 1794	Assigned 1 for No. 2 in Carrollsburg Assigned 2 for No. 5 in Carrollsburg Assigned 3 for No. 3 in Carrollsburg Assigned 6 for No. 7 in Carrollsburg Assigned 7 for No. 6 in Carrollsburg Assigned 11 for No. 8 in Carrollsburg United States: 4, 5, 8-10
S of S 667 2 lots	June 26, 1794	Assigned 2 for No. 1 in Carrollsburg United States: 1
E of S of S of 667, 1 lot	June 26, 1794	All to the United States
668 — 3 lots	July 28, 1796	Notley Young: All
669 — 26 lots	Aug. 9, 1796	Notley Young: 7-18 United States: 1-6, 19-26
670 — 1 lot	July 28, 1796	Notley Young: All
671 — 1 lot	July 28, 1796	Notley Young: All
672 — 34 lots	Aug. 9, 1796	Notley Young: 7-23 United States: 1-6, 24-34
673 — 24 lots	April 17, 1797	Benjamin Oden, Notley Young and Daniel Carroll of Duddington: 6-11, 18-23 United States: 1-5, 12-17, 24
674 — 24 lots	April 17, 1797	Benjamin Oden and Daniel Carroll of Duddington: 6-11, 18-23 United States: 1-5, 12-17, 24
675 — 28 lots	April 17, 1797	Benjamin Oden and Daniel Carroll of Duddington: 1-6, 14-20, 28 United States: 7-13, 21-27
676 — 8 lots	Oct. 21, 1796	Benjamin Oden and Daniel Carroll of Duddington: 2, 4, 6, 8 United States: 1, 3, 5, 7
677 — 8 lots	Oct. 21, 1796	Benjamin Oden and Daniel Carroll of Duddington: 2, 4, 6, 8 United States: 1, 3, 5, 7
678 — 12 lots	Jan. 25, 1797	Daniel Carroll of Duddington and Benjamin Oden: 2, 4, 6, 8, 10, 12 United States: 1, 3, 5, 7, 9, 11
679 — 2 lots	Nov. 5, 1796	Daniel Carroll of Duddington: 1 United States: 2

Square — No. of Lots	Date of Division	Original Owners, Lots Retained by Them, and Conveyed to the United States
680 — 10 lots	Nov. 5, 1796	Daniel Carroll of Duddington: 1-4, 10 United States: 5-9
681 — 16 lots	Nov. 5, 1796	Daniel Carroll of Duddington: 3-6, 12-15 United States: 1, 2, 7-11, 16
682 — 5 lots	Nov. 5, 1796	Daniel Carroll of Duddington: 2-4 United States: 1, 5
683 — 11 lots	Sept. 27, 1797	Daniel Carroll of Duddington: All
684 — 10 lots	Nov. 5, 1796	Daniel Carroll of Duddington: 3, 4, 7, 8, 9 United States: 1, 2, 5, 6, 10
685 — 19 lots	June 27, 1795	Daniel Carroll of Duddington: 1, 3, 4, 7-10, 13, 16, 17 United States: 2, 5, 6, 11, 12, 14, 15, 18, 19
686 — 17 lots	Oct. 2, 1799	Daniel Carroll of Duddington: 2, 5, 7, 9, 12, 13, 15, 17 United States: 1, 3, 4, 6, 8, 10, 11, 14, 16
687 — 24 lots	Oct. 10, 1792	Daniel Carroll of Duddington: All
688 — 24 lots	Oct. 10, 1792	Daniel Carroll of Duddington All to the United States
689 — 14 lots	Oct. 10, 1792	Daniel Carroll of Duddington: 6, 7, 9-14 United States: 1-5, 8
690 — 32 lots	June 27, 1795[48]	Daniel Carroll of Duddington: 1-4, 8-12, 15, 19-22, 25, 28, 32 United States: 5-7, 13, 14, 16-18, 23, 24, 26, 27, 29-31
re-division	May 11, 1800	Partial re-division by Thomas Law and Daniel Carroll of Duddington Daniel Carroll of Duddington: 1, 2, 4, 6, 8, 11 United States: 3, 5, 7, 9, 10
601 — 12 lots	Oct. 10, 1792	Daniel Carroll of Duddington: 4-10 United States: 1-3, 11, 12
re-division to 14 lots	Sept. 14, 1796	Re-divided on account of error. Daniel Carroll of Duddington: 1, 2, 7-10, 14 United States: 3-6, 11-13
692 — 14 lots	Sept. 14, 1796	Daniel Carroll of Duddington: 1, 2, 6-8, 13, 14 United States: 3-5, 9-12
693 — 30 lots	June 27, 1795	Daniel Carroll of Duddington: 3, 5, 7, 8, 11-13, 15, 16, 18, 19, 22, 25, 28, 29 United States: 1, 2, 4, 6, 9, 10, 14, 17, 20, 21, 23, 24, 26, 27, 30
694 — 11 lots	June 27, 1795	Daniel Carroll of Duddington: 2, 5-7, 10, 11 United States: 1, 3, 4, 8, 9
695 — 1 lot	Sept. 15, 1796	Daniel Carroll of Duddington All to the United States

---

[48] See proceedings of the Commissioners, 1791-1795, folio 398.

Square — No. of Lots	Date of Division	Original Owners, Lots Retained by Them, and Conveyed to the United States
NW of 695 5 lots	Nov. 5, 1796	Daniel Carroll of Duddington: All
W of 695 12 lots	Nov. 5, 1796	Daniel Carroll of Duddington All to the United States
W of W of 695		No record
696 — 18 lots	Sept. 14, 1796	Daniel Carroll of Duddington: All
697 — 18 lots	Sept. 14, 1796	Daniel Carroll of Duddington: All
N of 697, 18 lots	Nov. 5, 1796	Daniel Carroll of Duddington: All
698 — 20 lots	Sept. 14, 1796	Daniel Carroll of Duddington: All
699 — 10 lots	Sept. 15, 1796	Daniel Carroll of Duddington: All
N of 699 18 lots	Sept. 15, 1796	Daniel Carroll of Duddington All of the United States
700 — 32 lots	Sept. 14, 1796	Daniel Carroll of Duddington: All
701 — 32 lots	Sept. 14, 1796	Daniel Carroll of Duddington: All
702 — 20 lots	June 20, 1794	Assigned 1 for No. 241 in Carrollsburg Assigned 2 for No. 240 in Carrollsburg Assigned 3 for No. 256 in Carrollsburg Assigned 10 for No. 112 in Carrollsburg Assigned 11 for No. 110 in Carrollsburg Assigned 19 for No. 257 in Carrollsburg Assigned 20 for No. 249 in Carrollsburg United States: 4-9, 12-18
703 — 20 lots	June 26, 1794	Assigned 1 for No. 119 in Carrollsburg Assigned 2 for No. 243 in Carrollsburg Assigned 3 for No. 259 in Carrollsburg Assigned 4 for No. 258 in Carrollsburg Assigned 9 for No. 111 in Carrollsburg Assigned 14 for No. 114 in Carrollsburg Assigned 15 for No. 117 in Carrollsburg Assigned 16 for No. 113 in Carrollsburg Assigned 17 for No. 121 in Carrollsburg Assigned 18 for No. 116 in Carrollsburg Assigned 19 for No. 251 in Carrollsburg United States: 5-8, 10-13, 20
704 — 10 lots	June 26, 1794	Assigned 2 for No. 217 in Carrollsburg Assigned 6 for No. 264 in Carrollsburg Assigned 7 for No. 235 in Carrollsburg Assigned 8 for No. 229 in Carrollsburg Assigned 10 for No. 223 in Carrollsburg United States: 1, 3, 4, 5, 9

Square — No. of Lots	Date of Division	Original Owners, Lots Retained by Them, and Conveyed to the United States
705 — 14 lots	June 26, 1792	Assigned 1 for No. 43 in Carrollsburg Assigned 3 for No. 242 in Carrollsburg Assigned 4 for No. 248 in Carrollsburg Assigned 5 for No. 250 in Carrollsburg Assigned 6 for No. 266 in Carrollsburg Assigned 8 for No. 42 in Carrollsburg Assigned 9 for No. 46 in Carrollsburg Assigned 10 for No. 45 in Carrollsburg Assigned 11 for No. 41 in Carrollsburg Assigned 12 for No. 40 in Carrollsburg Assigned 13 for No. 38 in Carrollsburg Assigned 14 for No. 44 in Carrollsburg United States: 2, 7
706 — 5 lots	June 26, 1794	Assigned 2 for Nos. 267 and 234 in Carrollsburg Assigned 3 for No. 197 in Carrollsburg Assigned 4 for No. 139 in Carrollsburg Assigned 5 for No. 107 in Carrollsburg United States: 1
707 — 2 lots	Sept. 19, 1797	Assigned 1 for No. 37 in Carrollsburg United States: 2
708 — 13 lots	June 26, 1794	Assigned 1 for No. 31 in Carrollsburg Assigned 2 for No. 215 in Carrollsburg Assigned 3 for No. 213 in Carrollsburg Assigned 6 for No. 122 in Carrollsburg Assigned 8 for No. 123 in Carrollsburg Assigned 9 for No. 33 in Carrollsburg Assigned 12 for No. 32 in Carrollsburg Assigned 13 for No. 30 in Carrollsburg United States: 4, 5, 8, 10, 11
S of 708, 1 lot	June 27, 1794	All to the United States
E of 708 11 lots	June 26, 1794	Assigned 1 for No. 31 in Carrollsburg Assigned 2 for No. 30 in Carrollsburg Assigned 3 for No. 32 in Carrollsburg Assigned 6 for No. 33 in Carrollsburg Assigned 7 for Nos. 4 and 39 in Carrollsburg Assigned 9 for No. 34 in Carrollsburg Assigned 10 for No. 35 in Carrollsburg Assigned 11 for No. 36 in Carrollsburg United States: 4, 5, 8
709 — 1 lot	Aug. 9, 1796	Notley Young: All
710 — 20 lots	Aug. 9, 1796	Notley Young: 5-14 United States: 1-4, 15-20
E of 710, 1 lot	July 28, 1796	Notley Young All to the United States
711 — 26 lots	Nov. 18, 1796	Notley Young: 12-24 United States: 1-11, 25, 26
E of 711, 1 lot	July 28, 1796	Notley Young All to the United States

Square — No. of Lots	Date of Division	Original Owners, Lots Retained by Them, and Conveyed to the United States
712 — 18 lots	May 11, 1802	Daniel Carroll of Duddington and heirs of Notley Young. Daniel Carroll of Duddington: 1 Heirs of Notley Young: 7-11, 16-18 United States: 2-6, 12-15
713 — 12 lots	Sept. 27, 1797	Daniel Carroll of Duddington All to the United States
714	Sept. 27, 1797‡ Sept. 7, 1797†	Daniel Carroll of Duddington: All
715 — 9 lots	Sept. 7, 1797† Sept. 27, 1797‡	Daniel Carroll of Duddington All to the United States
716 — 5 lots	Sept. 7, 1797† Sept. 27, 1797‡	Daniel Carroll of Duddington: All
717 — 4 lots	Sept. 27, 1797	Daniel Carroll of Duddington All to the United States
718 — 10 lots	Sept. 27, 1797	Daniel Carroll of Duddington: All
719 — 16 lots	Sept. 30, 1796	Daniel Carroll of Duddington: 1-3, 8-10, 15, 16 United States: 4-7, 11-14
720 — 22 lots	Sept. 30, 1796	Daniel Carroll of Duddington: 1-4, 10-13, 20-22 United States: 5-9, 14-19
721 — 22 lots	Sept. 30, 1796	Daniel Carroll of Duddington: 5-10, 16-20 United States: 1-4, 11-15, 21, 22
722 — 2 lots	Sept. 30, 1796	Daniel Carroll of Duddington: 1 United States: 2
723 — 11 lots	Sept. 30, 1796	Daniel Carroll of Duddington: 5-10 United States: 1-4, 11
724 — 28 lots	Oct. 10, 1792	Daniel Carroll of Duddington: 4, 5, 8-10, 13, 14, 18, 19, 22-24, 27, 28 United States: 1, 2, 3, 6, 7, 11, 12, 15, 16, 17, 20, 21, 25, 26
725 — 32 lots	Oct. 10, 1792	Daniel Carroll of Duddington: 4, 5, 8-10, 14-16, 20, 21, 24-26, 30-32 United States: 1-3, 6, 7, 11-13, 17-19, 22, 23, 27-29
726 — 1 lot	Sept. 14, 1796	Daniel Carroll of Duddington: All
727 — 1 lot	Sept. 14, 1796	Daniel Carroll of Duddington All to the United States
728 — 30 lots	Oct. 10, 1792	Daniel Carroll of Duddington: 1, 3, 4, 7, 8, 11-13, 19-21, 24, 25, 29, 30 United States: 2, 5, 6, 9, 10, 14-18, 22, 23, 26-28
729 — 30 lots	Oct. 10, 1792	Daniel Carroll of Duddington: 1, 2, 5, 6, 10-14, 17, 20, 21, 24, 25, 30 United States: 3, 4, 7-9, 15, 16, 18, 19, 22, 23, 26-29
730 — 4 lots	Nov. 5, 1796	Daniel Carroll of Duddington: 3, 4 United States: 1, 2

Square — No. of Lots	Date of Division	Original Owners, Lots Retained by Them, and Conveyed to the United States
731 — 4 lots	Nov. 5, 1796	Daniel Carroll of Duddington: 3, 4 United States: 1, 2
732 — 44 lots	June 27, 1795	Daniel Carroll of Duddington: 1-5, 13-19, 32-34, 38-44 United States: 6-12, 20-31, 35-37
733 — 30 lots	Sept. 14, 1796	Daniel Carroll of Duddington: 7-21 United States: 1-6, 22-30
734 — 18 lots	Sept. 14, 1796	Daniel Carroll of Duddington: 6-14 United States: 1-5, 16-18
735 — 8 lots	Sept. 14, 1796	Daniel Carroll of Duddington: All
736 — 1 lot	July 26, 1798	Daniel Carroll of Duddington: All for improvements.
737 — 1 lot	Sept. 15, 1796	Daniel Carroll of Duddington: All
738 — 5 lots	Sept. 14, 1796	Daniel Carroll of Duddington All to the United States
739 — 1 lot	Sept. 15, 1796	Daniel Carroll of Duddington: All
740 — 1 lot	April 11, 1797	Daniel Carroll of Duddington All to the United States
741 — 11 lots	April 11, 1797	Daniel Carroll of Duddington All to the United States
742 — 1 lot	Sept. 15, 1796	Daniel Carroll of Duddington All to the United States
743 — 23 lots	Sept. 14, 1796	Daniel Carroll of Duddington: All
N of 743, 9 lots	Sept. 15, 1796	Daniel Carroll of Duddington All to the United States
744 — 2 lots	April 11, 1797	Daniel Carroll of Duddington All to the United States
S of 744, 9 lots	June 26, 1794	Assigned 5 for No. 118 in Carrollsburg Assigned 8 for No. 48 in Carrollsburg United States: 1-4, 6, 7, 9
745		No such Square
746		No such Square
747 — 7 lots	July 28, 1796	Notley Young: All
N of 747, 1 lot	July 28, 1796	Notley Young: All
748 — 16 lots	May 11, 1802	Daniel Carroll of Duddington and heirs of Notley Young. Daniel Carroll of Duddington: 11, 12 Heirs of Notley Young: 8-10, 13, 14 United States: 1-7, 15, 16
749 — 12 lots	Sept. 27, 1797	Daniel Carroll of Duddington All to the United States
750 — 12 lots	Sept. 27, 1797‡ Sept. 7, 1797†	Daniel Carroll of Duddington: All

Square — No. of Lots	Date of Division	Original Owners, Lots Retained by Them, and Conveyed to the United States
751 — 12 lots	Sept. 27, 1797	Daniel Carroll of Duddington: 3-8 United States: 1, 2, 9-12
752 — 14 lots	Sept. 30, 1796	Daniel Carroll of Duddington: 1, 2, 10-14 United States: 3-9
753 — 24 lots	Sept. 30, 1796	Daniel Carroll of Duddington: 1-3, 16-24 United States: 4-15
754 — 18 lots	Sept. 30, 1796	Daniel Carroll of Duddington: 4-12 United States: 1-3, 13-18
755 — 9 lots	Sept. 30, 1796	Daniel Carroll of Duddington: 3-6 United States: 1, 2, 7-9
756 — 11 lots	Sept. 30, 1796	Daniel Carroll of Duddington: 3-8 United States: 1, 2, 9-11
757 — 10 lots	Sept. 27, 1797	Daniel Carroll of Duddington: 1, 8-10 United States: 2-7
758 — 17 lots	Sept. 14, 1796	Daniel Carroll of Duddington: 4-11 United States: 1-3, 12-17
759 — 18 lots	Oct. 11, 1792	Daniel Carroll of Duddington All to the United States
760 — 18 lots	Oct. 10, 1792	Daniel Carroll of Duddington All to the United States
761 — 18 lots	Oct. 10, 1792	Daniel Carroll of Duddington: 1, 2, 4, 8-11, 13, 18 United States: 3, 5-7, 12, 14-17
762 — 15 lots	Sept. 14, 1796	Daniel Carroll of Duddington: 4-11 United States: 1-3, 12-15
763 — 16 lots	Sept. 14, 1796	Daniel Carroll of Duddington: 4-11 United States: 1-3, 12-16
764 — 14 lots	Sept. 14, 1796	Daniel Carroll of Duddington: 4-10 United States: 1-3, 11-14
765 — 12 lots	Sept. 14, 1796	Daniel Carroll of Duddington: All
766 — 9 lots	Sept. 15, 1796	Daniel Carroll of Duddington All to the United States
767 — 4 lots	Sept. 15, 1796	Daniel Carroll of Duddington All to the United States
768 — 4 lots	Sept. 15, 1796	Daniel Carroll of Duddington All to the United States
769 — 6 lots	Sept. 15, 1796	Daniel Carroll of Duddington All to the United States
770 — 16 lots	Sept. 14, 1796	Daniel Carroll of Duddington All to the United States
771 — 14 lots	June 8, 1795	Daniel Carroll of Duddington: 1, 10-14 United States: 2-9

Square — No. of Lots	Date of Division	Original Owners, Lots Retained by Them, and Conveyed to the United States
re-division to 7 lots	April 12, 1797	Daniel Carroll of Duddington: 5-7 James Barry: 1 United States: 2-4
772 — 18 lots	July 28, 1796	Notley Young: 1, 2, 12-18 United States: 3-11
N of 772, 1 lot	July 28, 1796	Notley Young: All
773 — 20 lots	July 28, 1796	Notley Young: 1, 2, 13-20 United States: 3-12
774 — 12 lots	July 28, 1796	Notley Young All to the United States
775 — 12 lots	July 28, 1796	Notley Young: All
776 — 12 lots	Aug. 9, 1796	Notley Young: 1, 2, 9-12 United States: 3-8
777 — 14 lots		Daniel Carroll of Duddington, heirs of Notley Young, and William Prout: 3-9 United States: 1, 2, 10-14
re-division	May 11, 1802	William Prout: 5 Heirs of Notley Young: 3, 4, 6-9
778 — 24 lots	Sept. 30, 1796	Daniel Carroll of Duddington and William Prout Daniel Carroll of Duddington: 1, 2, 24 William Prout: 3, 16-23 United States: 4-15
779 — 18 lots	Sept. 30, 1796	Daniel Carroll of Duddington and William Prout Daniel Carroll of Duddington: 1, 2, 3, 18 William Prout: 13-17 United States: 4-12
780 — 24 lots	Sept. 30, 1796	Daniel Carroll of Duddington and William Prout Daniel Carroll of Duddington: 4-7 William Prout: 8-15 United States: 1-3, 16-24
781 — 2 lots	Sept. 11, 1795	William Prout: 2 United States: 1
782 — 5 lots	Sept. 30, 1796	Daniel Carroll of Duddington and William Prout All to the United States
783 — 5 lots	Sept. 30, 1796	Daniel Carroll of Duddington and William Prout All to Daniel Carroll of Duddington
784 — 5 lots	Sept. 30, 1796	Daniel Carroll of Duddington and William Prout William Prout: 1, 3, 4 United States: 2, 5
785 — 18 lots	Sept. 30, 1796	Daniel Carroll of Duddington and William Prout William Prout: 1-3, 13-18 United States: 4-12

Square — No. of Lots	Date of Division	Original Owners, Lots Retained by Them, and Conveyed to the United States
786 — 16 lots	Sept. 30, 1796	Daniel Carroll of Duddington and William Prout Daniel Carroll of Duddington: 4-11 United States: 1-3, 12-16
787 — 16 lots	Sept. 30, 1796	Daniel Carroll of Duddington and William Prout William Prout: 4-11 United States: 1-3, 12-16
788 — 20 lots	Sept. 30, 1796	Daniel Carroll of Duddington and William Prout Daniel Carroll of Duddington: 4-13 United States: 1-3, 14-20
789 — 5 lots	April 7, 1797	Daniel Carroll of Duddington and William Prout All to the United States
790 — 5 lots	April 7, 1797	Daniel Carroll of Duddington and William Prout Daniel Carroll of Duddington: 5 William Prout: 3 United States: 1, 2, 4
791 — 5 lots	April 7, 1797	Daniel Carroll of Duddington and William Prout Daniel Carroll of Duddington: 3-5 William Prout: 1, 2
792 — 11 lots	April 7, 1797	Daniel Carroll of Duddington and William Prout Daniel Carroll of Duddington: 3-7 William Prout: 10 United States: 1, 2, 8, 9, 11
793 — 14 lots	Sept. 30, 1796	Daniel Carroll of Duddington and William Prout William Prout: 1, 2, 14 Daniel Carroll of Duddington: 10-13 United States: 3-9
794 — 5 lots	Sept. 30, 1796	Daniel Carroll of Duddington and William Prout Daniel Carroll of Duddington: 1, 2 William Prout: 5 United States: 3, 4
795 — 24 lots	June 27, 1795	Daniel Carroll of Duddington: All
796 — 15 lots	June 27, 1795	Daniel Carroll of Duddington and William Prout All to the United States
797 — 5 lots	Sept. 14, 1796	Daniel Carroll of Duddington All to the United States
798 — 18 lots	Sept. 14, 1796	Daniel Carroll of Duddington: All
799 — 18 lots	Sept. 14, 1796	Daniel Carroll of Duddington All to the United States
800 — 20 lots	Sept. 15, 1796	Daniel Carroll of Duddington All to the United States
801 — 32 lots	Sept. 14, 1796	Daniel Carroll of Duddington: All
802 — 9 lots	June 8, 1795	Daniel Carroll of Duddington: 1-3, 8, 9 United States: 4-7

Square — No. of Lots	Date of Division	Original Owners, Lots Retained by Them, and Conveyed to the United States
803 — 1 lot		Water lot
804 — 9 lots	July 28, 1796	Notley Young: All
805 — 16 lots	July 28, 1796	Notley Young: All
806 — 8 lots	July 28, 1796	Notley Young: All
807 — 8 lots	July 28, 1796	Notley Young: All
808 — 8 lots	July 28, 1796	Notley Young: All
809 — 10 lots	Oct. 24, 1799	Notley Young, George Walker and William Prout: 2, 3, 7-9 United States: 1, 4-6, 10
810 — 20 lots	Sept. 11, 1795	William Prout: 3-12 United States: 1, 2, 13-20
811 — 14 lots	Sept. 11, 1795	William Prout: 3-9 United States: 1, 2, 10-14
812 — 16 lots	Sept. 11, 1795	William Prout: 3-10 United States: 1, 2, 11-16
813 — 4 lots	Sept. 11, 1795	William Prout: 2, 3 United States: 1, 4
814 — 14 lots	Sept. 11, 1795	William Prout All to the United States
815 — 14 lots	Sept. 11, 1795	William Prout: All
816 — 12 lots	Sept. 11, 1795	William Prout All to the United States
817 — 12 lots	Sept. 11, 1795	William Prout: All
818 — 14 lots	Oct. 8, 1792	William Prout: 3-5, 10-13 United States: 1, 2, 6-9, 14
819 — 14 lots	Oct. 8, 1792	William Prout: 1, 2, 6-9, 14 United States: 3-5, 10-13
820 — 16 lots	July 25, 1795	William Prout: All
821 — 14 lots	July 25, 1795	William Prout: 3-9 United States: 1, 2, 10-14
822 — 17 lots	July 25, 1795	William Prout: All
823 — 18 lots	July 25, 1795	William Prout: All
824 — 11 lots	July 25, 1795	William Prout: All
825 — 4 lots	July 2, 1800[49]	Daniel Carroll of Duddington and William Prout: 1, 4 United States: 2, 3

---

[49] See proceedings of the Commissioners, 1798-1800, folio 386.

Square — No. of Lots	Date of Division	Original Owners, Lots Retained by Them, and Conveyed to the United States
S of 825 4 lots	July 2, 1800	Daniel Carroll of Duddington and William Prout William Prout: 1, 4 United States: 2, 3
826 — 26 lots	April 7, 1797	Daniel Carroll of Duddington: 3-15 United States: 1, 2, 16-26
827		Water lots
828 — 5 lots	July 28, 1796	Notley Young All to the United States
829 — 16 lots	July 28, 1796	Notley Young All to the United States
830 — 8 lots	July 28, 1796	Notley Young All to the United States
831 — 8 lots	July 28, 1796	Notley Young All to the United States
832 — 8 lots	July 28, 1796	Notley Young All to the United States
833 — 10 lots	Oct. 29, 1799	Notley Young and George Walker: 2-4, 7, 8 United States: 1, 5, 6, 9, 10
834 — 20 lots	Sept. 29, 1796	George Walker and William Prout William Prout: 3-7 George Walker: 13-17 United States: 1, 2, 8-12, 18-20
835 — 14 lots	Sept. 29, 1796	George Walker and William Prout William Prout: 3-6 George Walker: 10-12 United States: 1, 2, 7-9, 13, 14
836 — 16 lots	Sept. 29, 1796	George Walker and William Prout George Walker: 1, 2, 15, 16 William Prout: 7-10 United States: 3-6, 11-14
837 — 4 lots	Sept. 29, 1796	George Walker and William Prout George Walker: 4 William Prout: 2 United States: 1, 3
838 — 14 lots	Sept. 11, 1795	William Prout: All
839 — 14 lots	Sept. 11, 1795	William Prout All to the United States
840 — 12 lots	Sept. 11, 1795	William Prout: All
841 — 12 lots	Sept. 11, 1795	William Prout All to the United States
842 — 14 lots	Oct. 8, 1792	William Prout: 3-5, 10-13 United States: 1, 2, 6-9, 14

Square — No. of Lots	Date of Division	Original Owners, Lots Retained by Them, and Conveyed to the United States
843 — 14 lots	Oct. 8, 1792	William Prout: 1, 2, 6-9, 14 United States: 3-5, 10-13
844 — 16 lots	July 25, 1795	William Prout All to the United States
re-division	May 25, 1801[50]	William Prout: 1-3 United States: 4-16
845 — 10 lots	Sept. 11, 1795	William Prout: 2-7 United States: 1, 8-10
846 — 20 lots	July 25, 1795	William Prout All to the United States
847 — 20 lots	July 25, 1795	William Prout All to the United States
848		No such Square
849 — 7 lots	July 25, 1795	William Prout All to the United States
850		No such Square
851		No such Square
852		No such Square
853 — 4 lots April 1797		Daniel Carroll of Duddington: 1, 3 United States: 2, 4
re-division	Feb. 12, 1800	All to Daniel Carroll of Duddington
N of 853 4 lots	Jan. 27, 1800	Daniel Carroll of Duddington: 2, 4 United States: 1, 3
854		Water lots
855 — 35 lots	Aug. 9, 1795	Notley Young: 5-24 United States: 1-4, 25-35
N of 855, 1 lot	July 28, 1796	Notley Young All to the United States
856 — 20 lots	July 28, 1796	Notley Young: 5-14 United States: 1-4, 15-20
857 — 20 lots	July 28, 1796	Notley Young All to the United States
858 — 20 lots	July 28, 1796	Notley Young: All
859 — 22 lots	Oct. 24, 1799	Notley Young and George Walker: 5-10, 16-20 United States: 1-4, 11-15, 21, 22
860 — 32 lots	July 8, 1795	George Walker All to the United States

---

[50] See proceedings of the Commissioners, 1800-1802, folio 157.

Square — No. of Lots	Date of Division	Original Owners, Lots Retained by Them, and Conveyed to the United States
861 — 28 lots	July 8, 1795	George Walker: All
862 — 1 lot	June 12, 1795	George Walker: All for improvements.
863 — 2 lots	Sept. 5, 1795	George Walker: All
864 — 11 lots	Sept. 29, 1796	George Walker: 1-3, 8-11 United States: 4-7
865 — 15 lots	Sept. 29, 1796	George Walker and William Prout William Prout: 4-10 United States: 1-3, 11-15
866 — 7 lots	Sept. 11, 1795	William Prout: 1-3 United States: 4-7
867 — 26 lots	Sept. 11, 1795	William Prout: 6-18 United States: 1-5, 19-26
868 — 26 lots	Sept. 11, 1795	William Prout All to the United States
869 — 26 lots	Sept. 11, 1795	William Prout: All
870 — 26 lots	Oct. 8, 1792	William Prout: 3-5, 9-11, 16-18, 22-25 United States: 1, 2, 6-8, 12-15, 19-21, 26
871 — 8 lots	Sept. 11, 1795	William Prout: All
872 — 15 lots	Sept. 11, 1795	William Prout All to the United States
873 — 15 lots	Sept. 11, 1795	William Prout: All
874 — 15 lots	Sept. 11, 1795	William Prout All to the United States
875 — 12 lots	Sept. 11, 1795	William Prout All to the United States
876 — 18 lots	Sept. 11, 1795	William Prout: All
877 — 34 lots	July 25, 1795	William Prout: 6-22 United States: 1-5, 23-34
878 — 12 lots	July 25, 1795	William Prout: 1-8, 30-42 United States: 9-29
879 — 2 lots	April 7, 1795	William Prout: All
880 — 2 lots	April 7, 1797	William Prout All to the United States
881 — 14 lots	April 7, 1797	William Prout: 3-9 United States: 1, 2, 10-14
882 — 26 lots	Aug. 7, 1800	Daniel Carroll of Duddington and William Prout: 6-18 United States: 1-5, 19-26
883 — 2 lots	Dec. 3, 1799	Daniel Carroll of Duddington All to the United States

Square — No. of Lots	Date of Division	Original Owners, Lots Retained by Them, and Conveyed to the United States
884	Dec. 3, 1799	Daniel Carroll of Duddington All to the United States
885		Water lots
886 — 10 lots	July 28, 1796	Notley Young All to the United States
887 — 10 lots	July 28, 1796	Notley Young All to the United States
888 — 10 lots	July 28, 1796	Notley Young All to the United States
889 — 10 lots	July 27, 1796	Notley Young All to the United States
890 — 16 lots	July 8, 1795	George Walker: All
891 — 20 lots	July 8, 1794	George Walker: All
892 — 16 lots	July 8, 1795	George Walker All to the United States
893 — 7 lots	June 22, 1795	George Walker: All
S of 893, 1 lot	June 22, 1795	George Walker: All
894 — 16 lots	June 22, 1795	George Walker All to the United States
895 — 16 lots	Sept. 5, 1795	George Walker: 1, 10-16 United States: 2-9
896 — 8 lots	Sept. 9, 1796	George Walker and William Prout George Walker: 5, 6 William Prout: 3, 4 United States: 1, 2, 7, 8
897 — 14 lots	Sept. 29, 1796	George Walker and William Prout William Prout: 1, 2, 10-14 United States: 8-9
898 — 16 lots	Oct. 8, 1792	William Prout: 4-6, 11-15 United States: 1-3, 7-10, 16
899 — 10 lots	Sept. 11, 1795	William Prout: 3-7 United States: 1, 2, 8-10
900 — 18 lots	Sept. 11, 1795	William Prout and Daniel Carroll of Duddington All to William Prout
901 — 17 lots	Sept. 11, 1795	William Prout All to the United States
902 — 14 lots	July 25, 1795	William Prout All to the United States
903 — 22 lots	July 25, 1795	William Prout All to the United States

Square — No. of Lots	Date of Division	Original Owners, Lots Retained by Them, and Conveyed to the United States
904 — 30 lots	July 25, 1795	William Prout: 3-17 United States: 1, 2, 18-30
905	Feb. 16, 1802	William Prout: All for improvements.
906 — 6 lots	July 25, 1795 Feb. 16, 1802	William Prout All to the United States William Prout: All for improvements.
907 — 4 lots	Feb. 16, 1802	William Prout: All for improvements.
908 — 1 lot	July 28, 1796	Notley Young: All
909 — 10 lots	July 28, 1796	Notley Young: All
910 — 10 lots	July 28, 1796	Notley Young: All
911 — 10 lots	July 28, 1796	Notley Young and George Walker All to Notley Young
912 — 16 lots	July 8, 1795	George Walker All to the United States
913 — 20 lots	July 8, 1795	George Walker: All
914 — 16 lots	June 22, 1795	George Walker All to the United States
915 — 1 lot	June 22, 1795	George Walker All to the United States
S of 915, 1 lot	June 22, 1795	George Walker All to the United States
916 — 1 lot	June 22, 1795	George Walker: All
917 — 18 lots	Oct. 13, 1792	George Walker: 1, 2, 8-12, 17, 18 United States: 6-7, 13-16
S of 917, 2 lots	Sept. 5, 1795	George Walker: 2 United States: 1
918 — 2 lots	Sept. 5, 1795	George Walker: 2 United States: 1
919 — 14 lots	Sept. 5, 1795	George Walker: 3-9 United States: 1, 2, 10-14
920 — 14 lots	Sept. 29, 1796	George Walker and William Prout George Walker: 10-13 William Prout: 3-5 United States: 1, 2, 6-9, 14
921 — 2 lots	Sept. 29, 1796	George Walker and William Prout William Prout: 1 United States: 2
922 — 2 lots	Sept. 29, 1796	George Walker and William Prout William Prout: 1 United States: 2

Square — No. of Lots	Date of Division	Original Owners, Lots Retained by Them, and Conveyed to the United States
923 — 22 lots	Sept. 30, 1796	Daniel Carroll of Duddington: 1-3, 15-22 United States: 4-14
924 — 20 lots	Sept. 30, 1796	Daniel Carroll of Duddington: 8-12 William Prout: 3-7 United States: 1, 2, 13-20
925 — 12 lots	July 25, 1795	William Prout: All
926 — 22 lots	July 25, 1795	William Prout: All
927 — 30 lots	July 25, 1795	William Prout: 1, 2, 18-30 United States: 3-17
re-division	May 25, 1801	All to the United States
928 — 12 lots	July 25, 1795	William Prout: All
929	July 25, 1795	William Prout: All
930	July 25, 1795	William Prout: All
931	July 28, 1796	Notley Young: All
932 — 10 lots	July 28, 1796	Notley Young: All
933 — 10 lots	July 28, 1796	Notley Young: All
934 — 16 lots	No Date	George Walker All to the United States
935 — 20 lots	July 8, 1795	George Walker All to the United States
936 — 18 lots	June 22, 1795	George Walker: All
937 — 12 lots	June 22, 1795	George Walker All to the United States
938 — 16 lots	Oct. 13, 1792	George Walker: 1, 2, 7-10, 15, 16 United States: 3-6, 11-14
939 — 20 lots	Oct. 13, 1792	George Walker: 1-3, 10-15, 20 United States: 4-9, 16-19
940 — 8 lots	Sept. 5, 1795	George Walker: 1, 2, 6-8 United States: 3-5
941 — 10 lots	June 13, 1795	George Walker: 3-5, 9 United States: 1, 2, 6-8, 10
942 — 10 lots	June 30, 1795	George Walker: 2-4, 8-10 United States: 1, 5-7
943 — 8 lots	Sept. 30, 1796	Daniel Carroll of Duddington and George Walker George Walker: 1, 2, 6-8 United States: 3-5
944 — 20 lots	Sept. 27, 1797	Daniel Carroll of Duddington: All
945 — 7 lots	Sept. 30, 1795	Daniel Carroll of Duddington: 2-5 United States: 1, 6, 7

Square — No. of Lots	Date of Division	Original Owners, Lots Retained by Them, and Conveyed to the United States
946 — 2 lots	April 17, 1797	Daniel Carroll of Duddington: 2 United States: 1
947 — 4 lots	Sept. 27, 1797	Daniel Carroll of Duddington All to the United States
948 — 4 lots	Sept. 30, 1796	Daniel Carroll of Duddington and William Prout Daniel Carroll of Duddington: 2 William Prout: 1 United States: 3, 4
re-division	May 26, 1801	William Prout: 3, 4
949 — 2 lots	Sept. 30, 1796	Daniel Carroll of Duddington and William Prout William Prout: 4-14 United States: 1-3, 15-22
950 — 30 lots	Sept. 11, 1795	William Prout: 11-25 United States: 1-10, 26-30
951 — 12 lots	Sept. 11, 1795	William Prout All to the United States
S of 951 4 lots	Sept. 11, 1795	William Prout All to the United States
952 — 3 lots	July 25, 1795	William Prout All to the United States
953 — 28 lots	April 7, 1797	Daniel Carroll of Duddington, William Prout and William King: 10-23 United States: 1-9, 24-28
954 — 20 lots	April 29, 1800	Daniel Carroll of Duddington and William Prout Daniel Carroll of Duddington: 1-4 William Prout: 5-7, 18-20 United States: 8-17
955 — 5 lots	April 17, 1797	Daniel Carroll of Duddington: All
956 — 6 lots	July 28, 1796	Notley Young All to the United States
957 — 10 lots	July 28, 1796	Notley Young All to the United States
958 — 10 lots	July 28, 1796	Notley Young All to the United States
959 — 16 lots	Oct. 29, 1800	George Walker, Notley Young and heirs of Abraham Young Heirs of Abraham Young: 1, 2, 15, 16 Notley Young: 7-10 United States: 3-6, 11-14
960 — 20 lots	Oct. 29, 1800	George Walker and heirs of Abraham Young George Walker: 3-7, 13-17 United States: 1, 2, 8-12, 18-20
961 — 4 lots	Sept. 5, 1795	George Walker: 1, 2 United States: 3, 4

Square — No. of Lots	Date of Division	Original Owners, Lots Retained by Them, and Conveyed to the United States
962 — 16 lots	June 22, 1795	George Walker: All
N of 962 2 lots	Aug. 19, 1799	George Walker: 2 United States: 1
963 — 16 lots	Oct. 13, 1792	George Walker: 3-6, 11-14 United States: 1, 2, 7-10, 15, 16
964 — 20 lots	Oct. 13, 1792	George Walker: 3-7, 13-17 United States: 1, 2, 8-12, 18-20
965 — 14 lots	Sept. 5, 1795	George Walker: 3, 4, 9-12 United States: 1, 2, 5-8, 13, 14
966 — 3 lots	June 22, 1795	George Walker: All
967 — 3 lots	June 22, 1795	George Walker All to the United States
968 — 14 lots	Sept. 30, 1795	William Prout and George Walker George Walker: 3-8 United States: 1, 2, 9-14
969 — 20 lots	Sept. 27, 1797	Daniel Carroll of Duddington All to the United States
970 — 5 lots	Sept. 30, 1796	Daniel Carroll of Duddington: 1-5 United States: 2-4
971 — 2 lots	Sept. 30, 1796	Daniel Carroll of Duddington: 2 United States: 1
972 — 5 lots	Sept. 30, 1796	Daniel Carroll of Duddington: 1, 4, 5 United States: 2, 3
973 — 22 lots	May 30, 1800	Daniel Carroll of Duddington, William Prout, Robert Morris and John Nicholson. Morris and Nicholson: 1-8, 20-22 United States: 9-19
re-division	May 25, 1801	William Prout: 9-19
974 — 30 lots	Aug. 4, 1809	William Prout, Robert Morris, and John Nicholson Thomas Tingey, assignee of William Prout: 4, 18 United States: 1-3, 19-30
975 — 12 lots	Sept. 11, 1795	William Prout: All
S of 975, 6 lots	Sept. 11, 1795	William Prout: All
976 — 4 lots	Sept. 11, 1795	William Prout: 2, 3 United States: 1, 4
977 — 28 lots	Mar. 23, 1797	Daniel Carroll of Duddington, William Prout and William King: 3-16 United States: 1, 2, 17-28
978 — 20 lots	April 29, 1800	Daniel Carroll of Duddington, William Prout and William King Daniel Carroll of Duddington: 3-10 William Prout: 11, 12 United States: 1, 2, 13-20

Square — No. of Lots	Date of Division	Original Owners, Lots Retained by Them, and Conveyed to the United States
979 — 5 lots	July 2, 1800	Daniel Carroll of Duddington, William Prout and William King All to the United States
980 — 12 lots	Aug. 9, 1796	Notley Young All to the United States
981 — 12 lots	Aug. 9, 1796	Notley Young and Abraham Young All to Notley Young
982 — 12 lots	Sept. 22, 1797	Notley Young and Abraham Young All to Abraham Young
983	Sept. 22, 1797	Abraham Young and George Walker All to Abraham Young
984 — 4 lots	Oct. 29, 1800‡ Oct. 9, 1800†	George Walker and heirs of Abraham Young George Walker: 3 Heirs of Abraham Young: 1 United States: 2, 4
985 — 18 lots	Oct. 29, 1800	George Walker and heirs of Abraham Young George Walker: 3-7, 13-16 United States: 1, 2, 8-12, 17, 18
986 — 18 lots	Oct. 13, 1792	George Walker: 3-7, 13-16 United States: 1, 2, 8-12, 17, 18
987 — 22 lots	Oct. 13, 1792	George Walker: 1-3, 9-13, 20-22 United States: 4-8, 14-19
988 — 22 lots	Oct. 13, 1792	George Walker: All
989 — 22 lots	Oct. 13, 1792	George Walker All to the United States
990 — 26 lots	Sept. 30, 1796	Daniel Carroll of Duddington and George Walker Daniel Carroll of Duddington: 1-3, 24-26 George Walker: 17-23 United States: 4-16
S of 990 6 lots	Oct. 10, 1801	William Prout and George Walker William Prout: 2, 4 George Walker: 1 United States: 3, 5
991 — 14 lots		Daniel Carroll of Duddington: 1, 2, 10-14 United States: 3-9
992 — 18 lots		Daniel Carroll of Duddington: 1, 2, 12-18 United States: 3-11
993		No such Square
994 — 8 lots [51]	Sept. 30, 1796†	Daniel Carroll of Duddington, Morris and Nicholson: 3-6 United States: 1, 2, 7, 8

---

[51] This Square has been divided, and is signed by Daniel Carroll, and Robert Morris by his attorney William Cranch, and is among the unsigned Squares, wanting signature of the Commissioners and John Nicholson.

Square — No. of Lots	Date of Division	Original Owners, Lots Retained by Them, and Conveyed to the United States
995 — 30 lots	Aug. 4, 1809	William Prout, Robert Morris and John Nicholson Morris and Nicholson: 4-18 United States: 1-3, 19-30
996 — 13 lots	Aug. 4, 1809	William Prout, Robert Morris and John Nicholson William Prout: 3-6 United States: 1, 2, 7-13
997 — 2 lots	June 16, 1800	William Prout, Robert Morris and John Nicholson: 1 United States: 2
998		No such Square
999 — 4 lots	Sept. 11, 1795	William Prout: 3, 4 United States: 1, 2
1000 — 28 lots	April 7, 1797	William Prout and William King: 3-16 United States: 1, 2, 17-28
1001 — 20 lots	May 15, 1800	William Prout and William King: 3-7, 14-18 United States: 1, 2, 8-13, 19, 20
S of 1001		No record
1002 — 14 lots	Aug. 9, 1796	Notley Young: 1-4, 11-14 United States: 5-10
1003 — 16 lots	Sept. 26, 1797	Notley Young and Abraham Young All to the United States
1004 — 18 lots	Sept. 22, 1797	Abraham Young All to the United States
1005 — 14 lots	Sept. 22, 1797	Abraham Young All to the United States
1006 — 1 lot	Sept. 22, 1797	Abraham Young All to the United States
1007 — 18 lots	Sept. 22, 1797	Abraham Young All to the United States
1008 — 20 lots	Sept. 22, 1797	Abraham Young and George Walker All to the United States
1009 — 18 lots	Oct. 24, 1799	George Walker and heirs of Abraham Young United States: 4-7, 13-17 Proprietors: 1-3, 8-12, 18
1010 — 18 lots	Oct. 24, 1799	George Walker and heirs of Abraham Young United States: 1, 2, 8-11, 16-18 Proprietors: 3-7, 12-15
1011 — 10 lots	Sept. 29, 1796	George Walker: 5-10 United States: 1-4
1012 — 2 lots	Sept. 29, 1796	George Walker: 1 United States: 2
1013 — 2 lots	Sept. 29, 1796	George Walker: 1 United States: 2

Square — No. of Lots	Date of Division	Original Owners, Lots Retained by Them, and Conveyed to the United States
1014 — 10 lots	Sept. 29, 1796	George Walker: 6-9 United States: 1-5, 10
1015 — 34 lots	Sept. 5, 1795	George Walker: 5-16, 25-28 United States: 1-4, 17-24, 29-34
E of 1015 4 lots	Aug. 19, 1799	George Walker: 1, 2 United States: 3, 4
1016		No such Square
1017 — 28 lots	Sept. 30, 1796	Daniel Carroll of Duddington and George Walker George Walker: 6-18 United States: 1-4, 19-28
1018 — 28 lots	Sept. 30, 1796	Daniel Carroll of Duddington and George Walker Daniel Carroll of Duddington: 5-11 George Walker: 12-18 United States: 1-4, 19-28
1019 — 10 lots	Sept. 27, 1796	Daniel Carroll of Duddington, George Walker, Robert Morris and John Nicholson George Walker: 4, 5 Daniel Carroll of Duddington: 3, 6, 7 United States: 1, 2, 8-10
S of 1019 4 lots	Sept. 7, 1796	Robert Morris and John Nicholson: 1, 2 United States: 3, 4
1020 — 38 lots	Sept. 7, 1796	Robert Morris and John Nicholson: 1-5, 25-38 United States: 6-24
1021 — 2 lots	Sept. 7, 1796	Robert Morris and John Nicholson: 1 United States: 2
1022 — 2 lots	Sept. 7, 1796	Robert Morris and John Nicholson: 2 United States: 1
1023 — 14 lots	Sept. 17, 1796	Robert Morris and John Nicholson: 4-10 United States: 1-3, 11-14
NE of 1023		No such Square
1024 — 7 lots	Aug. 4, 1809	William Prout, Robert Morris and John Nicholson: 1-3, 7 United States: 4-6
1025	No Date	Morris and Nicholson, George Walker, William Prout, and Widow Wheeler (One of the unsigned Squares.)
S of 1025	No Date	William Prout and Elizabeth Wheeler. Water lots
E of 1025 8 lots	Dec. 5, 1798† Dec. 6, 1798‡	George Walker and Elizabeth Wheeler: 1, 3, 5, 7 United States: 2, 4, 6, 8

Square — No. of Lots	Date of Division	Original Owners, Lots Retained by Them, and Conveyed to the United States
1026 — 1 lot	Sept. 22, 1797	Abraham Young and Notley Young All to the United States
N of 1026 2 lots	Aug. 9, 1796	Notley Young All to the United States
1027 — 22 lots	Sept. 22, 1797	Notley Young and Abraham Young: All
S of 1027 1 lot	Sept. 22, 1797	Abraham Young: All
1028 — 22 lots	Sept. 22, 1797	Abraham Young: All
1029 — 26 lots	Sept. 22, 1797	Abraham Young All to the United States
1030 — 21 lots	Sept. 22, 1797	Abraham Young: All
1031 — 10 lots	Aug. 28, 1797	Abraham Young: 6-10 United States: 1-5
1032 — 5 lots	Aug. 28, 1797	Abraham Young: 1, 3, 4 United States: 2, 5
1033 — 13 lots	Aug. 28, 1797	Abraham Young: 1-3, 8, 9, 13 United States: 4-7, 10-12
NW of 1033 6 lots	Oct. 29, 1800	Heirs of Abraham Young: All
1034 — 10 lots	Oct. 24, 1799	George Walker and heirs of Abraham Young United States: 1-4, 10 Proprietors: 5-9
1035 — 17 lots	Oct. 29, 1799	Heirs of William Young, heirs of Abraham Young, and George Walker Proprietors: 5-11 United States: 1-4, 12-17
N of 1035 3 lots	Oct. 29, 1800	Abraham Young's heirs: All
1036 — 17 lots	Oct. 22, 1799	George Walker, heirs of William Young, and heirs of Abraham Young: 3, 4, 7-9, 14-16 United States: 1, 2, 5, 6, 10-13, 17
S of 1036 2 lots	Mar. 28, 1798	William Young's heirs All to the United States
1037 — 10 lots	Oct. 29, 1799	William Young's heirs and George Walker United States: 1-4 Proprietors: 5-10
1038 — 14 lots	Oct. 29, 1799	George Walker and William Young's heirs Proprietors: 1-4, 11-14 United States: 5-10
SW of 1038		No record

Square — No. of Lots	Date of Division	Original Owners, Lots Retained by Them, and Conveyed to the United States
1039 — 8 lots	Sept. 5, 1795	George Walker: 4, 5, 7 United States: 1-3, 6, 8
S of 1039 3 lots	Aug. 17, 1799	George Walker: 1 United States: 2, 3
1040 — 6 lots	Sept. 5, 1795	George Walker: 2-5 United States: 1-6
1041 — 18 lots	Sept. 5, 1795	George Walker: 5-9, 15-17 United States: 1-4, 10-14, 18
SE of 1041		No such Square
1042 — 34 lots	Sept. 5, 1795	George Walker: 7-23 United States: 1-6, 24-34
E of 1042, 1 lot	Aug. 19, 1799	George Walker: All
1043 - 36 lots	Sept. 5, 1795	George Walker: 11-23, 27-33 United States: 1-10, 24-26, 34-36
1044 — 2 lots	Sept. 30, 1796	George Walker: 1 United States: 2
1045 — 15 lots	Oct. 12, 1796	Robert Morris, John Nicholson and George Walker Morris and Nicholson: 9, 10, 12 George Walker: 1, 13-15 United States: 2-8, 11
1046 — 18 lots	Oct. 12, 1796	Robert Morris, John Nicholson and George Walker Morris and Nicholson: 2, 14, 15 George Walker: 1, 16-18 United States: 3-13
1047 — 28 lots	Sept. 30, 1796	Robert Morris, John Nicholson and George Walker Morris and Nicholson: 7-13, 19, 20 George Walker: 14-18 United States: 1-6, 21-28
1048 — 32 lots	Sept. 30, 1796	Robert Morris, John Nicholson and George Walker Morris and Nicholson: 7-9, 15-23 George Walker: 10-14 United States: 1-6, 24-32
S of 1048		Elizabeth Wheeler: For improvements.
1049 — 2 lots	Aug. 9, 1796	Notley Young: All
N of 1049 1 lot	Aug. 9, 1796	Notley Young All to the United States
1050 — 6 lots	Aug. 9, 1796	Notley Young: 1, 2, 6 United States: 3-5
1051 — 19 lots	Sept. 26, 1797	Notley Young and Abraham Young All to Notley Young
1052 — 5 lots	Sept. 22, 1797	Notley Young and Abraham Young All to the United States

Square — No. of Lots	Date of Division	Original Owners, Lots Retained by Them, and Conveyed to the United States
1053 — 14 lots	Sept. 22, 1797	Abraham Young: All
N of 1053	No Date	Notley Young's heirs and Abraham Young One-half to Notley Young for improvements. One-half to Abraham Young.
1054 — 16 lots	Sept. 22, 1797	Abraham Young: All
1055 — 18 lots	Aug. 28, 1797	Abraham Young: All
1056 — 13 lots	Aug. 28, 1797	Abraham Young All to the United States
1057 — 20 lots	Sept. 30, 1796	Abraham Young: 5-14 United States: 1-4, 15-20
1058 — 19 lots	No Date	Notley Young's heirs: 1-4, 10-14 United States: 5-9, 15-19
1059 — 13 lots	Sept. 28, 1797	William Young's heirs: 4-8 United States: 1-3, 9-13
S of 1059 3 lots	Mar. 28, 1798	William Young's heirs: All
1060 — 14 lots	Oct. 2, 1800‡ Oct. 20, 1800†	George Walker and William Young's heirs: 1-3, 7, 8, 11, 12 United States: 4-6, 9, 10, 13, 14
1061 — 24 lots	Oct. 29, 1799	George Walker and William Young's heirs: 1-3, 11-16, 22-24 United States: 4-10, 17-21
1062 — 14 lots	Sept. 5, 1795	George Walker: 1-4, 12-14 United States: 5-11
S of 1062, 1 lot	Aug. 19, 1799	George Walker: All
1063 — 22 lots	Sept. 5, 1795	George Walker: 5-10, 13-18 United States: 1-4, 11, 12, 19-22
1064 — 2 lots	Sept. 30, 1796	George Walker: 1 United States: 2
1065 — 4 lots	Nov. 17, 1796	George Walker: 2, 4 United States: 1, 3
NE of 1065 6 lots	Sept. 5, 1795	George Walker: 2-4 United States: 1, 5, 6
1066 — 18 lots	Mar. 22, 1796	George Walker: 5-13 United States: 1-4, 14-18
1067 — 18 lots	Mar. 22, 1796	George Walker: 1-3, 7-9, 15-18 United States: 4-6, 10-14
S of 1067 4 lots	Dec. 2, 1800	Elizabeth Wheeler: 2, 4 United States: 1, 3
1068 — 2 lots	Aug. 28, 1797	Abraham Young: 2 United States: 1

Square — No. of Lots	Date of Division	Original Owners, Lots Retained by Them, and Conveyed to the United States
SE of 1068 7 lots	Oct. 29, 1800	Abraham Young All to the United States
1069 — 18 lots	Sept. 30, 1796	Abraham Young: 1, 2, 12-18 United States: 3-11
1070 — 16 lots	No Date	Abraham Young's heirs and William Young's heirs: 4-11 (Not signed by W. Young's heirs.) United States: 1-3, 12-16
1071 — 16 lots	Sept. 28, 1797	William Young's heirs: 1-3, 12-16 United States: 4-11
1072 — 18 lots	Sept. 28, 1797	William Young's heirs: 1-3, 13-18 United States: 4-12
S of 1072 5 lots	Mar. 28, 1798	William Young's heirs All to the United States
1073 — 12 lots	Mar. 28, 1798	William Young's heirs: 1, 9-12 United States: 2-8
1074 — 20 lots	Sept. 28, 1797	William Young's heirs: 1-3, 14-20 United States: 4-13
1075 — 22 lots	Oct. 29, 1799	George Walker and William Young's heirs: 4-9, 15-19 United States: 1-3, 10-14, 20-22
1076 — 11 lots	Oct. 29, 1799	George Walker and William Young's heirs United States: 2, 8-11 Proprietors: 1, 3-7
1077 — 24 lots	Oct. 29, 1799	George Walker: 1-7, 20-24 United States: 8-19
1078 — 13 lots	Sept. 5, 1795	George Walker: 5-10 United States: 1-4, 11-13
1079 — 12 lots	Oct. 9, 1795	George Walker: 1, 3, 5, 6, 10, 11 United States: 2, 4, 7-9, 12
SE of 1079 1 lot	Nov. 25, 1797	George Walker
1080 — 2 lots	Oct. 9, 1795	George Walker: 1 United States: 2
S of 1080	Nov. 25, 1797	George Walker: 2 United States: 1
1081		No such Square
1082 — 12 lots	Aug. 28, 1797	Abraham Young: 1, 2, 8-12 United States: 1, 2, 12-18
1083 — 18 lots	Sept. 30, 1796	Abraham Young: 3-11 United States: 1, 2, 12-18
1084 — 16 lots	No Date	Abraham Young's heirs and William Young's heirs: 4-11 United States: 1-3, 12-16

Square — No. of Lots	Date of Division	Original Owners, Lots Retained by Them, and Conveyed to the United States
1085 — 16 lots	Sept. 28, 1797	William Young's heirs: 4-11 United States: 1-3, 12-16
1086 — 18 lots	Sept. 28, 1797	William Young's heirs: 4-12 United States: 1-3, 13-18
1087 — 9 lots	Sept. 28, 1797	William Young's heirs: 1, 6-9 United States: 2-5
1088 — 5 lots	Mar. 28, 1798	William Young's heirs: All
1089 — 20 lots	Mar. 28, 1798	William Young's heirs All to the United States
1090 — 22 lots	Mar. 28, 1798	William Young's heirs: All
1091 — 5 lots	Mar. 28, 1798	William Young's heirs: All
S of 1091 2 lots	Sept. 28, 1797	William Young's heirs All to the United States
1092 — 12 lots	Nov. 1, 1799	George Walker and William Young's heirs: 3-9 United States: 1, 2, 9-12
S of 1092 2 lots	Aug. 19, 1799	George Walker: 1 United States: 2
1093 — 24 lots	Sept. 30, 1796	Abraham Young: 1-4, 17-24 United States: 5-16
S of 1093		No such Square
1094 — 20 lots	Sept. 30, 1796	Abraham Young: 5-14 United States: 1-4, 15-20
1095 — 20 lots	Sept. 30, 1796	Abraham Young: 4-13 United States: 1-3, 14-20
1096 — 20 lots	Oct. 29, 1799	William Young's heirs and Abraham Young's heirs: 1-4, 14-20 United States: 5-13
1097 — 20 lots	Oct. 29, 1799	William Young's heirs and Abraham Young's heirs: 5-13 United States: 1-4, 14-20
1098 — 20 lots	Oct. 29, 1799	William Young's heirs and Abraham Young's heirs: 3-11 United States: 1, 2, 12-20
1099		No such Square
1100 — 16 lots	Mar. 28, 1798	William Young's heirs: All
1101		No such Square
1102 — 16 lots	Mar. 28, 1798	William Young's heirs All to the United States
1103		No such Square
1104 — 12 lots	Mar. 28, 1798	William Young's heirs: All
1105 — 20 lots	Sept. 28, 1797	William Young's heirs: 4-13 United States: 1-3, 14-20

Square — No. of Lots	Date of Division	Original Owners, Lots Retained by Them, and Conveyed to the United States
1106		William Young's heirs: All for improvements.
1107 — 24 lots	Sept. 30, 1796	Abraham Young: 5-16 United States: 1-4, 17-24
1108 — 20 lots	Sept. 30, 1796	Abraham Young: 4-13 United States: 1-3, 14-20
1109 — 20 lots	Sept. 30, 1796	Abraham Young: 5-14 United States: 1-4, 15-20
1110 — 20 lots	Sept. 30, 1796	Abraham Young: 5-14 United States: 1-4, 15-20
1111 — 20 lots	Sept. 30, 1796	Abraham Young: 5-14 United States: 1-4, 15-20
1112 — 26 lots	Oct. 29, 1799	William Young's heirs and Abraham Young's heirs: 4-9, 16-22 United States: 1-3, 10-15, 23-26
1113 — 6 lots	Oct. 28, 1797† Oct. 29, 1797‡	William Young's heirs All to the United States
NE of 1113	No Date	William Young: All
1114 — 6 lots	Sept. 28, 1797	William Young's heirs: All
SE of 1114 2 lots	Mar. 28, 1798	William Young's heirs: All
1115 — 28 lots	Mar. 28, 1798	William Young's heirs All to the United States
1116 — 20 lots	Sept. 28, 1797	William Young's heirs: 1-3, 14-20 United States: 4-13
1117 — 9 lots	Sept. 28, 1797	William Young's heirs: 4-8 United States: 1-3, 9
1118 — 16 lots	Sept. 30, 1796	Abraham Young: 3-10 United States: 1, 2, 10-14
1119 — 14 lots	Sept. 30, 1796	Abraham Young: 3-9 United States: 1, 2, 9-12
1120 — 12 lots	Sept. 30, 1796	Abraham Young: 3-8 United States: 1, 2, 9-12
1121 — 12 lots	Oct. 1, 1796	Robert Morris, John Nicholson, William Prout and Abraham Young Abraham Young: 3-8 United States: 1, 2, 9-12
1122 — 14 lots	Oct. 1, 1796	Robert Morris, John Nicholson, William Prout and Abraham Young Abraham Young: 3-9 United States: 1, 2, 10-14
1123 — 12 lots	Sept. 28, 1797	William Young's heirs: 1, 2, 9-12 United States: 3-8

Square — No. of Lots	Date of Division	Original Owners, Lots Retained by Them, and Conveyed to the United States
1124		No such Square
1125 — 16 lots	Oct. 1, 1796	Robert Morris, John Nicholson, William Prout and Abraham Young Morris and Nicholson: 7-10 William Prout: 3-6 United States: 1, 2, 11-16
1126 — 14 lots	Oct. 1, 1796	Robert Morris, John Nicholson, William Prout and Abraham Young William Prout: 3-5, half of 6 Morris and Nicholson: 7-9, half of 6 United States: 1, 2, 10-14
1127 — 12 lots	Sept. 7, 1796	Robert Morris, John Nicholson and William Prout Morris and Nicholson: 9-11 William Prout: 1, 2, 12 United States: 3-8
1128 — 12 lots	Sept. 7, 1796	Robert Morris, John Nicholson and William Prout Morris and Nicholson: 3-5 William Prout: 6-8 United States: 1, 2, 9-12
1129 — 4 lots	Sept. 7, 1796	Robert Morris, John Nicholson and William Prout Morris and Nicholson: 10-13 William Prout: 1, 2, 14 United States: 3-9
1130 — 12 lots	Sept. 28, 1797	William Young's heirs: 1, 2, 9-12 United States: 3-8
1131		No such Square
1132 — 16 lots	Sept. 7, 1796	Robert Morris, John Nicholson and William Prout Morris and Nicholson: 3-6 William Prout: 7-10 United States: 1, 2, 11-16
1133 — 14 lots	Sept. 7, 1796	Robert Morris, John Nicholson and William Prout Morris and Nicholson: 7-9 William Prout: 3-6 United States: 1, 2, 10-14
1134 — 12 lots	Sept. 7, 1796	Robert Morris, John Nicholson and William Prout Morris and Nicholson: 3-5 William Prout: 6-8 United States: 1, 2, 9-12
1135 — 12 lots	Sept. 7, 1796	Robert Morris, John Nicholson and William Prout Morris and Nicholson: 9-11 William Prout: 1, 2, 12 United States: 3-8
1136 — 14 lots	Sept. 7, 1796	Robert Morris, John Nicholson and William Prout Morris and Nicholson: 3-6 William Prout: 7-9 United States: 1, 2, 10-14

Square — No. of Lots	Date of Division	Original Owners, Lots Retained by Them, and Conveyed to the United States
1137 — 16 lots	Sept. 7, 1796	Robert Morris, John Nicholson and William Prout Morris and Nicholson: 7-10 William Prout: 3-6 United States: 1, 2, 11-16
1138 — 14 lots	Sept. 7, 1796	Robert Morris, John Nicholson and William Prout Morris and Nicholson: 3-5 William Prout: 6-9 United States: 1, 2, 10-14
1139 — 12 lots	Sept. 7, 1796	Robert Morris, John Nicholson and William Prout Morris and Nicholson: 6-8 William Prout: 3-5 United States: 1, 2, 9-12
1140 — 12 lots	Sept. 7, 1796	Robert Morris, John Nicholson and William Prout Morris and Nicholson: 3-5 William Prout: 6-8 United States: 1, 2, 9-12
S of 1140 14 lots	Sept. 7, 1796	Robert Morris, John Nicholson and William Prout Morris and Nicholson: 6-9 William Prout: 3-5 United States: 1, 2, 10-14
1141 — 16 lots	Sept. 7, 1796	Robert Morris, John Nicholson and William Prout Morris and Nicholson: 3-6 William Prout: 7-10 United States: 1, 2, 11-16
1142 — 14 lots	Sept. 7, 1796	Robert Morris, John Nicholson and William Prout Morris and Nicholson: 10-12 William Prout: 1, 2, 13, 14 United States: 3-9
1143 — 12 lots	Sept. 7, 1796	Robert Morris, John Nicholson and William Prout Morris and Nicholson: 3-5 William Prout: 6-8 United States: 1, 2, 9-12
1144 — 16 lots	No Date	Robert Morris, John Nicholson and William Prout: 7-14 United States: 1-6, 15-16
1145 — 13 lots	No Date	Robert Morris, John Nicholson and William Prout: 1-6 United States: 70-13
1146 — 12 lots	No Date	Robert Morris, John Nicholson and William Prout: 6-11 United States: 1-5, 12
1147		No such Square
1148 — 3 lots	No Date	William Young's heirs and Mrs. Elizabeth Wheeler All to the United States
1149 — 4 lots	No Date	William Young's heirs and Elizabeth Wheeler All to the United States

CONCLUSION

THE foregoing tabular statements were prepared with the greatest accuracy, as a faithful and systematic transcript from the public records, to serve as a manual of easy reference to all interested in the original titles or early conveyances of property in Washington city, and as such the compilers might consider their work completed. However, having briefly reviewed in the introduction the most important historical events which preceded the establishment of the seat of the General Government in this city, it is surely useful, if not necessary, to cast a passing glance upon occurrences succeeding that epoch, as far as they have any bearing upon present property relations.

By this it is not contemplated to render a history of succession in each piece of property, as this would be an attempt probably exceeding mortal powers, and certainly reaching beyond the means of a single life-time and private enterprise, but simply a chronological synopsis of legislative measures which gradually advanced property to its present development and value.

Congress assumed direct jurisdiction over the District of Columbia and the National Capital in the year 1801, and one of the earliest enactments within its precincts was to declare that, until future direction, the laws of Maryland and Virginia should remain in force within the respective portions ceded by these States.

In this measure, although it seems natural under the circumstances, many of the difficulties and grievances surrounding and retarding the subsequent growth and progress of our city find their origin and primary cause. At the very start three distinct codes of statutes ruled the fealty of landlords within an area inferior to some of the very smallest counties of our vast Republic, namely, those of Maryland and Virginia and the rapidly multiplying enactments of Congress; and to this triple legislation very soon were added the local laws passed by our municipal authorities under delegation of power from Congress.

Such a burden of complicated legislation (with the exception of the Virginia code, the operations of which ceased in 1846, with the retrocession of the territorial rights and limits originally yielded by that State,) continues until the present day to puzzle the proverbial Philadelphia lawyer, and it is surprising that it has not stifled ere now every vestige of development. It certainly has contributed much to impede our facilities for industrial and commercial expansion; and without the reflex of prestige from its share in national successors, Washington city would never have risen from the ignominious attitude which induced Moore, in 1804, to permit his Muse to indulge in the following satire:

In fancy not beneath the twilight gloom
Come, let me lead thee o'er this modern Rome,
Where Tribunes rule, where dusky Davi bow,
And what was Goose Creek once as Tiber now.

This famed metropolis, where fancy sees
Squares in morasses, obelisks in trees;
Which travelling fools and gazetteers adorn
With shrines unbuilt and heroes yet unborn;
Tho' naught but wood and — they see
Where streets should run, and sages ought to be.

We wonder what Moore thought that London was a few years after its foundation, when he wrote this lampoon, and whether he foresaw that neither local disadvantages nor narrow-sighted legislation could prevent the capital of a great nation from emerging out of mire and sloth, and that in seventy years, although still not a commercial emporium nor a manufacturing centre, it should rise in many other regards to an eminence which some of the proudest cities of Europe, with the means of tyrannical power and the treasures of centures at their command, might envy, and in vain attempt to emulate.

Before this digression our narration of historical events had advanced to the close of the year 1801, when, besides the public reservations previously enumerated, there were still 4,682 lots and 2,042 feet of water-front for navigation, unsold, in the possession of the General Government.

In the following year, viz., 1802, Congress reduced the number of Commissioners to one, and instructed him to cause the sale of as many lots as might suffice to pay off all liabilities incurred during the previous ten years. These instructions were obeyed, and most of the lots donated by the original landowners to the Government were thus sold; still, there are a few of them yet in charge of the present Commissioner of Public Buildings and Grounds.

However, the magnificent donation of 10,136 lots, over and above the 2,000 acres and more sold at a merely nominal price for public reservations, has never been appreciated or reciprocated by Congress with adequate liberality. Up to 1840, nearly all the contributions of the General Government towards educational and benevolent enterprises of the city, of which Congress received a large part of the benefit, were limited to the return of several such lots as aforesaid, valued at $70,000, of which the City Orphan, and the St. Vincent Female Orphan Asylums each received $10,000, and the Columbian and Georgetown Colleges each $25,000; and up to this date the share assumed by Congress, in expenditures by the city for public purposes and improvements, is anything but commensurate.

The most important act of Congress in relation to our city was "to incorporate the inhabitants of Washington, in the District of Columbia," passed March 3, 1802, by which Congress delegated part of its powers under the Constitution. This act divided the city in three wards, as previously the Levy Court of the county of Washington had done for the purposes of assessment. It also provided for the election of councils in two chambers, the first with seven, the second with five members, to be elected annually by a general ticket, out of which the latter five were chosen by ballot among the twelve.

The first election took place June 17, 1802. The Mayor was then appointed by the President, and he, the Mayor, appointed all officers under him. By this act the Corporation was prohibited from ordering tax sales for default of payment on vacant and unimproved lots.

In 1804, a supplementary act was passed, enlarging the powers of the Corporation in some respects, yet still leaving with the Levy Court the authority of imposing taxes upon city property. This act reduced the councils to nine members, each branch to be elected by distinct ballot.

In 1812, another supplementary act was passed, by which the Mayor was elected also, the date of annual elections fixed, and the Mayor was only allowed to nominate officials, to be confirmed by a majority of the Board of Aldermen.

This Board was organized to consist of two, and the Board of Councilmen of three members, from each ward, the former to be elected for two, the latter for one year. The powers of the Corporation were again increased, among others, by the authority to sell property for non-payment of taxes.

On June 20, 1819, and Feb. 28, 1820, further amendatory acts were passed, mainly referring to the collection of taxes, and finally, on May 15, 1820, all previous acts were superseded by an act generally called, "The Charter of Washington," remaining in force, with but few and slight alterations (viz., acts of May 26, 1824, May 11, 1832, quieting titles, etc., May 5, 1864, and Resolution, June 1, 1864,) until Feb. 21, 1871, when an organic act radically changed the form of government, since when the events and legislation are of too recent date to escape the memory or means of information of persons interested.

The act of May 15, 1820, affected the property relation and interests only in regard to the mode of levying and collecting taxes, tax sales, and a few other provisions, easily within the reach of any one by reference either to the publication of laws, by Andrew Rothwell, 1833, and other authors of digests and other publications.

There were altogether 21 Mayors from 1802-1871; viz:

    1802, Robert Brent
    1812, Daniel Rapine
    1813, James H. Blake
    1817, Benjamin G. Orr
    1819, Samuel M. Smallwood
    1822, T. Carberry
    1824, Richard C. Weightman
    1827, Joseph Gales, Jr.
    1830, John P. Van Ness
    1834, William A. Bardley
    1836, Peter Force
    1840, W.W. Seaton
    1850, Walter Lennox
    1852, J.W. Maury
    1854, J.T. Towers
    1856, W.B. Magruder
    1858, J.G. Berret
    1862, Richard Wallach
    1868, S.J. Bowen
    1870, M.G. Emery

During the regime of these municipal authorities there was no lack of provisions which tended toward the improvement of the city, and the enhancement of real estate therein. The enactments for the partial grading, lighting, cleaning, and sewering of streets and avenues, the planting and preserving of trees therein, the erection of pumps and reservoirs, the establishment of markets, graveyards, educational and benevolent institutions, as schools, orphan and other asylums, infirmaries, homes for the poor, insane, or other wretched mortals, workhouses and places of restraint for criminals and other offenders of the law, the construction of wharves and river defences, the organization of health and police officers, and measures against the ravages of fire, epidemics, or other calamities, and literally numberless, and the most important among these laws in relation to property and its value were those referring to the mode of levying and collecting taxes, building regulations, tax sales, etc., easily to be found by reference to the statutes of the Corporation.

During all these seventy years, or at least sixty of them, Congress seems to have scarcely remembered that the Constitution has entrusted it with the exclusive power of legislation over the national capital and that Government was the sole owner of the streets and avenues therein, so few were the Congressional acts in those days interfering with the measures of the Corporation; and with the exception of some enactments bearing upon tax levies, the collection of taxes, and the quieting of titles, which, however, still need additional provisions, its legislation confined itself to sparing appropriations in aid of institutions from which the different branches of the Government and its numerous officers and employees derived a large share of benefit, and to the incorporation of canal, railroad, gas, and other companies, banks, and other powerful associations, from which the city received an arbitrary and sometimes even questionable pittance of advantage.

The effects of such a condition of affairs were inevitable. Inexperience, poverty, calamities like the destruction of the city by fire in its most tender infancy, and other embarrassments, retarded its progress to an alarming extent, so that for many years during the nearly miraculous expansion of nearly all other sections of our glorious Republic in growth and prosperity, the question was not improperly agitated whether the seat of Government should not be removed from the neglected place of which the country was almost ashamed. Nor was this surprising when looking back upon its past condition. Excepting the Government buildings and reservations, the city had no improvements of any consequence, and for nearly twenty-five years but few scores of houses and a very small standing population. The building of a city hall was not even commenced till 1822; the salary of the Mayor was $400 per annum till 1815, and $500 till 1820; and then for many years but $1,000. Only in 1819 it was possible to levy a tax of 50 cents on every hundred dollars, and this was thought ruinous; and then, in 1837, the tax was raised to 75 cents, the tax-payers considered their powers inadequate to pay such amount. In 1821 the entire police force of the city consisted of six men, and this was thought more than necessary. Pavements, roadways, and sidewalks, were limited to very primitive material and to the immediate vicinity of Government buildings, and one or two thoroughfares between them. Sewers were unknown, and even surface drainage was little regulated until within recent years. Many streets and vacant lots were unopened or without fencing, a favorite pasture and resort of cattle and animals of all descriptions, holding, in spite of corporation rules, the freedom of the city until very lately. The city had a vary scanty revenue from its small standing population, and the industrial and commercial resources of the citizens were crippled by the fact that only the few months of the Congressional sessions yielded reasonable returns to their efforts, whilst during the remainder of the year scarcely any business establishment, hotels not excepted, paid for current expenses. The city exchequer never knew a moment of freedom from debt from the earliest days to the present, and its liabilities steadily multiplied in quantity and quality. In brief, up to 1860 the city was, in regard to internal improvements, inferior to almost any of her equals in population, and surely far below the standard of all her equals in area and territorial capacity.

The most important events in the history of the District from its cession to that year were, first, the capture and destruction of Washington city by the British in 1812, and in 1846, the retrocession of Virginia of the territorial portion originally ceded by that State.

The outbreak of the civil war of course had its terrors and dark hours also for the national capital, yet however much lamented in every other respect, brought some blessings to her in this, that the repeated presence or passage of large military forces in and through her precincts and vicinity, and the necessary expansion and increase of the Government Departments and its branches, opened new avenues of business and enterprise in industrial and commercial pursuits, and naturally brought a large influx of population, and also capital, so that during the ten years from 1860 to 1870 a greater stride in growth of population and improvements has been perceptible than in half the time of her previous existence, and literally has opened a new era for her future prospects.

But unquestionably the greatest march of progress and the most telling development of her natural capacities has been realized, whatever errors may have been committed, during the brief administration of her affairs under the Territorial authorities established by the organic act of Congress, passed Feb. 21, 1871, so that the present improvements of the National Capital have fully redeemed her previous unflattering reputation, and have demonstrated that her capacities for improvement had been slandered, and were never inferior to those of other cities; and, on the contrary, that her broad avenues and streets were designed by our far-seeing ancestors in clear appreciation of what the National Capital of the greatest Republic should be, and that they are by far superior to the thoroughfares of the proudest metropolis of any country, and by a wise and liberal policy on the part of Congress may be made the pride of our nation and the marvel of the world.

That this will be realized, is the destiny of Washington city and the wish of the authors.

E.F.M. FAEHTZ
F.W. PRATT
1874

APPENDIX A

At the request of the Commissioners appointed under the Act of Congress entitled "An Act for Establishing the Temporary and Permanent Seat of the Government of the United States," certificates of purchase were recorded. A number of these are found beginning in District of Columbia Deed Book B2 Part A. A typical record shows the transaction from the Commissioners to a lot purchaser. Unfortunately, not many of the certificates are found to have been recorded.

Date	Certificate Holder	Square	Lot(s)	Fee	Book	Page
Dec. 24, 1793	Robert Morris and James Greenleaf[52]	0001	1, 3, 17, 18, 20		B2B	150
May 18, 1793	Leonard Harbaugh	0001	8, 10		B2B	145
May 18, 1793	Leonard Harbaugh	0001	9	75 cm[53]	B2B	175
June 24, 1793	Heinrich Konig, George Town, Md.	0001	12	$266⅔	B2A	430
June 24, 1793	Henry Konig[54]	0001	12	100 Md.[55]	B2B	141
May 18, 1793	Leonard Harbaugh[56]	0001	13		B2B	145
Oct. 1, 1792	Richard Ober	0004	1	transfer	B2A	462
Oct. 9, 1792	Richard Ober, George Town, Md.	0004	1	$178⅔	B2A	407
Oct. 9, 1792	Richard Bland Lee, of Va.	0004	2	$202⅔	B2A	405
Oct. 9, 1792	Richard B. Lee, of Va.[57]	0004	2	76 Md.	B2B	161
Mar. 5, 1795	Thomas Johnson, Frederick Co., Md.	0004	3, 15-19	$3992.15	G7A	93
Oct. 1791	George Warley	0004	12	£86	B2A	457
Dec. 24, 1793	Robert Morris and James Greenleaf[58]	0004 W	Public	$437.19	G7A	92
Oct. 8, 1792	Richard Ober, George Town, Md.	0005	8	$189⅓	B2A	404
Oct. 1, 1792	Richard Ober	0005	8	transfer	B2A	462
Oct. 9, 1792	Richard A. Contee[59]	0005	11, 17	80 Md.	B2B	165
— Oct. 1791	George Warley[60]	0005	12	60 cm	B2A	457
Oct. 19, 1792	William Deakins, Jr.[61]	0005	18	78 Md.	B2B	147
June 22, 1793	Tobias Lear	0009	3	$266⅔	B2B	156
June 22, 1793	Tobias Lear, Philadelphia, Pa.	0009	3	$266⅔	B2A	430
Dec. 24, 1793	Robert Morris and James Greenleaf[62]	0015	1-3, 13-16	30 cm/ea	B2B	139
Oct. 9, 1792	Walter Hellen	0016	15, 16	164 Md.	B2A	465
Oct. 9, 1792	James Hoban and Pierce Purcell	0016	17	$269⅓	B2A	406

[52] Since transferred to Robert Peter.
[53] "cm" indicates current money. This reference was for 75 pounds current money.
[54] Since transferred by Konig to Thomas Cook and Joseph E. Rowles.
[55] Maryland currency.
[56] Since transferred to Thomas Cook.
[57] Since transferred to [Sabret] Scott.
[58] Since assigned to Thomas Johnson of Frederick Co., Md.
[59] Since transferred to David Crawford.
[60] Transferred to William Deakins, Jr. on 10 FEB 1794.
[61] Since transferred to Clotworthy Stephenson of the City of Washington.
[62] Since transferred to Thomas Johnson, Esq., of Frederick County.

Date	Certificate Holder	Square	Lot(s)	Fee	Book	Page
Oct. 9, 1792	Richard Ober, George Town, Md.	0016	22	$168	B2A	407
Oct. 1, 1792	Richard Ober	0016	22, 23	transfer	B2A	462
Oct. 9, 1792	Richard Ober, George Town, Md.	0016	23	$216	B2A	406
Jun. 23, 1794	George Washington, Esq.	0021	1	200 Md.	B2B	175
April 23, 1794	George Washington, Esq.	0021	4	200 Md.	B2B	175
Dec. 10, 1794	Dr. William Thornton	0033	5, 6	200 cm	B2B	168
Feb. 12, 1795	Uriah Forrest, Montgomery Co., Md.	0038	All		B2B	166
Feb. 12, 1795	Uriah Forrest, Montgomery Co., Md.	0038	All		B2B	169
Sept. 19, 1793	Marsham Warring, George Town, Md.	0057	4	$176	B2A	441
Sept. 21, 1799	Thomas Corcoran, George Town, Md.	0063	10	$360	E5	91
Dec. 24, 1793	Robert Morris and James Greenleaf[63]	0074	5, 12-13		K10	396
Oct. 19, 1791	Joseph Hodgson	0077	3	transfer	B2A	462
Dec. 11, 1794	William O'Neale	0078	1		B2B	157
Dec. 1, 1794	William O'Neale	0078	2	89.6.8 Md.	B2A	469
Oct. 18, 1791	James Gilchrist, Philadelphia, Pa.	0078	8, 19, 22		B2A	398
Oct. 18, 1791	James Gilchrist	0078	8, 19, 22	427 Md.	F6	40
Jan. 25, 1797	William O'Neale, City of Washington	0078	9	125 cm	B2B	159
Oct. 18, 1791	Jacob Welsh, Lunenburg, Mass.	0078	9, 10	165 Md.	B2A	400
June 1, 1797	William O'Neale, City of Washington	0078	10	200 cm	B2B	159
Oct. 19, 1791	John Davidson	0079	5	61 Md.	B2A	470
Oct. 19, 1791	Thomas Peirce, Smithfield, Va.	0079	7, 19	176 Md.	B2A	399
Oct. 19, 1791	Jacob Welch, Lunenburg, Mass.	0079	10	61 Md.	B2A	399
Aug. 15, 1793	Cornelius Cunningham	0088 E	10	10 cm	B2B	174
Oct. 19, 1791	Thomas Pierce	0101	7, 19	176 Md.	B2A	466
Feb. 12, 1795	Uriah Forrest, Montgomery Co., Md.[64]	0101	18		B2B	166
Feb. 12, 1795	Uriah Forrest, Montgomery Co., Md.	0101	18		B2B	169
Sept. 19, 1793	Richard Ross	0102	2	71 Md.	B2B	144
Sept. 19, 1793	Richard Ross, Bladensburg, Md.	0102	2	$189⅓	B2A	441
Sept. 16, 1800	Henry Gaither	0104	2, 3	$1920.06	F6	31
Oct. 18, 1791	Tobias Lear	0104	4	112 Md.	B2A	463
Oct. 18, 1791	Francis Cabot[65]	0105	3	111 Md.	B2B	155
Oct. 18, 1791	Tobias Lear, Portsmouth, N.H.	0105	4	112 Md.	B2A	398
Oct. 18, 1791	Nicholas Sluby	0105	7, 8	228 Md.	B2A	464

[63] Since transferred to Isaac Polock.
[64] Since transferred to William Campbell.
[65] Since transferred to Richard Harrison of Philadelphia, Pa.

Date	Certificate Holder	Square	Lot(s)	Fee	Book	Page
Oct. 18, 1791	Jacob Stiner, Jr.	0105	14	105 Md.	B2A	468
Oct. 18, 1791	James Gilchrist, Philadelphia, Pa.	0107	4		B2A	398
Oct. 18, 1791	James Gilchrist	0107	4	427 Md.	F6	40
Dec. 24, 1793	Robert Morris and James Greenleaf[66]	0118	1, 2, 13, 3 (part)	$264.71	B2B	166
Aug. 28, 1797	Frederick May and Samuel Eliot, Jr.	0119	13		B2B	170
Jan. 4, 1800	Henry O'Reily[67]	0122	1	$506.16	F6	83
Nov. 6, 1799	John Kearney, City of Washington	0122	9	$552.03	E5	359
Dec. 24, 1793	Robert Morris and James Greenleaf	0123	1, 7		B2B	149
Oct. 17, 1791	Jacob Welsh, Lunenburg, Mass.	0125	22, 23	150 Md.	B2A	397
Oct. 17, 1791	Peter Casanave of George Town, Md.	0126	28	101 Md.	B2A	395
Oct. 17, 1791	Thomas Lee Shippen, Phila., Pa.	0126	29	115 Md.	B2A	396
Oct. 9, 1791	Henry Carroll	0126	31	201 Md.	B2A	467
Oct. 1, 1799	Samuel Smith, Baltimore, Md.	0127	14-16	$1892.06	F6	54
Sept. 16, 1800	Henry Gaither	0127	22, 23	$1920.06	F6	31
Oct. 19, 1791	Thomas Sim Lee	0127	28, 29	122 Md.	B2A	463
Dec. 24, 1793	Robert Morris and James Greenleaf	0128	3-8		B2B	149
Mar. 14, 1793	Henry Nicholls	0128	14, 15	$533.33	B2A	466
Oct. 1, 1799	Samuel Smith, Baltimore, Md.	0142	3, 10	$1892.06	F6	54
June 21, 1796	Richard Gridley	0143	10	$260	B2B	152
Dec. 24, 1793	Robert Morris and James Greenleaf[68]	0168	4	$71	E5	158
Dec. 24, 1793	Robert Morris and James Greenleaf[69]	0168	21		B2B	164
Aug. 28, 1799	Solomon Etting, Esq., Baltimore, Md.	0169	6-10	$2188.11	G7A	237
April 19, 1800	George Andrews, City of Washington	0169	15	$346.07	H8	115
Jan. 4, 1800	William McCreery, Baltimore, Md.	0169	16	$484.47	G7A	116
June 26, 1794	Philip Gadsden (see 169)	0169	19, 20	600 Md.	B2B	142
July 28, 1796	James Brown, Queen Anne's Co., Md.	0169	21	$482.85	B2B	176
Dec. 24, 1793	Robert Morris and James Greenleaf[70]	0170	7, 8	60 Md.	B2B	146
Dec. 24, 1793	Robert Morris and James Greenleaf[71]	0170	15, 16		B2B	150
Sept. 17, 1793	Dr. John Weems, George Town, Md.	0172	1	$193⅓	B2A	434
Oct. 22, 1792	Samuel Blodget, Jun., Boston, Mass.	0200	1	$266⅔	B2A	414
Oct. 22, 1792	John Templeman, Boston, Mass.	0200	2	$206⅔	B2A	410

---

[66] Since transferred to William Deakins, Jr. and Uriah Forrest.
[67] Since transferred to Walter S. Chandler of George Town, Md.
[68] Since transferred to Cuthbert Powell.
[69] Since transferred to Uriah Forrest.
[70] Since transferred to Gustavus Scott.
[71] Since transferred to Robert Peter.

Date	Certificate Holder	Square	Lot(s)	Fee	Book	Page
Oct. 22, 1792	Thomas Ketland	0200	3	100 Md.	B2B	173
Oct. 22, 1792	[blank] Ketland, Philadelphia, Pa.	0200	3	$266⅔	B2A	415
Mar. 31, 1793	Walter Stuart, Philadelphia, Pa.	0200	8	$266⅔	B2A	425
Mar. 31, 1793	Walter Stuart, Philadelphia, Pa.	0200	9	$266⅔	B2A	424
Mar. 31, 1793	Walter Stuart, Philadelphia, Pa.	0200	10	$266⅔	B2A	422
Mar. 31, 1793	Walter Stuart, Philadelphia, Pa.	0200	11	$266⅔	B2A	424
Dec. 5, 1792	James Hoban and Pierce Purcell	0200	16	$266⅔	B2A	420
Dec. 5, 1792	James Hoban and Pierce Purcell	0200	17	$266⅔	B2A	419
Oct. 1792	Samuel Davidson	0221	All (24)	£2,040	B2A	454
Oct. 11, 1792	Samuel Davidson	0221	All (24)	£85 ea.	B2A	429
Oct. 8, 1802	Thomas J. Beatty, George Town, Md.	0224	1	$301.33	B2B	138
Oct. 8, 1792	Thomas J. Beatty, George Town, Md.	0224	1	$301⅓	B2A	403
Oct. 8, 1792	James Hoban and Peirce Purcell	0224	4	$293⅓	B2A	403
Oct. 18, 1792	William Coglan, lately Charleston, S.C.[72]	0224	5	105 cm	B2B	169
Oct. 8, 1792	David Burnes, Pr. George's Co., Md.	0224	8	$533⅓	B2A	400
Oct. 8, 1792	David Burnes, Pr. George's Co., Md.	0224	9	$400	B2A	402
Oct. 22, 1792	Thomas Metcalf	0224	11	100 Md.	B2B	140
Oct. 8, 1792	William A. Washington, of Va.	0224	12	$333⅓	B2A	401
Oct. 8, 1792	William Augustine Washington	0224	12	transfer[73]	B2A	468
Oct. 8, 1792	William Augustine Washington, of Va.	0224	13	$266⅔	B2A	401
Oct. 8, 1792	William Augustine Washington	0224	13	transfer	B2A	469
Oct. 8, 1792	Thomas J. Beatty, George Town, Md.	0224	16	$313.33	B2B	138
Oct. 8, 1792	Thomas J. Beatty, George Town, Md.	0224	16	$313⅓	B2A	402
Mar. 31, 1793	Walter Stuart, Philadelphia, Pa.	0225	1	$266⅔	B2A	423
Mar. 31, 1793	Walter Stewart, Philadelphia, Pa.	0225	2	$266⅔	B2A	421
Mar. 31, 1793	Walter Stuart, Philadelphia, Pa.	0225	3	$226⅔	B2A	425
Mar. 31, 1793	Thomas L. Moore, Philadelphia, Pa.	0225	4	$266⅔	B2A	422
Mar. 31, 1793	Thomas L. Moore, Philadelphia, Pa.	0225	5	$266⅔	B2A	423
Oct. 22, 1792	Peter Gilman, Boston, Mass.	0225	6	$266⅔	B2A	413
Oct. 22, 1792	Samuel Blodget, Jun., Boston, Mass.	0225	7	$266⅔	B2A	412
Oct. 22, 1792	Benjamin Blodget, Boston, Mass.	0225	8	$266⅔	B2A	414

[72] Since assigned to James Hoban of the City of Washington.
[73] Transfer to Arnauld Gouges in fee simple.

Date	Certificate Holder	Square	Lot(s)	Fee	Book	Page
Oct. 13, 1792	Patrick McDermott Roe[74]	0225	10	75 cm	G7B	569
Nov. 3, 1792	Patrick McDermott Roe, G.T., Md.	0225	10	$225	B2A	417
Oct. 22, 1792	Thomas Metcalf, Philadelphia, Pa.	0225	11	$266⅔	B2A	410
Dec. 24, 1793	Robert Morris and James Greenleaf[75]	0225	12-15		B2B	162
Mar. 31, 1793	Walter Stuart, Philadelphia, Pa.	0225	16	$226⅔	B2A	426
Mar. 31, 1793	Nathaniel Philips, Philadelphia, Pa.	0228	6	$226⅔	B2A	427
Dec. 24, 1793	Robert Morris and James Greenleaf[76]	0228	All		B2B	162
Dec. 24, 1793	Robert Morris and James Greenleaf[77]	0229	2-4		B2B	162
Dec. 24, 1793	Robert Morris and James Greenleaf[78]	0231	19, 20		B2B	157
Oct. 13, 1792	Patrick McDermott Roe, G.T., Md.	0253	6	$200	B2A	409
Oct. 22, 1792	John Templeman, Boston, Mass.	0253	7	$266⅔	B2A	417
Oct. 22, 1792	John Templeman	0253	7	$266⅔	B2A	471
Oct. 22, 1792	John Templeman, Boston, Mass.	0253	8	$266⅔	B2A	417
Oct. 22, 1792	John Templeman, Boston, Mass.	0253	9	$266⅔	B2A	416
Oct. 22, 1792	John Templeman[79]	0253	9	$266⅔	B2B	166
Jun. 26, 1800	William Lovell, City of Washington[80]	0253	12	4¢/sq.ft.	G7A	10
Oct. 13, 1792	Cornelius McDermot Roe, G.T., Md.	0254	1	$293⅓	B2A	409
Oct. 8, 1792	Samuel Davidson	0254	2	£86	B2A	429
Oct. 1792	Samuel Davidson	0254	2	£86	B2A	454
Oct. 8, 1792	Leonard Harbaugh	0254	5	135 Md.	B2B	144
Oct. 8, 1792	Gabriel P. Van Horne, Pr. G. Co., Md.	0254	7	$320	B2A	404
Oct. 8, 1792	Clotworthy Stephenson	0254	10	102 Md.	B2B	147
Oct. 8, 1792	Colin Williamson, George Town, Md.	0254	11	$280	B2A	405
Oct. 8, 1792	Collin Williamson	0254	11	105 Md.	B2A	477
Dec. 24, 1793	Robert Morris and James Greenleaf[81]	0254	24, 25		B2B	162
Dec. 24, 1793	Robert Morris and James Greenleaf[82]	0260	1, 3, 5, 7		B2B	162
Oct. 27, 1797	Frederick May and Samuel Eliot, Jr.	0288	14		B2B	171
Dec. 24, 1793	Robert Morris and James Greenleaf[83]	0289	1		B2B	148

[74] Patrick McDermott Roe having in his life time, to wit on the 12th March in the year 1795, transferred all his interest in said lot to Owen McDermott Roe, and the said Owen McDermott Roe having this day [Dec. 11, 1801] transferred all his interest therein to Bernard McDermott Roe.
[75] Since transferred to Thomas Law.
[76] Ibid.
[77] Ibid.
[78] Since transferred to William Mayne Duncanson who was charged with building at least one brick house two stories high on every third lot with four years after contract for sale.
[79] Since transferred to Richard Gridley of the City of Washington.
[80] Since transferred in the south half of the lot to Jonathan Pancost who has assigned the same to John Burchan.
[81] Since transferred to Thomas Law.
[82] Ibid.
[83] Since transferred to Henry Edwards of the City of Washington.

Date	Certificate Holder	Square	Lot(s)	Fee	Book	Page
July 31, 1793	Henry Edwards, City of Washington	0290	12	$266⅔	B2A	431
July 1, 1793	Henry Edwards[84]	0290	12	$266⅔	B2A	473
July 31, 1793	Charles Jones, City of Washington	0290	13	$266⅔	B2A	431
July 31, 1793	Charles Jones[85]	0290	13	$266⅔	B2B	148
Oct. 22, 1792	[blank] Ketland, Philadelphia, Pa.	0290	13	$266⅔	B2A	411
May 29, 1800	Nicholas and Elias E. Traverse	0291	2	$400.05	F6	68
Jun. 18, 1800	Nicholas Voss, City of Washington[86]	0291	6	$315	G7A	106
May 21, 1799	Lewis Movin, Baltimore, Md.	0292	1	$569.77	E5	324
Dec. 24, 1793	Robert Morris and James Greenleaf[87]	0294	1, 3		B2B	162
Dec. 24, 1793	Robert Morris and James Greenleaf[88]	0295	1, 3, 5		B2B	162
Oct. 13, 1792	Cornelius McDermot Roe, G.T., Md.	0323	8	$173⅓	B2A	408
Oct. 13, 1792	Cornelius McDermot Roe, G.T., Md.	0323	9	$173⅓	B2A	408
Dec. 24, 1793	Robert Morris and James Greenleaf[89]	0324	1, 2, 6-8, 12		B2B	162
Dec. 24, 1793	Robert Morris and James Greenleaf[90]	0350	1, 2, 6-8, 12		B2B	162
Nov. 6, 1797	Frederick May and Samuel Eliot, Jr.	0351 N	2		B2B	170
April 19, 1794	Rev. Anthony Caffray, City of Wash.	0376	5, 6	80 cm	B2B	172
Jun. 23, 1794	Rev. Anthony Caffray, City of Wash.	0376	7	60 cm	B2B	172
Dec. 24, 1793	Robert Morris and James Greenleaf[91]	0377	1	$80	B2B	155
Dec. 24, 1793	Robert Morris and James Greenleaf[92]	0379	1, 2, 4, 6, 7, 9		B2B	162
Dec. 24, 1793	Robert Morris and James Greenleaf[93]	0381	3, 4, 5		B2B	162
Dec. 24, 1793	Robert Morris and James Greenleaf[94]	0382	2, 3, 5, 7		B2B	162
Nov. 6, 1702	Andrew Estave	0406	4	100 Md.	B2A	471
April 6, 1796	William Deakins, Jr.	0406	5, 6	$500	B2A	476
Dec. 24, 1793	Robert Morris and James Greenleaf[95]	0407	12, 13	$132	B2B	155
Oct. 22, 1792	Nathan Bond, Boston, Mass.	0408	1	$266⅔	B2A	475
Oct. 22, 1792	Nathan Bond, Boston, Mass.	0408	1	$266⅔	B2A	411

---

[84] Since transferred to Thomas Johnson, Jr., now deceased, by Edwards, and by Johnson during his lifetime transferred to Christopher Richmond who has paid the principal and interest to receive lot in fee simple.
[85] Since transferred to Mary Sweeny of the City of Washington, who conveyed in fee to her children George Sweeny and Sarah Sweeny; they are entitled to same in fee simple as tenants in common and not as joint tenants.
[86] Since assigned to David Williamson of the City of Baltimore, merchant.
[87] Since transferred to Thomas Law.
[88] Ibid.
[89] Ibid.
[90] Ibid.
[91] Since transferred to John Crocker.
[92] Since transferred to Thomas Law.
[93] Ibid.
[94] Ibid.
[95] Since transferred to Isaac Philips, Paul Grout and Joel West.

Date	Certificate Holder	Square	Lot(s)	Fee	Book	Page
Oct. 22, 1792	Nathan Bond, Boston, Mass.	0408	2	$266⅔	B2A	476
Oct. 22, 1792	Nathan Bond, Boston, Mass.	0408	2	$266⅔	B2A	416
Dec. 24, 1793	Robert Morris and James Greenleaf[96]	0408	6-8, 12		B2B	162
Dec. 24, 1793	Robert Morris and James Greenleaf[97]	0430	6-8, 11		B2B	162
Dec. 24, 1793	Robert Morris and James Greenleaf[98]	0431	3, 4, 9, 17, 18		B2B	162
Sept. 19, 1793	James R. Dermott	0431	7, 8	139 Md.	B2A	472
Sept. 19, 1793	James R. Dermott, City of Washington	0431	7	$286⅔	B2A	440
Sept. 19, 1793	James R. Dermott, City of Washington	0431	8	$284	B2A	439
Sept. 18, 1793	Robert Kid, Philadelphia, Pa.	0431	12	$189⅓	B2A	439
Sept. 18, 1793	Robert Kid, Philadelphia, Pa.	0431	12	$189⅓	E5	230
Jun. 3, 1795	James R. Dermott, City of Washington	0432	1, 2 [?]	$1443.44	G7A	331
Dec. 24, 1793	Robert Morris and James Greenleaf[99]	0456	17, 18	30 cm/ea	B2B	140
Sept. 19, 1793	John Maitland[100]	0457	18	82 Md.	B2B	143
Sept. 13, 1799	Robert Brent	0459	2	$440.02	F6	69
Sept. 13, 1799	Robert Brent, City of Washington[101]	0459	4	$321.51	H8	192
Dec. 24, 1793	Robert Morris and James Greenleaf[102]	0460	2, 4, 5		B2B	162
July 22, 1791	John Crookshank and Geo. Thomson	0461	5	$720.24	G7B	589
Sept. 1793	Samuel Davidson	0487	1	£57	B2A	454
Feb. 4, 1797	Rev. George Ralph[103]	0488	2, 3	$604.62	B2B	171
Nov. 5, 1792	James Hoban and Pierce Purcell	0489	1	$216	B2A	419
Nov. 5, 1792	James Hoban and Pierce Purcell	0489	2	$229⅓	B2A	418
Oct. 10, 1792	Samuel Davidson	0489	13	£67	B2A	429
Oct. 1792	Samuel Davidson	0489	13	£67	B2A	454
Dec. 24, 1793	Robert Morris and James Greenleaf	0490	1-3, 12-18, 22, 24, 25		B2B	149
May 11, 1798	William Bayly	0514	2, 20, 22	$300	D4	284
Oct. 15, 1793	Edward Burrows, Pr. George's Co., Md.	0531	1	$266⅔	B2A	442
June 15, 1793	Edward Burrows	0532	1	100 Md.	B2B	153
Oct. 22, 1792	Nathan Bond, Boston, Mass.	0533	5	$266⅔	B2A	474

---

[96] Since transferred to Thomas Law.
[97] Ibid.
[98] Ibid.
[99] Since transferred to Robert Morris and John Nicholson.
[100] Part of which has since been transferred to Andrew Jamieson of Alexandria, Va.
[101] On March 17, 1801, Brent conveyed all his interest in lot before conveyed to John C. Willson of Princess Anne, Md., now to Thomas Herty of the City of Washington.
[102] Since transferred to Thomas Law.
[103] Since assigned and transferred to William Penrose Matthews of Baltimore, Md.

Date	Certificate Holder	Square	Lot(s)	Fee	Book	Page
Oct. 22, 1792	Nathan Bond, Boston, Mass.	0533	5	$266⅔	B2A	415
Oct. 22, 1792	Nathan Bond, Boston, Mass.	0533	6	$266⅔	B2A	475
Oct. 22, 1792	Nathan Bond, Boston, Mass.	0533	6	$266⅔	B2A	413
Dec. 24, 1793	Robert Morris and James Greenleaf	0573	1, 3, 5		B2B	149
Dec. 24, 1793	Robert Morris and James Greenleaf[104]	0575	3-5, 8-10		B2B	162
	Robert Morris and James Greenleaf	0590	½		B2A	473
Dec. 24, 1793	Robert Morris and James Greenleaf	0629	2		B2B	149
Dec. 24, 1793	Robert Morris and James Greenleaf	0631	2, 4, 6, 8		B2B	149
Dec. 24, 1793	Robert Morris and James Greenleaf[105]	0633	3-6, 11, 12		B2B	162
June 26, 1794	Philip Gadsden (see 634)	0634	2, 3	600 Md.	B2B	143
Dec. 24, 1793	Robert Morris and James Greenleaf[106]	0637	1-3, 7-9, 14		B2B	162
Mar. 23, 1795	James Barry (see north of 708)	0662	1	1478.6.8	B2A	478
Nov. 20, 1798	James Barry, Baltimore, Md.	0662	3, 4	$599	D4	369
Jan. 15, 1799	James Barry, Baltimore, Md.	0662	7, 8	$658	D4	369
Sept. 17, 1793	Tobias Lear & Co., City of Washington	0664	4	$266⅔	B2A	433
Sept. 16, 1793	T. Lear, T. Dalton, J. Greenleaf[107]	0664	4, 5	200 Md.	E5	152
Sept. 17, 1793	Tobias Lear & Co., City of Washington	0664	5	$266⅔	B2A	432
Sept. 17, 1793	Daniel Carroll of Duddington	0665	22	$213⅓	B2A	433
Jan. 14, 1795	Lewis Deblois, City of Washington	0665	14	180 cm	E5	356
Sept. 18, 1793	Daniel Carroll of Duddington	0665	15-18, 22		B2B	151
Sept. 17, 1793	Daniel Carroll of Duddington	0665	16	$258⅔	B2A	435
Sept. 17, 1793	Daniel Carroll of Duddington	0665	17	$258⅔	B2A	434
Sept. 17, 1793	Daniel Carroll of Duddington	0665	18	$258⅔	B2A	436
Sept. 18, 1793	Daniel Carroll of Duddington	0666	2, 6-8		B2B	151
Jan. 14, 1795	Lewis Deblois, City of Washington	0666	10	180 cm	E5	356
Jan. 5, 1795	James Barry (see south of 708)	0667 S	1	$3,600	B2B	137
Sept. 18, 1793	Daniel Carroll of Duddington	0667 E	3		B2B	151
Sept. 17, 1793	George Washington, Esq.	0667 E	4, 5, 6		B2B	174
Sept. 18, 1793	George Washington, President	0667	5	$306⅔	B2A	436
Sept. 17, 1793	George Washington, Esq.	0667	5, 12-14		B2B	174
Sept. 18, 1793	George Washington, President	0667	12-14	$1066⅔	B2A	437

[104] Since transferred to Thomas Law.
[105] Ibid.
[106] Ibid.
[107] Since transferred to Francis Deakins, executor and residuary devisee of William Deakins, Jr.

Date	Certificate Holder	Square	Lot(s)	Fee	Book	Page
Sept. 17, 1793	Daniel Carroll of Duddington	0667	15	$224	B2A	433
Sept. 18, 1793	Daniel Carroll of Duddington	0667	15		B2B	151
Dec. 24, 1793	Robert Morris and James Greenleaf[108]	0685	2, 5, 6, 11, 12, 14, 15, 18, 19		B2B	162
Aug. 4, 1800	Mathew Brown, City of Baltimore	0686	1	$700	G7B	380
Mar. 10, 1800	Daniel Carroll of Duddington and Henry H. Carroll	0686	6	$735.90	G7A	87
May 16, 1800	Joseph Karrick and Joshua Percival	0686	8	$881.63	G7A	248
Oct. 10, 1792	Samuel Blodget[109]	0688	13	57 Md.	G7A	264
Oct. 10, 1792	Samuel Blodget, Jun.[110]	0688	22, 23	114 cm	G7A	357
	Robert Morris and James Greenleaf	0689	½		B2A	473
Dec. 24, 1793	Robert Morris and James Greenleaf[111]	0692	3-5, 9-12		B2B	162
	Robert Morris and James Greenleaf	0693	½		B2A	473
Dec. 24, 1793	Robert Morris and James Greenleaf[112]	0694	1, 3, 4, 8, 9		B2B	162
Dec. 24, 1793	Robert Morris and James Greenleaf[113]	0695	All		B2B	162
Dec. 24, 1793	Robert Morris and James Greenleaf[114]	0699 N	All		B2B	162
April 13, 1796	James Reed Dermott, City of Wash.	0705	2	$400	B2B	160
Sept. 19, 1797	Lewis Deblois, City of Washington	0706	1	$1196.92	E5	341
Jun. 7, 1794	Lewis [Deblois], City of Washington	0707	2	460.16.8	B2B	173
Mar. 23, 1795	James Barry (see 662)	0708 N	(slip)	1478.6.8	B2A	478
Jan. 5, 1795	James Barry (see south of 667)	0708 S	1	$3,600	B2B	137
Jun. 14, 1796	James Barry, Baltimore, Md., merchant	0708	4, 5, 10, 11	$720	B2B	161
April 19, 1796	James Barry	0708	4	$400	B2B	137
Mar. 29, 1796	James Barry	0708	5, 8	$900	B2A	478
Sept. 18, 1793	Daniel Carroll of Duddington	0708 E	8		B2B	151
Sept. 18, 1793	Daniel Carroll of Duddington	0725	1	$266⅔	B2A	437
Sept. 18, 1793	Daniel Carroll of Duddington	0725	1		B2B	151
Sept. 18, 1793	James R. Dermott, George Town, Md.	0725	2	$269⅓	B2A	439
Sept. 18, 1793	Peter Casanave[115]	0725	3	90 Md.	B2A	472

[108] Since transferred to Thomas Law.
[109] Since assigned to William Duane of the City of Philadelphia, editor of the *Aurora or General Advertiser*.
[110] Also subject to all claims which the holders of prize tickets in the lotteries commonly called the Hotel Lottery and Washington Lottery No. 2 may have therein as security for complying with the terms of the said Lotteries.
[111] Since transferred to Thomas Law.
[112] Ibid.
[113] Ibid.
[114] Ibid.
[115] Appearing that James R. Dermott has paid the principal and interest he is entitled to the said lot in fee simple.

Date	Certificate Holder	Square	Lot(s)	Fee	Book	Page
Sept. 18, 1793	Benjamin Dulany, of Va.	0725	6	$429⅓	B2A	438
Sept. 18, 1793	Benjamin Dulany, of Va.	0725	7	$426⅔	B2A	438
Sept. 22, 1797	Wilson Bryan	0728	2	$345.28	G7A	140
Mar. 31, 1799	Philip Nicklin, Philadelphia, Pa.	0728	5	$266⅔	E5	104
Mar. 31, 1793	Philip Nichlin, Philadelphia, Pa.	0728	5	$226⅔	B2A	427
Mar. 14, 1793	Henry Nicholls, Baltimore, Md.	0728	14	$266⅔	B2A	420
Mar. 14, 1793	Henry Nicholls, Baltimore, Md.	0728	15	$266⅔	B2A	421
Mar. 14, 1793	Henry Nicholls	0728	14, 15	$533.3	B2A	466
Feb. 20, 1796	James Reed Dermott, City of Wash.[116]	0728	16	$409.65	B2B	160
Oct. 17, 1793	James Hoban	0729	3, 9, 26	210 Md.	B2B	152
Mar. 31, 1793	James Watson, of N.Y.	0729	10	$226⅔	B2A	429
Mar. 31, 1793	James Watson, of N.Y.	0729	18	$226⅔	B2A	428
Mar. 31, 1793	James Crammond	0729	22	$266⅔	B2A	467
Mar. 31, 1793	James Cramm[o]nd, Philadelphia, Pa.	0729	22	$226⅔	B2A	428
Mar. 31, 1793	John Coles	0729	23	100 Md.	B2A	464
Mar. 31, 1793	[blank] Coles, Philadelphia, Pa.	0729	23	$226⅔	B2A	426
Sept. 17, 1793	John Henry, City of Washington[117]	0729	27	$266.66	B2A	477
Sept. 27, 1798	Edward Langley, City of Washington[118]	0731	1	$763	D4	368
Sept. 28, 1798	Adam Lynn, Alexandria, Va.	0731	2 (part)	$225.10	F6	10
Sept. 19, 1798	Richard Andrews and Henry Polkinhorn	0731	2 (part)		G7A	59
	Robert Morris and James Greenleaf	0732	½		B2A	473
Dec. 24, 1793	Robert Morris and James Greenleaf[119]	0738	1-5		B2B	162
	Robert Morris and James Greenleaf	0740	All		B2A	473
	Robert Morris and James Greenleaf	0741	All		B2A	473
Dec. 24, 1793	Robert Morris and James Greenleaf[120]	0742	All		B2B	162
Dec. 24, 1793	Robert Morris and James Greenleaf[121]	0743 N	All		B2B	162
	Robert Morris and James Greenleaf	0743	½		B2A	473
	Robert Morris and James Greenleaf	0744	All		B2A	473
Dec. 24, 1793	Robert Morris and James Greenleaf[122]	0766	All		B2B	162

---

[116] Since transferred to Lund Washington of the City of Washington.
[117] Since transferred by Henry to Alexander Robertson of the City of Washington who having paid the principal and interest is to receive lot in fee simple.
[118] Since transferred to John Shute, Sen., of Exeter in Great Britain.
[119] Since transferred to Thomas Law.
[120] Ibid.
[121] Ibid.
[122] Ibid.

Date	Certificate Holder	Square	Lot(s)	Fee	Book	Page
Dec. 24, 1793	Robert Morris and James Greenleaf[123]	0767	All		B2B	157
Dec. 24, 1793	Robert Morris and James Greenleaf[124]	0768	All		B2B	157
Dec. 24, 1793	Robert Morris and James Greenleaf[125]	0769	All		B2B	157
Dec. 24, 1793	Robert Morris and James Greenleaf[126]	0770	All[127]		B2B	162
	Robert Morris and James Greenleaf	0770	½		B2A	473
April 23, 1794	James Greenleaf[128]	0771	2, 3	400 Md.	B2B	141
Dec. 24, 1793	Robert Morris and James Greenleaf[129]	0771	2, 3, 4		B2B	162
Dec. 24, 1793	Robert Morris and James Greenleaf[130]	0800	All		B2B	157
April 23, 1794	James Greenleaf[131]	0802	4, 5, 6		B2B	165
Dec. 24, 1793	Robert Morris and James Greenleaf[132]	0802	7	30 Md.	B2B	146
Dec. 24, 1793	Robert Morris and James Greenleaf[133]	0875	1-12		B2B	157
Dec. 24, 1793	Robert Morris and James Greenleaf[134]	0878	9-14		B2B	149
Dec. 24, 1793	Robert Morris and James Greenleaf	0881	1, 2, 10-14		B2B	149
Dec. 24, 1793	Robert Morris and James Greenleaf	0902	1-14		B2B	149
Dec. 24, 1793	Robert Morris and James Greenleaf	0903	1-22		B2B	149
Dec. 24, 1793	Robert Morris and James Greenleaf	0904	1-2, 18-30		B2B	149
Dec. 24, 1793	Robert Morris and James Greenleaf	0949	1-3, 15-22		B2B	149
Dec. 24, 1793	Robert Morris and James Greenleaf	0950	1-10, 26-30		B2B	149
Dec. 24, 1793	Robert Morris and James Greenleaf[135]	0951	1-4		B2B	157
Dec. 24, 1793	Robert Morris and James Greenleaf	0951	1-12		B2B	149
Dec. 24, 1793	Robert Morris and James Greenleaf[136]	0953	1-9, 24-28		B2B	157
Dec. 24, 1793	Robert Morris and James Greenleaf[137]	0954	8-17		B2B	157
Dec. 24, 1793	Robert Morris and James Greenleaf	0974	1-3, 19-30		B2B	149
Dec. 24, 1793	Robert Morris and James Greenleaf	0976	1, 4		B2B	149

[123] Since transferred to William Mayne Duncanson who was charged with building at least one brick house two stories high on every third lot with four years after contract for sale.
[124] Ibid.
[125] Ibid.
[126] Since transferred to Thomas Law.
[127] Moiety thereof has been conveyed by the Commissioners to Thomas Law.
[128] Since transferred to James Barry of Baltimore, Md.
[129] Since transferred to Thomas Law.
[130] Since transferred to William Mayne Duncanson who was charged with building at least one brick house two stories high on every third lot with four years after contract for sale.
[131] Since transferred to Thomas Law.
[132] On November 3, 1796, sold and transferred to James Reed Dermott.
[133] Since transferred to William Mayne Duncanson who was charged with building at least one brick house two stories high on every third lot with four years after contract for sale.
[134] Since transferred to James Dunlop and Joseph Caleton of Georgetown.
[135] Since transferred to William Mayne Duncanson who was charged with building at least one brick house two stories high on every third lot with four years after contract for sale.
[136] Ibid.
[137] Ibid.

Date	Certificate Holder	Square	Lot(s)	Fee	Book	Page
Dec. 24, 1793	Robert Morris and James Greenleaf	0977	1, 2, 17-28		B2B	149
Dec. 24, 1793	Robert Morris and James Greenleaf	0994	1, 2, 7, 8		B2B	149
Dec. 24, 1793	Robert Morris and James Greenleaf	0995	1-3, 19-30		B2B	149
Dec. 24, 1793	Robert Morris and James Greenleaf	0996	1, 2, 10-13		B2B	149
Dec. 24, 1793	Robert Morris and James Greenleaf	0999	1, 2		B2B	149
Dec. 24, 1793	Robert Morris and James Greenleaf	1000	18-28		B2B	149
Dec. 24, 1793	Robert Morris and James Greenleaf	1001	8-13, 19, 20		B2B	149
Dec. 24, 1793	Robert Morris and James Greenleaf	1024	4		B2B	149
Sept. 22, 1796	Joseph Boone, Pr. George's Co., Md.	1044	2	$972.90	B2B	167

Wesley E. Pippenger
Arlington, Virginia
September 1999

INDEX

A

acquisition of property 1
Adams
   John 18, 20, 21
Addison
   Henry 41, 47
   Thomas 41, 43-45
aldermen 15, 128
Alexandria, Va. 6, 8, 9, 37, 38, 137, 140
   newspaper of 14
Allison
   Robert 27
Anacostia River 3, 6, 19
Andrews
   George 133
   Richard 140
animals 129
Annapolis, Md. 3, 16
architects
   President's House 17
archives 22
arsenals 3, 21
artisans 17
Assembly of Maryland 3-5, 9, 13
associations 128
asylums 128
Atlantic Ocean 3
Attorney-General 8, 20
Aurora or General Advertiser 139
authors 1
avenues 9-11, 18, 21

B

Bailey
   William 7, 51, 53, 54
Baker
   Walter 28
ballast
   from ships 15
Baltimore, Md. 16, 40-42, 133, 136-141
banks 128
Bardley
   William A. 128
Barnes & Redgate 37, 40, 42, 43, 45, 46
Barry
   James 104, 138, 139, 141
Bayley
   William 43
Bayly
   William 137
Beale
   George 7
   Thomas 7
Beall
   Brook 32
   George 9, 13, 18, 20
   James 27
   John 30
   Thomas 7, 9, 13, 14, 18, 20, 31
   William M. 27
   William Murdock 28
Beanes
   William 44, 46
Beard
   Margaret 27
Beatty
   Charles 7, 29, 32
   Thomas J. 134
   Thomas, Sr. 27, 28
benevolent institutions 128
Berret
   J.G. 128
Bitting
   Anthony 32
Black
   William 2
Bladensburg, Md. 13, 132
Blake
   James H. 128
Blodget
   Benjamin 134
   Mr. 12
   Samuel . 7, 17, 29, 51, 64-70, 72, 74-76, 78-80,
                             82-84, 86, 139
   Samuel, Jr. 133, 134, 139
Blodget's Hotel 17
Board of Aldermen 128
Board of Councilmen 128
Boarman
   Ralph 46
   Raphael 39
Bogue
   John J. 1
Bond
   Nathan 136-138
Boone
   Joseph 142
Bordley
   John B. 41, 42
   John Beall 46
Boston, Mass. 133-138
boundaries 1, 9
Bowen
   S.J. 128
Bowie
   F. 45
   Fielder 42
Boyd
   Washington 21
Boyer
   Jacob 28
Bradford
   H.J. 46
   Henry 40
Brent
   Robert 128, 137
Brice
   John 41
   John, Jr. 45

brick-work 15
Brogden
    William 41
    William, Jr. 47
Brooke
    Benjamin 39, 46
    Henry 1, 2
Brown
    James 37, 40, 41, 46, 133
    Mathew 139
    Robert 40, 42, 45
Bryan
    Wilson 140
Buchan
    Alex. 40, 41, 43
Buchanan
    George 46
    Robert 45
    Thomas 39, 41, 43, 46
Bucke
    Mathias 27
Buddicomb
    William 29
building materials 15, 17
building regulations 12, 18, 128
building specifications 11
buildings 3, 4, 6-12, 17, 129
Burchan
    John 135
Burch's Digest 8
Burnes
    David 7, 21, 64-66, 69-71, 73-75, 77, 78, 81-85, 87, 88, 134
    David, heirs 65
    Marcia 69
Burrows
    Edward 137
Butler
    Mr. 54

C

Cabot
    Francis 132
Caffray
    Anthony, Rev. 136
Caleton
    Joseph 141
Calvert
    Benedict 39, 40, 46
    Benjamin 46
Calvinist Society 28
Campbell
    John 37, 42, 45
    P. 46
    Peter 46
    William 132
canal companies 128
canals 18, 19, 128
Capital
    location of 18

Capitol 12, 17, 22
    building of 10
Capitol record 53
Capitol Square 20
Carberry
    T. 128
carpenters' work 15
Carr
    Overton 7
Carroll
    C., Jr. 46, 47
    Charles 40
    Charles, Jr. 1, 39, 40, 43, 47
    Charles, of Carrollton 37, 44, 45
    Daniel . 1-3, 5, 7-11, 38, 39, 41-43, 46, 47, 115
    Daniel, of Duddington 13, 21, 38, 42, 70, 71, 73, 75, 78, 80, 81, 83, 85, 88, 89, 92-94, 97-99, 101-110, 112-115, 117, 138, 139
    E. 46
    Elizabeth 38, 40, 43
    Henry 133
    Henry H. 139
    M. 46
    M.J. 46
    Mary 38
Carrollsburg 1, 2, 7-9, 13, 14, 16, 22, 44, 51, 89-91, 94-97, 99, 100, 102
    divided 1
    lottery for 45
Casanave
    Peter 42, 133, 139
Casey
    John, Jr. 41, 43, 45
Casner
    Martin 29
cattle 129
cellar-doors 11
cellars 15
Centre Market 21
certificates of purchase 131
cession 1, 3, 5, 12, 13, 17
Chandler
    Walter S. 133
Charleston 9
Charleston, S.C. 134
Charter of Washington 128
Chase
    S., Jr. 45
    Samuel 42
    Samuel, Jr. 45
Chesapeake Bay 3
Chiswell
    Joseph N. 30
city hall 129
City of Washington ... vi, 1, 10-14, 16, 18, 20, 51, 131-140
    plan of 49
Civil War 129
Clack
    Burton 46

INDEX

Clagett/Claggett
    William 38, 40, 46
Clagot
    Hezakiah 29
cleaning of streets 128
clerks 14
    Circuit Court 1
    County Court 15
    recording deeds 15, 16
climate 3
Cock
    Daniel 45
Coglan
    William 134
Coles
    John 140
Collard
    S. 46
    Samuel 38, 40
Collidge
    Samuel 38
Collin Dunlap & Son 45
Columbian College 127
Commissioner of Public Buildings and Grounds
    127
Commissioners 5-9, 11-17, 20, 21, 38, 41-43, 131
    appointed 20
    reduced to one 127
Comp
    John 30
Congress of U.S. . . 3-6, 8, 10, 12, 13, 15, 16, 18,
    20-22, 127-129, 131
Cono[c]ocheague River 3-5
Contee
    Richard A. 131
conveyances 16
    not made 13
Conway
    Richard 42, 47
Cook
    Daniel 41
    Thomas 131
Coolidge
    Judson 46
    Samuel 39, 43
Coontz
    Henry 28
Copper
    Cyrus 41, 43, 45, 46
copyright 1
Corcoran
    Thomas 132
corner-stones 9, 17
Cost
    Francis 27
courthouses 1, 6
Craig
    Dr. 45
    James, Dr. 37, 38
    John 37, 39, 41

Craiger
    Samuel 30
Crammond
    James 140
Cramphin
    Thomas 30, 31
Cranch
    William 3, 115
Crawford
    David 42, 43, 46, 131
Creigh
    John 46
criminals 128
Crookshank
    John 137
Cunningham
    Cornelius 132
Curts
    F. 29
    Frederick 30
    Peter 29

D

Dalton
    T. 138
Davidson
    John 40, 46, 132
    John, heirs 21, 69-72, 74-77
    Samuel . . 7, 21, 39, 45, 51, 63, 64, 66-69, 134,
    135, 137
Davison
    Elias 29
Deakins
    Francis 138
    Levi 31
    W. 45
    William 29
    William, Col. 31
    William, Jr. . . . 7, 30, 51, 82, 84, 85, 87, 131, 133,
    136, 138
Deblois
    Lewis 138, 139
debts 16
deeds 13
    acknowledgement of 15
    in trust 14
    recorded in book 15
    to be recorded 16
Delaware 3
Dermott
    James Reed 137, 139-141
Dick
    James 2
    Robert 47
    Thomas 43
Dick & Stuart 40, 43-45
Digges/Diggs
    Ignatius 40-42, 46
    Joseph 42, 44-46
    William 38, 41, 43, 46

distilled spirits 16
ditches 11, 22
dock-yards 3
Doll
   Conrad 28
   Joseph 30
Douglass
   Eliphas 7
dower
   release of 13
drainage 10
Duane
   William 139
Duddington Manor 1, 2
   division of 44
Duddington Pasture 1, 2
   division of 44
Dulany
   Benjamin 140
   Walter 46
Duncanson
   William Mayne 135, 141
Dunlap
   Collin 45
Dunlop
   James 141

E

Earle
   James 38, 45
Eastern Branch 4-6, 8, 10, 13, 15, 19
Eastern Branch ferry 13
Eastern Branch Market Square 21
Easton, Md. 16
eaves 11
Edelin
   Christian 31
Eden
   John 40, 43, 45
editor 139
educational institutions 128
Edwards
   Henry 135, 136
ejectment 14
Eliot
   Samuel, Jr. 133, 135, 136
Ellicott
   Andrew 7, 10, 11
Emery
   M.G. 128
epidemics 128
equestrian statue 17
Estave
   Andrew 136
Etting
   Solomon 133
Europe 127
   importations from 17
Evans
   J. 46

Ewing
   Thomas 45
exchequer 129
Exeter, Eng. 140

F

Faehtz
   Ernest F.M. . . . . vi, viii, 2, 27, 129
Fenwick
   Ignatius 38-40, 42, 44
fire 128
Fisher
   A., heirs 28, 31
Fitzhugh
   William, Col. 37, 42, 47
Fleak
   A. 29
Font
   Baltis 27
footways 11
Force
   Peter 128
foreigners 15
   holding land 13
Forrest
   Uriah . . 7, 9, 17, 37, 58, 61, 62, 70, 71, 73, 132,
        133
   Uriah, Col. 43, 44
Forster
   Ralph 38
Fort, The 21
forts 3
Foster
   Ralph 44, 46
foundations 15
Fountain Square 21
Fowler
   Job 37, 45
Franklin Square 21
Frederick Co., Md. 131
freeholders 14
French
   William 29, 32
French & Marr 27, 29
Funk
   Jacob . . . . vi, 2, 27
Funkstown 2

G

Gadsden
   Philip 133, 138
Gaither
   Henry 132, 133
Gales
   Joseph, Jr. 128
Galloway
   S. 37, 46
   Samuel 40-42

INDEX

Gangaware
  Michael 27
Gantt
  John M. 7, 9, 14, 18, 20
  John Mackall 13
Garlick
  Joseph 29
Garner
  Frederick 41
gas companies 128
Gay
  Ann 39, 47
Georgetown College 127
Georgetown, Md. 1, 6-10, 12-16, 131-136, 139, 141
Gerrard
  William 28
Gilchrist
  James 132, 133
Gilman
  Peter 134
Golden
  Frederick 29
  Rev. 29
Goose Creek 13, 127
Gouges
  Arnauld 134
Governor
  Thomas 46
grading 10
grading of streets 128
Graham
  Richard 41, 43
Grahame
  Charles 46
Grammar
  Frederick 38
graveyards 7, 21, 128
Greenleaf
  James 7, 17, 51, 58, 63, 73, 82, 84, 87,
                                131-133, 135-142
Greenleaf's Point 21, 22
Gridley
  Richard 133, 135
Gross
  Michael 27
Grout
  Paul 136

H

Hackett
  John 27
Hagar
  Jonathan 28
Hall
  Jonathan 43, 46
  Martha 41, 45
Ham
  Peter 32
Hamburgh 1, 2, 7, 13, 14, 16, 22, 51, 55-60, 62-65

Hamell
  John 29
Harbaugh
  Leonard 131, 135
Harrison
  Richard 132
Harry
  David 32
Hass
  John 30
Hatfield
  Mr. 30
hawking 12
Hawkins
  George F. 30
health officers 128
Hellen
  W. 29
  Walter 131
Hemersley
  William 37, 43, 45
Henderson
  Richard 41, 43, 45, 46
Henry
  John 140
Henry Co., Va. 29
Hepburn
  A. 46
  Ann 46
  J. 46
  J., Jr. 43
  Samuel 42
Herty
  Thomas 137
Hess
  Jacob 31
Hester
  Daniel 29
Hill
  H. 46
  Henry 37, 39, 40, 43
Hillary
  R. 46
  Rignold 38
Hilleary
  Henry, Jr. 29
Hindman
  William 41, 45
Hoban
  James 17, 131, 134, 137, 140
Hocandofer
  Frederick 28
Hodgson
  Joseph 132
Holliday
  James 41, 45
hollows 10
Hollyday
  James 44

Holmead
  Anthony 7, 27, 54-57, 60-62, 64
Holstine
  George 28, 29
Hooe
  Robert T. 42, 46
Hoof
  J. 28
  Valentine 29
Hoofman
  Martin 31
Hospital Square 21
Hotel Lottery 139
hotels 17
House of Representatives 5, 8
houses 129, 135
  building of 15
  building requirement 17
Hunting Creek 6, 8, 12

I

incorporation 127
infirmaries 128
insane 128
institutions 128
Isaac
  David 32

J

Jacques
  Samuel 45
Jacques & Johnson 45
James Creek 10
Jamieson
  Andrew 137
Jaques
  Denton 43
Jefferson
  Thomas 5, 6, 8, 17
Jennifer
  Daniel 40
  Daniel of St. Thomas 45
  Daniel, Jr. 38, 41
  Thomas 40
Jennings
  Thomas 37, 40, 45
Johns
  Thomas 2, 27, 32
Johnson
  James 45
  James, Jr. 38
  Joshua 30, 32
  Mr. 8
  Mrs. 31
  Roger 39, 45
  Thomas 3, 5, 7-11, 31, 38-39, 42-43, 51, 53, 131
  Thomas, Jr. 40, 42, 44, 45, 136
joiners' work 15

Jones
  Charles 136
Jones's Point, Va. 8, 12
Jordan
  Capt. 45
Judiciary Square 21
jurymen 14
justices of the peace 15, 16

K

Karrick
  Joseph 139
Kearney
  John 133
Kemp
  Christian 27, 30
  Frederick 29
  Gilbert 29, 31
  Lodowick 28
  Peter 31
Kephart
  John 27
Kesler
  Andrew 28
Ketland
  Thomas 134, 136
Kid
  Robert 137
Kilty's Laws of Maryland 2
King
  Josias W. 39
  William 7, 31, 113-116
Kingston, N.Y. 3
Kinsor
  Nicholas 28
Kirk
  James 28
Klinger
  Henry 27, 29, 31
Konig
  Heinrich 131
  Henry 131

L

L'Enfant
  Pierre Charles 7, 9-11
Laidler
  Eleanor 42
  Elizabeth 40
Laidlew
  E.W. 45
land records . . . . vi, 1, 2, 7, 11, 17, 53, 131
landholders 8, 9
landlords 127
Langley
  Edward 140
Law
  Patrick 27
  Thomas 20, 98, 135-141

laws of Maryland and Virginia 127
Lawson
    A. 40, 41, 47
lawyers 1
Leak/Leek
    Francis. 39, 41, 46
leaning walls 11
Lear
    Tobias 131, 132, 138
Lee
    Mr. 17
    Richard Bland 131
    Thomas Sim 133
Leitch
    A. 42, 45, 46
Lennox
    Walter 128
Leroy
    John J. 27, 29, 32
Levy Court 127, 128
licenses
    for building 15
Lick
    Ann 38
Liday
    Samuel 30
lighting of streets 128
Lingan
    James M. . 7, 9, 21, 27, 29, 31, 32, 51, 58-65, 67
    Robert 7, 51
Linginfetter
    George 31
Link
    Andrew 29
London, Eng. 2, 127
lot-holders 44
lots 7, 9, 14
    City of Washington 51
    division of 13, 16
    improvements on 11
    sale of 10, 12, 16, 17
lottery 1, 2, 14, 17, 44, 139
Lovell
    William 135
Lower
    Christian 29, 30, 32
Lunenburg, Mass. 132, 133
Lutheran Congregation 30
Lux
    Darby 37, 42, 46
    William 37, 46
Lynch
    Dominick 7, 51, 76-80, 82, 84, 85, 87
Lynch & Sands 21, 85
Lynn
    Adam 140

M
Macgakin/Magackin
    William 41, 46
    William, Capt. 38
Mackie
    Ebenezer 42
    El. 47
Macquaken
    Capt. 47
magazines 3, 21
Magrath
    William 28
Magruder
    J.R. 46
    John R. 37, 38
    W.B. 128
Maitland
    John 137
Maley
    Frederick 28
Mall, the 20
Maniville
    Mary 31
    Patrick 31
Mann
    Frederick 29
Mantz
    Caspar 31
    Casper 28
    J. 32
    John 30-32
    P. 32
Manual
    Patrick 31
maps 10, 11
Marine Barracks 21
markets 128
Marlborough, Md. 1
Marr
    John 29, 32
married women
    owning land 13
Maryland 3, 6, 8, 12, 17, 21, 127
Maryland Herald 14
Maryland Journal and Baltimore Advertiser . . . 14
Mason
    John 43
master-builders 15
Matthews
    William Penrose 137
Maury
    J.W. 128
Mawburn
    James 43, 45
May
    Frederick 133, 135, 136
Mayor of Washington 128, 129
McClary
    Henry 29

McCreery
    William 133
McDade
    John 28
McGrath
    William 31
McMahon
    P. 29
mechanics 12
Meddart
    Jacob 30
merchants 2, 136, 139
Merewhether/Meriwhether
    Reuben 41, 45
meridian line 10
Merkle
    Conrad 28, 32
Metcalf
    Thomas 134, 135
metes and bounds 4, 5, 8, 12, 22
Miller
    James 41
    John 46
    S. 29
    Samuel 32
minors
    owning land 13
Mires
    Philip H 27
money
    advancement 4
    lack of 18
Montgomery Co., Md. 132
Moore
    Mr. (author) 127
    Thomas L. 134
Morris
    Robert 7, 17, 51, 55-58, 61, 63, 64, 84, 86, 114-
        117, 119, 123-125, 131-133, 135-142
Morris & Nicholson 84, 115
mortgages 15
Morton
    Thomas, Jr. 43, 46
Mount Vernon, Va. 8
Mountz
    John 27
Movin
    Lewis 136
Moylan/Moyland
    S. 46
    Stephen 39, 40
Murdock
    George 28

N

name of the city determined 9
National Church Square 21
national monument 17
Naval Observatory 55
navigation 3, 127

Navy Yard Square 21
Neal (also see Neill)
    B. 47
Neill (also see Neal)
    Bennet 37, 43
    James 37, 43
New England 18
New Jersey 3
New York 3, 5, 140
newspapers 14, 16
Nicholls
    Henry 133, 140
Nichols
    Michael 27
Nicholson
    John 7, 17, 51, 55-58, 61, 63, 64, 84, 86, 114-117,
        119, 123-125, 137
Nicklin
    Philip 140

O

oaths 14
obelisks 127
Ober
    Richard 131, 132
Observatory Place 21
Oden
    Benjamin 7, 51, 82, 84, 85, 87, 88, 92, 97
Offutt
    N. 46
Organic Act (1871) 129
Orindorf
    Christian 27, 28
Orphan Asylum, The 127
orphan asylums 128
Orr
    Benjamin G. 128
Ott
    Adam 29
O'Neal
    Lawrence 32
O'Neale
    William 132
O'Reily
    Henry 133

P

P. Campbell and Clagett 46
Pancost
    Jonathan 135
Parkinson
    Ed/Edward 41, 46
party-walls 11
passages 10
pastures 129
Patent Office 17, 21
Pauling
    Henry 28
pavements 129

INDEX

Peirce (also see Pierce)
    Edward 7
    James 7
    Thomas 132
Pennack
    James 46
Pennsylvania 3, 37, 39-43
Penrose
    I. 39
Percival
    Joshua 139
Peter
    Robert 7, 9, 28, 30, 31, 53-58, 61, 63, 65-68, 70, 72-76, 78, 79, 131, 133
petitions 3
Philadelphia lawyer 127
Philadelphia, Pa. .. 4-6, 9, 11, 17, 20, 22, 131-137, 139, 140
Philips
    Isaac 136
    Nathaniel 135
Pickering
    Timothy 20
Pierce (also see Peirce)
    Thomas 132
plan
    defect in 10
    Executive offices 20
    of the Capitol 17
    President's House 17
    streets and reservations 20
Plater
    George 37, 43, 44, 46, 47
plats 1
police officers 128, 129
Polkinhorn
    Henry 140
Polock
    Isaac 132
poor 128
population 129
porches 11
Porter
    Samuel 28
Portsmouth, N.H. 132
Post Office 17
Potomac River .. 3, 5, 6, 8, 10, 12, 13, 15, 19, 21
poverty 128
Powell
    Cuthbert 133
Pratt
    F.W. 2
President's House 12, 17, 21, 22
President's Square 20
Price
    Thomas 30
Prince George's Co., Md. 1, 14, 134, 135, 137, 142
Princess Anne, Md. 137
property-holders 1, 7, 9, 12, 18

Prout
    William 7, 21, 104-117, 123-125
public appropriations 19
public auction 10, 16
public reservations 127
pumps
    erection of 128
Purcell
    Pierce 131, 134, 137

Q

Queen Anne's Co., Md. 133

R

Ragan
    Daniel 30
Ragh
    Benath 47
railroad companies 128
Ralph
    George, Rev. 137
Ramer
    Michael 27, 30
Randolph
    Gov., of Va. 9
Rap
    Dr. 47
Rapell
    William 46
Rapine
    Daniel 128
ravines 10
Raymer
    Michael 31
Reed
    Leonard 32
Reedy Branch 13
Regan
    Joshua 27
    W. 27
Reintzel/Reintzell
    Daniel 28
    Valentine 32
Rench
    A. 28, 31, 32
    John 28, 31, 32
Reservation No. 6 2
reservations 20, 129
reservoirs 128
retrocession 127, 129
Rhorer
    John 28
Richardson
    Thomas 39, 42, 44-46
Richmond
    Charles 45
    Christopher 39, 136
Richmond, Va. 9

Ridley
  M. 46
  Matthew 37, 39, 42
Ringold
  Thomas 45, 46
  Thomas, Jr. 40, 42
Ritenover
  Aaron 27
  Mathias 29
roadways 129
Robertson
  Alexander 140
  William 7
Rock Creek 10, 13
Roe
  Bernard McDermott 135
  Cornelius McDermott 135, 136
  Owen McDermott 135
  Patrick McDermott 135
Rome, Italy 127
Ross
  David 38, 41
  Richard 132
Rothwell
  Andrew 128
Rover
  John 29
Rowles
  Joseph E. 7, 131
Rozer
  H. 46
  H.T. 45
  Henry 1, 2, 38, 41
Russell
  William 37, 40, 41, 44, 47

S

Sands
  Comfort 7, 51, 76-80, 82, 84, 85, 87
Sayle
  John 30
Schell
  Chas. 31
  Christ., heirs 31
schools 128
Scott
  Dr. 45
  Gustavus 3, 20, 133
  Sabret 131
  Upton, Dr. 39, 43
seal
  office for recording deeds 16
seat of government .. 3-6, 8, 12, 20, 127, 128, 131
Seaton
  W.W. 128
sewering of streets 128
Shell
  Charles 27, 28, 31
sheriffs 14
  Prince George's Co., Md. 14

Shillman
  John 32
Shippen
  Thomas Lee 133
ships and vessels 15
Sholman
  John 30
Shute
  John, Sr. 140
Sidebottom
  William 30, 38, 42, 46
sidewalks 22, 129
Skinner
  Edward 31
Slater
  David 38
  Jonathan 38, 41, 45
  Sarah 40, 47
slaves 17
Sluby
  Nicholas 132
Slye
  George 39, 45
Smallwood
  Samuel M. 128
Smith
  Amos 30
  John 38
  John, Capt. 1
  John, Sr. 40-42
  Samuel 133
  Secretary 46
Smithfield, Va. 132
Sneberly
  Henry 29
Snowden
  Richard 32
  S. 46, 47
  Samuel 31, 39
soil 3, 4, 13
Spiker
  Benjamin 28, 30
spirits 16
Spoor
  John 28
Spriggs
  E., Jr. 43
squares 7, 9, 10, 14, 18, 20, 127
  access to 11
  public 18
  shape of 10
St. Elizabeth Asylum 2
St. Vincent Female Orphan Asylum 127
Stall
  Henry 32
statutes of the Corporation 128
Stephenson
  Clotworthy 131, 135
steps 11

INDEX

Sterrett
    James 28
Stewart
    Charles 45
    Dr. 45, 46
    Sarah 42
    Walter 134
Stiner
    Jacob, Jr. 133
Stoddert
    Benjamin . 7, 9, 17, 27-30, 58, 61, 62, 70, 71, 73
Stoddert & Deakins 30-32
Stoker
    Michael 29
Stone
    John H. 7, 51, 54-56
stoops 11
streets 7, 9-11, 17, 18, 20, 21, 128, 129
    15th 18
    15th, West 19
    17th, West 18
    1st, East 18, 19
    1st, West 18
    20th, West 19
    21st, West 19
    23rd, West 19
    25th, West 19
    2nd, West 19, 21
    3rd, East 19
    3rd, West 19, 21
    4th, West 19
    4½, West 19, 21
    5th, East 19
    5th, West 19
    6th, East 19
    7th, East 19
    7th, West 19
    9th, East 19
    9th, West 19
    B, North 18, 19, 21
    B, South 18
    C, North 19, 21
    Canal 18, 19
    E, North 19
    E, South 19, 20
    G, North 19
    Georgia Avenue 19
    H, North 18
    K, South 19
    L, South 19
    M, South 19
    Maryland Avenue 18
    naming of 10
    ownership of 18
    Pennsylvania Avenue 18, 19, 21
    T, South 19
Streeves
    Joakim 28
Striker
    George 31

Stuart
    Charles 38
    David 3, 5, 8-11
    John, Dr. 38, 39, 43
    Walter 134, 135
surveyors 7
Surveyor's office 53
surveys 5
Suter
    John 7
Sweeny
    Mary 136
    Sarah 136
Swingle
    George 30
Sybert
    Philip 30

T

taxes 128
Templeman
    John 133, 135
Terrell
    James 31
Territory of Columbia 10, 13, 16
Thomas
    Evan 28, 42, 46
    P., Dr. 28
    Philip, Dr. 30, 32
Thomas Richardson & Co. 39, 42, 44, 46
Thomson
    George 137
Thornton
    William 3, 17, 20
    William, Dr. 132
Tiber Creek 10, 20, 127
Tilghman
    Ed. 45
    Edward 42, 44
    James 40, 42, 45
    Matthew 38, 40, 42, 43, 45
    Peregrine 40, 42
    Perry 45
    Richard 38, 40, 42, 45
    Richard, Jr. 45
Tilley
    John 31
Tingey
    Thomas 114
titles 12, 13
Tobias Lear & Co. 138
Tomton
    Jacob 27
Toner
    Joseph M. 1
Torrin
    A. 47
    Anne 43
Towers
    J.T. 128

INDEX

Town-House Square 21
Traverse
   Elias E. 136
   John 38
   Nicholas 136
treasurer 15
Treasury
   Secretary of the 18
Treasury building 22
trees
   planting and preserving 128
Trenton, N.J. 3
Trustees
   lots divided by 53
Turkey Buzzard Point 21
Turner
   Thomas 41

U

Umhults
   Henry 31
undertakers 15
United States Naval Observatory 2
University Place 21
Upper Marlborough, Md. 2

V

valleys 10
Van Horne
   Gabriel P. 135
Van Ness
   John P. 7, 51, 82, 88, 128
vaults
   prohibited 11
Virginia 3, 5, 6, 8, 17, 27, 29, 127, 129, 131, 134, 140
Virginia code 127
Voss
   Nicholas 136

W

Walgamot
   John 29
Walker
   George 7, 21, 51, 106-112, 114-122
Wallach
   Richard 128
walls of houses 16
Walter
   Henry 32
War of 1812 129
Ward
   William H. 1
wards of the city 127
Warley
   George 131
Warman
   Henry 29

Warner
   B.H. 1
Warren
   James 7
   W. 7
Warring
   Basil/Bazil 46, 47
   Basil, 3d 40
   Henry 42
   John 7
   Marsham 28, 132
Washington
   George 4-10, 12, 17, 18, 20, 21, 132, 138
   Lund 140
   William Augustine 37, 39-44, 134
Washington Lottery No. 2 139
water lots 39, 91, 106-108, 110, 117, 127
water-courses 9
Watson
   Henry 2
   James 140
   John 40
   Lucy 2
Waugh
   Eliza 28, 31
   William 28, 31
Weems
   John, Dr. 133
Weightman
   Richard C. 128
Welch
   Jacob 132
Wells
   James 27
wells (water) 15
Welsh
   Jacob 132, 133
West
   Joel 136
West Market 21
Wharton
   J. 45, 46
   James 37, 38
   Joseph 41
   William 47
wharves 128
   building of 15
Wheeler
   Elizabeth 7, 117, 119, 120, 125
   Elizabeth, Mrs. 9, 125
   Widow 117
White
   Alexander 20
   [blank] 3
Whitehair
   Appelona 31
   George 31
Widow's Mite 2, 17

INDEX

Wigell/Wigill
   B. 28
   B., heirs 31
Williams
   James 37, 38
   Thomas O. 27, 31
Williamson
   Colin 135
   David 136
Willson
   John C. 137
Wilmore
   John, Jr. 30
Winder's Building 21
windows 11
Winter
   John 31
Winters
   George 31
wood 7
Wooten/Wootten
   William 40, 41
workhouses 128
Worthington
   Charles 30
writ of inquiry 14

Y

Yoel
   Henry 27
Youhman
   Elias 29
Young
   A.C. 7
   Abraham 7, 21, 115, 116, 118-124
   Abraham, heirs ... 113, 115, 116, 118, 121-123
   Jacob 31
   Joseph 39, 45
   Mary 38, 40, 43
   Notley 1, 2, 7, 9, 13-14, 21, 38-41, 43-45, 47, 70,
      71, 73-81, 83, 85-87, 89, 90, 92, 97, 100-102,
      104, 106-108, 110-113, 115, 116, 118-120
   Notley, heirs 101, 102, 104, 120
   Ruth Ann 21
   William 7
   William, heirs 118, 120-124
Youst
   Casper 28, 29

Z

Zetter
   Jacob 30, 32

ABOUT THE AUTHOR

Wesley E. Pippenger is an active member in a number of historical and genealogical societies in Virginia, and is past-President of the Board of Governors of the Virginia Genealogical Society. He has been employed by the Federal Government for over 27 years, and is a management analyst with the Office of Inspector General, National Aeronautics and Space Administration in Washington, D.C. He resides in Arlington, Virginia.

Mr. Pippenger has been active in genealogical research since 1970. Shortly after moving from Colorado to Virginia in 1982, he began to locate, study, catalog, and have data published about cemeteries in the Alexandria, Virginia area. Subsequent published works, now numbering upwards of 60 items, include abstracts of court records, vital records, acts of the Virginia Assembly, newspapers, land, probate, and legislative petition records, and more. His current landmark project, published in series by the Virginia Genealogical Society, is to inventory all estate-related documents for the period 1800-1865, for the entire state of Virginia.

Other Heritage Books by Wesley E. Pippenger:

Alexandria (Arlington) County, Virginia Death Records, 1853-1896

Alexandria City and Arlington County, Virginia Records Index: Vol. 1

Alexandria City and Arlington County, Virginia Records Index: Vol. 2

Alexandria County, Virginia Marriage Records, 1853-1895

Alexandria Virginia Marriage Index, January 10, 1893 to August 31, 1905

Alexandria, Virginia Marriages, 1870-1892

Alexandria, Virginia Town Lots, 1749-1801, Together with the Proceedings of the Board of Trustees, 1749-1780

Alexandria, Virginia Wills, Administrations and Guardianships, 1786-1800

Alexandria, Virginia 1808 Census (Wards 1, 2, 3, and 4)

Alexandria, Virginia Death Records, 1863-1896

Alexandria, Virginia Hustings Court Orders, Volume 1, 1780-1787

Connections and Separations: Divorce, Name Change and Other Genealogical Tidbits from the Acts of the Virginia General Assembly

Daily National Intelligencer Index to Deaths, 1855-1870

Daily National Intelligencer, Washington, District of Columbia Marriages and Deaths Notices (January 1, 1851 to December 30, 1854)

Dead People on the Move: Reconstruction of the Georgetown Presbyterian Burying Ground, Holmead's (Western) Burying Ground, and other Removals in the District of Columbia

Death Notices from Richmond, Virginia Newspapers, 1841-1853

District of Columbia Ancestors, A Guide to Records of the District of Columbia

District of Columbia Death Records: August 1, 1874-July 31, 1879

District of Columbia Foreign Deaths, 1888-1923

District of Columbia Guardianship Index, 1802-1928

District of Columbia Interments (Index to Deaths), January 1, 1855 to July 31, 1874

District of Columbia Marriage Licenses, Register 1: 1811-1858

District of Columbia Marriage Licenses, Register 2: 1858-1870

District of Columbia Marriage Records Index, 1877-1885

District of Columbia Marriage Records Index, October 20, 1885 to January 20, 1892: Marriage Record Books 21 to 30

District of Columbia Probate Records, 1801-1852

District of Columbia: Original Land Owners, 1791-1800

Early Church Records of Alexandria City and Fairfax County, Virginia

Georgetown, District of Columbia 1850 Federal Population Census (Schedule I) and 1853 Directory of Residents of Georgetown

Georgetown, District of Columbia Marriage and Death Notices, 1801-1838

Husbands and Wives Associated with Early Alexandria, Virginia (and the Surrounding Area), 3rd Edition, Revised

Index to Virginia Estates, 1800-1865 Volumes 4, 5 and 6

John Alexander, a Northern Neck Proprietor, His Family, Friends and Kin

Legislative Petitions of Alexandria, 1778-1861

Pippenger and Pittenger Families

Proceedings of the Orphan's Court, Washington County, District of Columbia, 1801-1808

The Georgetown Courier Marriage and Death Notices: Georgetown, District of Columbia, November 18, 1865 to May 6, 1876

The Georgetown Directory for the Year 1830: to which is appended, a Short Description of the Churches, Public Institutions, and the Original Charter of Georgetown, and Extracts of the Laws Pertaining to the Chesapeake and Ohio Canal Company

The Virginia Gazette and Alexandria Advertiser: Volume 1, September 3, 1789 to November 11, 1790

The Virginia Journal and Alexandria Advertiser: Volume I (February 5, 1784 to January 27, 1785)

Volume II (February 3, 1785 to January 26, 1786)

Volume III (March 2, 1786 to January 25, 1787)

Volume IV (February 8, 1787 to May 21, 1789)

The Washington and Georgetown Directory of 1853

Tombstone Inscriptions of Alexandria, Volumes 1-4

www.ingramcontent.com/pod-product-compliance
Lightning Source LLC
Chambersburg PA
CBHW082040230426
43670CB00016B/2721